GCSE
Humanities
for WJEC

John Clarke, Gregg Coleman
Damien Lane, Dave Lewis
Rob Quinn and Layla Taylor

Series Editor: Dave Lewis

HODDER
EDUCATION
AN HACHETTE UK COMPANY

Although every effort has been made to ensure that website addresses are correct at time of going to press, Hodder Education cannot be held responsible for the content of any website mentioned in this book. It is sometimes possible to find a relocated web page by typing in the address of the home page for a website in the URL window of your browser.

Hachette UK's policy is to use papers that are natural, renewable and recyclable products and made from wood grown in sustainable forests. The logging and manufacturing processes are expected to conform to the environmental regulations of the country of origin.

Orders: please contact Bookpoint Ltd, 130 Milton Park, Abingdon, Oxon OX14 4SB. Telephone: (44) 01235 827720. Fax: (44) 01235 400454. Lines are open 9.00–5.00, Monday to Saturday, with a 24-hour message answering service. Visit our website at www.hoddereducation.co.uk

© John Clarke, Gregg Coleman, Damien Lane, Dave Lewis, Rob Quinn & Layla Taylor, 2011
First published in 2011 by
Hodder Education,
An Hachette UK Company
338 Euston Road
London NW1 3BH

Impression number   5 4 3 2 1
Year   2015 2014 2013 2012 2011

Cover photo Milinz/Veer
Illustrations by Barking Dog
Typeset in Trade Gothic Medium 10.5pt by DC Graphic Design Ltd., Swanley Village, Kent.
Printed in Italy

A catalogue record for this title is available from the British Library

ISBN: 978 1444 12424 8

Contents

Acknowledgements

The publishers would like to thank the following for permission to reproduce copyright material:

Photo credits:

p.2 *tl* © Andrew Fox/Alamy; **p.5** © Colin Shepherd/Rex Features; **p.6** © Sipa Press/Rex Features; **p.7** © Scott Olson/Getty Images; **p.8** © jack ruston – Fotolia; **p.9** Gregg Coleman; **p.11** © KBImages/Alamy; **p.13** © Andrew Fox/Alamy; **p.19** © John Stanmeyer/VII/Corbis; **pp.20–21** © Debbie Allen; **p.22** © Debbie Allen; **p.23** *l* Victor Englebert/Time Life Pictures/Getty Images, *r* © Debbie Allen; **p.26** © Paul Cowan – Fotolia **p.29** © macky_ch – Fotolia; **p.30** © Images of Africa Photobank/Alamy; **p.32** © Victor M. Vicente Selvas/publicdomain/ http://commons.wikimedia.org/wiki/File:Contour_line_8_gener_2007.jpg; **p.33** *l* George Steinmetz/Corbis, *r* © Imagestate Media; **p.43** © Lloyd Cluff/Corbis; **p.44** © Fukushima Minpo/AFP/Getty Images; **p.51** *All* © Dave Lewis; **p.52** © Stephen Dowle, http://www.flickr.com/photos/fray_bentos/174359462/; **p.53** *tr* © Photofusion Picture Library/Alamy , *cl* © Christopher Pillitz/In Pictures/Corbis, *bl* © fazon – Fotolia; **p.54** © So-Shan Au; **p.55** *c* © Fundación Salvadoreña de Desarrollo y Vivienda Mínima, *b* © Jonathan McIntosh/http://commons.wikimedia.org/wiki/File:Jakarta_slumhome_2.jpg/http://creativecommons.org/licenses/by/2.0/deed.en; **p.60** © Alexander – Fotolia; **p.64** © So-Shan Au; **p.68** US National Archives, 306-NT-3163V; **p.69** © Associated Newspapers/Daily Mail/Rex Features; **p.70** © Topham Picturepoint/Press Association Images; **p.71** © Rex Features; **p.73** Library of Congress Prints & Photographs division/LC-DIG-fsa-8e11165; **p.74** © Mary Evans Picture Library 2011; **p.78** © Popperfoto/Getty Images; **p.79** © Lebrecht Music and Arts Photo Library/Alamy; **p.83** © Topham Picturepoint/Press Association Images; **p.88** © Trinity Mirror/Mirrorpix/Alamy; **p.90** US National Archives and Records Administration; **p.96** Campaign for Nuclear Disarmament/http://www.flickr.com/photos/cnduk/4820883302/http://creativecommons.org/licenses/by/2.0/deed.en_GB; **p.97** © Daily Mail/Rex Features; **p.100** © Blue Lantern Studio/Corbis; **p.101** Photograph by Robert Knudsen, White House, in the John F. Kennedy Presidential Library and Museum, Boston.; **p.104** US National Archives,193927; **p.105** © Bettmann/Corbis; **p.108** © Bettmann/Corbis; **p.110** Library of Congress, Prints & Photographs Division, Russell Lee, FSA/OWI Collection, LC-USZ62-80126; **p.112** © Bettmann/Corbis; **p.114** © Francis Miller/Time & Life Pictures/Getty Images; **p.116** © FPG/Hulton Archive/Getty Images; **p.121** © Douglas R. Gilbert/Redferns/Getty Images; **p.122** © Everett Collection/Rex Features; **p.124** © Bettmann/Corbis; **p.128** © Everett Collection/Rex Features; **p.130** © SuperStock/Alamy; **p.133** © Giuliano Bevilacqua/Rex Features; **p.134** *l* © James Steidl – Fotolia, *r* © TravelStockCollection – Homer Sykes/Alamy; **p.135** U.S. Navy photo by Mass Communication Specialist 2nd Class Jason T. Poplin; **p.136** *l* © vivien monument – Fotolia, *c* © Digipic – Fotolia, *r* © Robert Young – Fotolia; **p.137** *t* © fotosergio – Fotolia, *b* © Viorika Prikhodko/iStockphoto.com; **p.139** *t* © Rex Features, *b* © Piotr Marcinski – Fotolia; **p.141** © Tony Canon; **p.142** *l* © Layla Taylor, *r* © Glenda Powers – Fotolia; **p.144** © Layla Taylor; **p.145** *t* © Monkey Business – Fotolia.com, *bl* © SUNSET/Rex Features, *br* © Imagestate Media; **p.147** © Christian Aid, 2011, www.christianaid.org.uk; **p.148** © Jean-Claude Francolon/Gamma-Rapho via Getty Images; **p.151** © Doreen Lawrence OBE; **p.152** US National Archives, NWDNS-306-SSM-4C(51)13; **p.153** © Stockbyte/Photolibrary Group Ltd; **p.154** Mehak/World Vision/Photo Voice; **p.155** © Garo/Phanie/Rex Features; **p.156** © John Downing/Rex Features; **p.157** © Getty Images/Stockbyte Silver; **p.162** 'The Good Samaritan' by Dr. He Qi (www.heqigallery.com); **p.164** © DXfoto.com – Fotolia; **p.165** © Debbie Allen; **p.166** © Emir Obolan – Fotolia.com; **p.167** © Layla Taylor; **p.168** © Getty Images/Asia Images; **p.169** © Robert Harding Picture Library Ltd/Alamy; **p.170** © Poppy/Alamy; **p.172** © geewhiz – Fotolia; **p.176** © Sipa Press/Rex Features; **p.177** with thanks to Barbara Davies, CAFOD Programme Officer for Peru and Colombia; **p.181** © Dragos Iliescu – Fotolia; **p.182** © TheFinalMiracle – Fotolia.com; **p.184** © Richard Gardner/Rex Features; **p.186** © Stephen Simpson/Rex Features; **p.188** © S.Meltzer/Photodisc/Getty Images; **p.189** © SFG – Fotolia; **p.191** © Robert Mulder/Alamy; **p.193** © Howard Sandler – Fotolia; **p.194** © Oli Scarff/Getty Images; **p.197** © World Jewish Relief.

Text acknowledgements

p.68 quote by Alan Hartley from Stephen Moss, 'Remembering the blitz: "They bombed in straight lines, east to west, south to north"', *The Guardian* (7 September 2010), © Guardian News & Media Ltd 2010; quote from an ARP warden in *GCSE Bitesize Revision: Modern World History* (BBC Books, 2002); **p.72** quotes by Betty Taylor and June Fryer from David Garmston, 'Surviving World War Two: The Bristol Evacuees' from *www.bbc.co.uk/history/british/britain_wwtwo/bristol_evacuees_01.html* (Last updated 2011-02-17); **p.73** quote by Nellie Brook from Carol Harris, 'Women Under Fire in World War Two' from *www.bbc.co.uk/history/british/britain_wwtwo/women_at_war_01.shtml* (Last updated 2011-02-17); **p.74** Winston Churchill, quote from 'I have nothing to offer but blood, toil, tears and sweat', a speech delivered in the House of Commons, 13 May 1940; **p.75** quote from the diary of Edna Davies in A. G. Veysey, *Clwyd at War, 1939–45* (Clwyd Record Office, 1989); **p.78** quote by Renie Lester from *Yesterday's Britain: The Illustrated Story of How We Lived, Worked and Played in this Century* (Reader's Digest, 1998); **p.81** extract from Philip Sauvain, *British Economic and Social History* (Nelson Thornes, 1987); **p.82** quote by Mrs Ford from *Yesterday's Britain: The Illustrated Story of How We Lived, Worked and Played in this Century* (Reader's Digest, 1998); **p.84** extract from the *Beeching Report* (HMSO,1963); **p.92** extract from Keith Farley, *At the Flicks* from *www.localhistory.scit.wlv.ac.uk/articles/AtTheFlicks/Page14.htm*; **p.94** lyrics by Pete Townshend from 'My Generation' by *The Who*, © 1965 Fabulous Music Ltd, of Suite 2.07, Plaza 535 Kings Road, London SW10 0SZ. International Copyright Secured. All Rights Reserved. Used by Permission; **p.98** quote from an interview with Phil Bradley in 'Forty years ago pictures of Mods and Rockers shocked polite society. But were they staged by the press?', *The Independent* (4 April 2004); quote from '1964: Mods and Rockers jailed after seaside riots', *BBC News, On This Day*, 18 May 1964; **p.105** quote from John F. Kennedy's Cuban Missile address, Washington D.C., 22 October 1962; **p.114** quotes from Martin Luther King's 'I have a dream' speech, Washington D.C., 28 August 1963, copyright 1963 Dr Martin Luther King Jr; copyright renewed 1991 Coretta Scott King; **p.116** quote from Malcolm X's 'We go for separation' speech, *Comment*, 3 April 1964; **p.117** quote from Stokely Carmichael's 'Black Power' speech, October 1966, Berkeley, California; **p.119** examiner's tips from the WJEC GCSE Humanities Specimen Assessment Materials taken from WJEC website; extract from Neil de Marco, *The USA: a divided nation* (Longman, 1992); **p.121** Bob Dylan, a verse from 'The Times They Are a-Changin', © 1963 Warner Bros, Inc.; **p.151** extract from 'Loved with Everlasting Love', George Wade Robinson (1838–1877); **p.154** Case Study, text with kind permission of World Vision, *www.worldvision.org.uk*; **p.176** website text from *www.islamic-relief.org.uk*, by permission of Islamic Relief; **p.177** CAFOD, website text from *www.cafod.org.uk/about-us/where-we-work/lebanon*.

Every effort has been made to trace or contact all copyright holders, but if any have been inadvertently overlooked the Publishers will be pleased to make the necessary arrangements at the first opportunity.

How do people have an impact on natural systems?

How do humans affect the movement of water within a drainage basin?

Drainage basins are the areas of land surrounding a stream or river. The **precipitation** that falls anywhere in that drainage basin feeds the stream or river. Drainage basins come in a vast array of different sizes and contain different river patterns. The mighty Amazon drainage basin is over 6 million km² and contains many smaller basins, which surround the Amazon's many tributaries.

Drainage basins are separated from each other by a line of higher ground called a watershed – whichever side of the watershed a drop of water falls will determine which river it will eventually feed. Figure 1 shows the main pathways that a drop of water can take on its journey through its drainage basin.

Water enters the drainage basin through precipitation (input) and then either moves through the basin (transfer) or stays where it is (store). Most water typically leaves the drainage basin as the river flows into the sea, lake or another river, although some is lost back to the atmosphere through **evaporation** and **transpiration** (output).

The route water takes to get to the river determines how fast it gets there. Water that falls directly into the river obviously gets there quickest. **Overland flow** is the second quickest route, followed by **through flow** and finally **groundwater flow**, which is the slowest. This is very important as the quicker the water gets into a river, the less time the river has to move this water and the more chance there is of it flooding. It may be helpful here to think of the river as a conveyor belt. The speed of the belt (river) and how quickly you put things on it (how quickly rain gets into the river) will determine whether the things pile up and fall off (flood) or not.

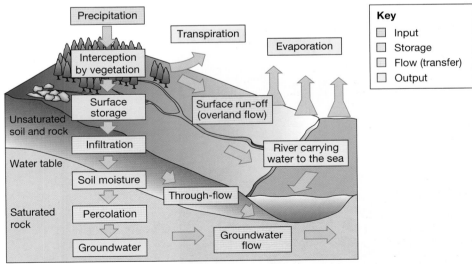

Figure 1 Diagram to show drainage basin water processes

Activity

1 In Figure 1, the movement of water is shown as a flow diagram. Imagine a water droplet as a person. Create a diary extract or story describing the different 'choices' a droplet could make on its journey and what experiences they might face.

Temperature and rainfall can affect the movement of water in a drainage basin. If temperatures fall low enough to freeze the ground, water would tend not to infiltrate. It would stay on the surface and so get into rivers more quickly (overland flow is quicker than through flow). High rainfall can **saturate** the ground so additional water cannot infiltrate (think of a sponge that is already full of water) and it too would move on the surface rather than through the ground.

Now consider the impact humans may have on the movement of water through the drainage basin. Our top two activities are **deforestation** and **urbanisation**, but any change in land use can have an effect, such as heavy modern farming machines compacting the soil and reducing **infiltration**.

Look back at Figure 1 (page 1). Without trees, there will be less **interception**, water will not evaporate off leaves or return back to the atmosphere through transpiration so more water will reach the river. Soil will be denser and more compact without roots to break it up, so water will find it harder to infiltrate and will travel to rivers faster on the surface.

Urbanisation is the growth of towns and cities. More urban areas mean more tarmac and concrete, **impermeable** surfaces that water cannot infiltrate. Drains work like water motorways, transporting rainwater very quickly into streams and rivers. Water getting to rivers quickly means more chance of a flood.

A hydrograph (see Figure 3 on the following page) shows us how a river responds to rainfall. Water falling directly into the river and water travelling by overland flow get to the river first and cause an increase in water discharge shown on the graph as the rising limb. The highest point is called the peak discharge and the time between the rain falling and peak discharge is called the lag time. A short lag time means water is reaching the river quickly and so increasing the chance of flooding.

The falling limb is not as steep as the rising limb due to throughflow which, because it is slower, enters the river later than the overland flow and continues to feed the river after the overland flow has had its effect.

River discharge is the amount of water carried by the river and is usually measured in m³ per second, so an increase in discharge will refer to an increase in river level *and* speed.

Figure 2 Rain in an urban environment

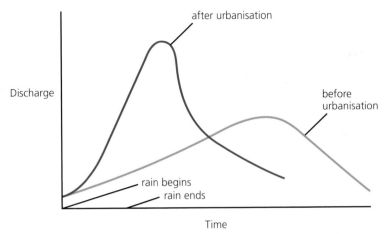

Figure 3 A simple hydrograph to show how urbanisation affects how a river responds to rainfall

How does water pollution in rivers affect the quality of human life?

What are the causes of river pollution?

Water covers over 70 per cent of the earth's surface, and yet only around 3 per cent of that is fresh water that is so essential to life. Furthermore, only about 1 per cent of this fresh water is accessible, the rest being locked in icecaps or hidden deep underground. This means that only about 0.003 per cent of the water in the world is available to us as fresh water.

To put it another way, if all of the world's water was contained in a two-litre bottle then less than a single drop would be available for all the humans, plants and animals on the planet to use for their survival. The UN estimate that the population of the world will increase from 6.2 billion to 9.7 billion people between 2000 and 2050, putting further strain on the world's fresh water supply. And do we look after this resource? Do we protect it and care for it, save it and use it sparingly? The answer is, unbelievably, no.

River pollution is not a recent problem. In ancient Roman times, their amazing sewage systems dumped the city's waste directly into the Tiber and made the water downstream very bad for people's health. The dumping of raw sewage into rivers has caused diseases such as cholera, typhoid and dysentery throughout history and is still killing thousands of people without access to clean water today.

The **industrial revolution** put further strain on our rivers. Factories often saw them as a convenient means of disposing of waste materials such as animal carcasses and poisonous chemicals. Old industries are still polluting today. Rainwater moving through abandoned mines washes dangerous polluting materials into local rivers.

Apart from being unsightly and smelly, which has an effect on locals' standard of living, cleaning up water pollution in England and Wales is estimated to cost over £1 billion a year. That's about a quarter of annual Welsh education spending. Heavy metals and other industrial wastes poison fish and shellfish, which can cause humans who eat them to become very ill, and they can even cause cancers and birth defects.

Sewage

In richer countries such as the UK the vast majority of the population has access to flushing toilets where waste is transported cleanly and safely away from living areas to sewage treatment works before being returned to our waterways. However, leaking pipes, blockages in sewer pipes caused by people flushing various sanitary items down the toilet and floodwater can all cause raw sewage to overflow and re-enter our water system.

A good example is the River Thames where Combined Sewage Overflows (CSOs) collect sewage from homes and industry but also from road runoff. Torrential rain creates huge volumes of road runoff which is too much for the system to deal with and the excess road runoff mixed with sewage from homes and local industries is discharged into the river.

Some water treatment plants allow water to re-enter waterways after only basic cleaning, so water can still contain harmful bacteria.

Farming

Point source pollution is pollution that comes from one particular location or point. Examples of this include milk spillage, silage liquor and cattle and pig slurry from farms. These contaminants can carry harmful parasites and feed algae which grow and use up the oxygen in the water, causing other river life to die. Algae block the sunlight, killing water plant life and further reducing the supply of oxygen in the water. This process is called **eutrophication**.

Diffuse source pollution is harder to trace and therefore control. It includes fertilisers and pesticides being washed into the water cycle and entering rivers.

Industrial

Chemical waste products such as cyanide, lead and mercury can kill river life instantly or collect, accumulate and poison the whole food chain. Warm water from power stations entering rivers contains less oxygen than cold and affects river life. Detergents cause protective mucus layers of fish to dissolve, so they are more susceptible to bacteria and parasites.

How is sewage water treated?

In order for sewage water to be safely introduced back into the environment, impurities must be removed. Larger solids including grit and sand are removed by physical processes such as filters and screens, then remaining solids are passed through settlement tanks where they sink to the bottom and are removed. This is known as primary treatment.

Secondary treatment involves percolating filters, which slowly trickle the sewage water over gravel beds full of micro-organisms that feed on the bacteria and purify the water before it is released back into rivers.

Sometimes a final treatment like sand filters, reed beds or ultra-violet light is used to clean the sewage even more. This is known as tertiary treatment. Ultra-violet light kills micro-organisms in the water without being harmful to the environment and is increasingly used instead of chlorine in the UK.

Activity

1 Research a specific case study of eutrophication. Find out where it happened, why it happened and what effects it had on the quality of human life.

2 Find an example of industrial pollution that happened close to where you live.

3 What effect might river pollution have on the following:

   a) value of riverside houses

   b) farm irrigation and animal watering

   c) drinking-water treatment costs

   d) recreational use of the river

   e) tourist industries

   f) the food chain and human health?

4 Describe the different processes used to clean up sewage water in a treatment plant.

5 'Water pollution is the worst effect we have on our environment.' How far do you agree with this statement?

How do people respond to the threat posed by natural disasters?

What effects does a flood have on people's lives?

Although we have seen how human activity can increase the likelihood of flooding, it is still heavy and/or prolonged rainfall that causes the majority of flood disasters around the world. Flash floods are one of the most devastating natural disasters that occur in the UK. They are typically caused by large amounts of rain falling in short periods.

Examiner's Tips

Although **flash floods** can be caused by dam failure, this method of flash flood is not mentioned in the specification and so will not appear on exam papers, nor will case studies relating solely to this cause be fully credited in answers. Dam failure should only be used as an example of a disadvantage of flood control. Furthermore, your flooding case studies should focus on floods caused directly by rainfall and not **storm surges**, etc.

We can separate the effects of a flood into long and short-term effects:

- Short-term effects are caused directly by the flood itself, such as crops being washed away or buildings destroyed.
- Long-term effects continue to be felt even when the flood has subsided, and are often linked to short-term effects.

- Crops being washed away (short-term) links with people starving (long-term). Buildings destroyed (short-term) leads to homelessness, loss of business revenue, etc. (long-term).
- By linking long and short-term effects in your exam, you will ensure the higher level marks.
- Short-term effects of flooding are usually similar whether it happens in rich, developed countries or poorer ones. Often the most striking difference can be seen in the long-term effects, with developing countries suffering much more as they do not have the resources available to deal as quickly and effectively with the short-term effects. Crop failure always affects the poorest in society most.

Case Study

Boscastle, 2004

On Monday 16 August 2004 a very localised storm dropped 200 mm of rain on the steep slopes surrounding the river Valency in Cornwall and caused a flash flood to rip through the village of Boscastle.

Although nobody was killed, the flood caused an estimated £15 million of damage and it took many hours to rescue tourists and residents trapped by the rising water as roads were blocked and rescue services had to use helicopters. People waiting on rooftops risked hypothermia. Sewage from old pipes mixing with the floodwater also caused other health concerns. Hospitals were immediately put on standby and local hotels were used as temporary accommodation. After several days, residents were allowed to return and salvage possessions. Work began on repairing roads, water and electricity supply, etc. to allow most residents to return home.

Figure 4 Boscastle flood, 2004

Case Study

Pakistan, 2010

Figure 5 Pakistan floods, 2010

Pakistan is a useful case study in that it can be seen as almost the opposite type of flood to Boscastle. Unlike Boscastle, it flooded huge areas, occurred in an **LEDC**, killed an estimated 2000 people and forced around 14 million from their homes. Half a million hectares of farmland was flooded, causing thousands of job losses and soaring inflation as food prices rose.

The government was overwhelmed by the scale of the disaster and the United Nations made an appeal for a $460 million aid package.

With millions homeless and exposed to the elements, dirty floodwaters spreading disease and a lack of food and clean water, a second wave of disease and misery followed. Even a year on, thousands of families still needed support to rebuild their lives.

Activity

1 Research the floods in Boscastle and Pakistan or two other contrasting floods. List all the short-term effects you can find. What are the main differences and similarities? You can use Figures 4 (page 5) and 5 to help you. What are the differences in the long-term effects?

2 'A flood in an LEDC will be worse than one in an **MEDC** because they have less money.' How far do you agree with this statement?

How can we try to control floods?

Flood defences come in two groups: hard and soft. Hard flood defences use technology and structures to reduce the effects of floods, whilst soft flood defences include managing the river basin to reduce flood effects.

Levees: Water, as we have already seen, is a vital requirement of life and this is why many settlements are built on or close to rivers. Being close means they are often at risk from flooding. A simple solution is to raise the natural river banks, allowing water levels to rise without spilling over the top of the banks. These artificial river banks are also known as dykes or embankments.

Dams: Probably the most well-known and recognisable method of flood defences, the dam is a wall across a river which controls the rate at which water can flow downstream.

Channel alteration (deepening and straightening): If you can increase the speed with which a river transports water, then you reduce the chances of water building up and causing a flood. By straightening a river you shorten the distance and so increase the slope of the river, which speeds it up. Channel clearing will also help increase a river's ability to move water quickly. By deepening a river's channel, we increase the amount of water it can hold and thus reduce flood risks.

Afforestation: We've already seen how **deforestation** can increase the chance of flooding and so it stands to reason that planting trees would reduce this risk. Trees break up soil, allowing better infiltration so water takes longer to get to rivers. Trees also use water in the process of photosynthesis, returning it to the atmosphere before it has the chance to enter the river. Less water getting into the river means less chance of a flood.

Land-use zoning: A flood is only a problem if it affects us. If we prevent people building houses, factories and roads, etc. in flood-risk areas and keep the land empty or for farming where occasional floods might bring benefits (nutrient-rich deposits of silt left behind, for example) then the flood loses its ability to cause damage.

Figure 6 Levee holds back floodwater

Flood defence	Additional benefits	Problems/costs
Levees	Allow flood plains to be built on right up to the river itself.	Expensive to build. If they fail, the flood is many times worse than it would have been as there is so much more water contained in the river.
Dams	Can be adapted to provide hydroelectricity. The man-made lake created behind the dam can be used as a water store or for recreation. Level of the river downstream can be kept constant, helping with irrigation.	Costs a fortune to build. Land is deliberately flooded behind the dam – people are forced to move, farmland is destroyed. Loss of plant and animal life. Requires high levels of technology and skill to build. Affects fish spawning journeys. Sediment trapped behind the dam can build up and cause the dam to fail.
Channel engineering	Rivers can be navigated more quickly because they are shorter.	Environments are destroyed. You increase flood risk further downstream where the river slows again. Increasing the river's speed increases its ability to erode.
Afforestation	Provides additional recreational opportunities. Reduces soil erosion. Cheap.	Requires large areas of land.
Land use zoning	Provides recreational opportunities, such as building football fields, etc. Doesn't cost money.	Restricts development and the areas where you can construct essential buildings such as housing. Useless in areas already developed.
Flood warning systems	Cheap. Gives people time to save themselves and possessions.	Doesn't stop the flood. Some people may not have access to communication.

Key

☐ Hard defences   ☐ Soft defences

Figure 7 The benefits and problems of flood defences

Activity

1 Which do you think is the best single type of flood defence? Give reasons for your answer.

2 According to the government's chief scientific adviser, Sir David King, the number of people at high risk of flooding in Britain is expected to more than double to nearly 3.5 million by 2080. Use Figure 8 and your own knowledge to explain why this might be.

3 Use Figure 6 (on page 7) and your own knowledge to explain how a levee might cause a more damaging flood if it broke.

4 Research an example of a river flood defence. How successful was it? What effect has it had on local people and the environment?

5 'The most effective way to protect against flooding is to build more dams.' To what extent do you agree with this statement?

Figure 8 A new housing development built on a river floodplain

Why is the management of natural resources necessary?

Why does water supply and demand in the UK vary?

The population of the UK was 61,792,000 in mid-2009. This is an increase of 394,000 (0.6 per cent) on mid-2008 and is equivalent to an average increase of over 1,000 people a day. On average, each person in the UK uses 150 litres of water every day, considerably more than many developing countries, where around 20 litres is used (equivalent to UK usage in the nineteenth century). Figure 10 shows some of the reasons for this difference. Our growing population is expected to need 15 per cent more water by 2030.

Our average use of 150 litres of water is not taking into account the water needed to produce the food we eat, the clothes we wear and the cars we drive. This is sometimes called virtual water and, taking it into account, we use more like 4645 litres per person per day.

Around 20 per cent of UK water use is domestic, with agriculture and fisheries using 14 per cent, manufacturing using 14 per cent and energy production around 44 per cent. As our population grows and our standard of living continues to increase, so does demand for all the things produced by these industries.

There is more precipitation on the northern and western areas of the UK due to prevailing winds coming in off the North Atlantic and being forced to rise over the highland found here. This is known as **relief rainfall**. The moist air cools and condenses as it rises to form rain clouds. Rocks in these regions tend to be impermeable so water travels back to the sea via streams and rivers. This impermeable rock, high rainfall and large numbers of valleys due to the mountains make these areas very attractive sites for dams and reservoirs.

The south and east gets less rain although its geology means that the rocks absorb more water and keep it hidden deep underground in large **aquifers**. Water is therefore stored naturally for us to dig down and use. Unfortunately the demand for water means the water available in these aquifers is falling all the time and not having time to be replaced. While we think of the UK as quite a wet country, the south east of England has less water available per person than Sudan and Syria.

The flatter land and more fertile soils of the south-east lend themselves to arable farming, which requires more water for irrigation of the crops than the pastoral farming found in hillier areas.

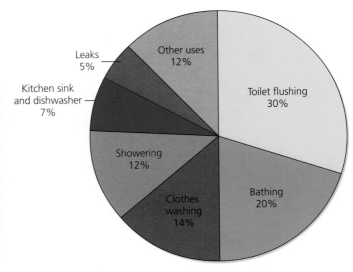

Figure 9 Family fun in the garden

Figure 10 Domestic water use in the UK

Pie chart labels:
- Other uses 12%
- Leaks 5%
- Kitchen sink and dishwasher 7%
- Toilet flushing 30%
- Showering 12%
- Clothes washing 14%
- Bathing 20%

Activity

6 Use Figures 9 and 10 and your own knowledge to explain why MEDCs use more water per person than a century ago.

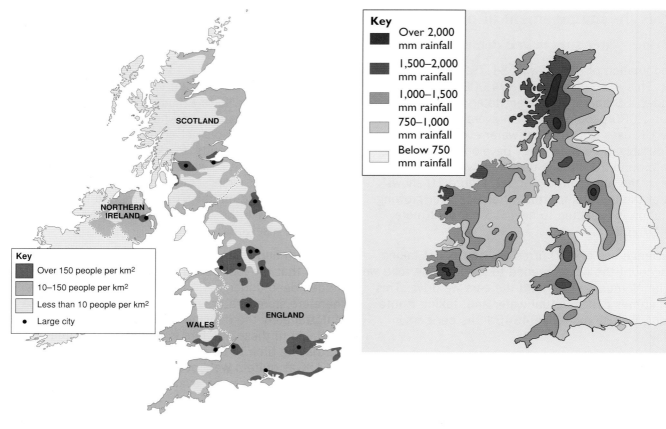

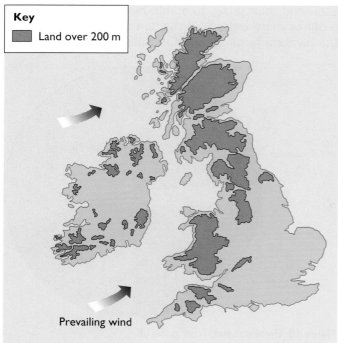

Figure 11 UK maps showing population distribution, rainfall and relief of land

Activity

1 Explain why the north and west of the UK receive higher rainfall than the south and east.

2 Where would you be most likely to find reservoirs in the UK? Why?

3 Use Figure 11 and your own knowledge to explain why demand for water is higher in the south-east of England than Scotland.

4 'It's always raining in the UK. There is no problem with me using as much water as I like.' How far do you agree with this statement?

Why do we build dams?

Dams provide defence against flooding, storage of water for domestic and industrial use and create excellent opportunities for recreational activities with the creation of huge man-made lakes behind them. Some even produce power in the form of hydroelectricity. However, there are many who feel the disadvantages of environmental destruction, caused by a whole valley being flooded, and the effects on locals forced to move from their homes and often their livelihood, far outweigh the advantages, particularly as these locals are often not the ones to benefit from the advantages of the dam.

Case Study

Trywern, Wales

In 1965, the River Tryweryn was dammed to form the Llyn Celyn reservoir in order to provide water to the industry growing in the city of Liverpool and the surrounding area. Capel Celyn was a small rural village located in the Afon Tryweryn valley, the location for the new reservoir. Nobody from the village wanted to move but the then Liverpool Council brought a bill before parliament to develop the reservoir and get permission to forcibly move the villagers.

When voted upon, 35 of the 36 Welsh MPs voted against the bill but it was passed anyway. Eight years of further struggle proved unsuccessful and the entire village (including its chapel and graveyard), surrounding area and twelve farmsteads were flooded.

The effects of this decision are still felt today and the strain put on Welsh–English relations were such that in 2005 the city of Liverpool officially apologised for the hurt caused.

Figure 12 A message urging people to 'remember Tryweryn'

Today the dam provides excellent recreational opportunities such as white-water rafting and canoeing as the water level of the river is kept constant by the dam and so can be used throughout the year when other rivers cannot.

Internet Research Activity

www.llgc.org.uk/ymgyrchu/Dwr/Tryweryn/index-e.htm

Visit this site for more details on the history of the village and reservoir and further links.

Case Study

The Three Gorges Dam, China

The Yangtze River, China, is the third largest river in the world and so big that ocean-going ships can easily sail up it for hundreds of miles, right into the heart of China, (providing the water is deep enough). One-third of China's population lives in its valley, an estimated 1.3 billion people, and over 30 industrial cities have grown on its banks. By damming the river, the Chinese government hoped to protect its people and cities from disastrous floods, create thousands of new jobs, allow ships access all year round to China's interior industrial cities and produce electricity equivalent to eighteen power stations, 10 per cent of China's annual need.

The Three Gorges Dam is 2 kilometres long and over 250 metres tall and created a reservoir over 600 kilometres long, flooding 62,000 acres of land, thirteen major cities and hundreds of large and smaller villages. It is estimated that over one million people have been forced to move from their homes. The Chinese government promised those forced to move a better life with higher wages but many of these farmers had no other skills and are finding it difficult to adapt to new ways of life.

Conflict is rising as **displaced** farmers fight over what small amounts of farmland are left, and rising water is eroding land and causing devastating landslides. Fears are rising that a natural disaster, such as an earthquake, could cause immense damage to the dam, and potentially kill millions in a resulting flood.

Concerns have been raised over pollution collecting in the reservoir behind the dam, creating major health issues and spreading diseases. There is a worry that silt will build up behind the dam and block the turbines. Fish stocks including the baiji dolphin, river sturgeon and finless porpoise are being wiped out due to pollution and blocked food and migration patterns.

Thousands of sites of ancient tombs, inscriptions and other cultural treasures have been lost as the water levels rose, flooding the breathtakingly beautiful cliffs and mountainsides of the area.

Internet Research Activity

www.internationalrivers.org
www.geographypages.co.uk/3gorges.htm

There are online news reports about the Three Gorges Dam posted frequently on news sites, which offer great information, but also try those above.

Activity

1 Who do you think wrote the message in Figure 12 (on page 11)? Why did they write it?

2 Research has shown that moving house is one of the most stressful life events, right up at the top with divorce and bereavement. Imagine you were living in Capel Celyn or were a farmer on the shores of the Yangtze. How would you feel? What effects would the move have on you and your family? Would the effects be different in Wales and China?

3 What are the advantages of hydroelectricity production over a more traditional coal-fired power station?

4 Work in pairs. One takes the role of a Chinese government spokesperson in favour of the dam, the other a foreign news reporter against the dam. Research the advantages and disadvantages of the Three Gorges project and feed back to each other.

Examiner's Tips

To help with your preparation of the exam, make sure that you know:

- the main routes water takes from when it falls to earth to when it flows back to the sea, and how human activity can change the speed in which water reaches rivers
- the causes and effects of water pollution, including specific examples and how sewage is treated before returning to rivers
- the primary and secondary effects of flooding, including specific examples from different countries and the ways these countries try to prevent them

- why the supply and demand for water varies around the UK
- why we need reservoirs and how they affect the people and environment around them.

Wherever you can, always try to use actual examples to support your answers. Use the case studies given in this chapter or other examples that you have covered in class.

When asked to use a source, try to pick out details from it to answer the question and then expand on these details with your own knowledge.

Sample question

How much water is needed to produce 1kg of food (litres)

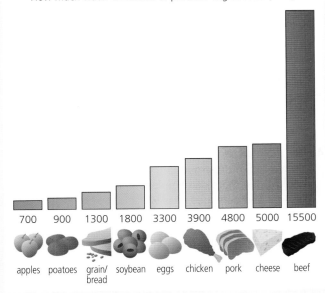

| 700 | 900 | 1300 | 1800 | 3300 | 3900 | 4800 | 5000 | 15500 |

apples poatoes grain/bread soybean eggs chicken pork cheese beef

Source A Amount of water needed in production

Source B Rainwater in an urban environment

What the examiner has to say!

1 What does Source A tell you about water use? [2]

1 A simple statement from the source will get you one mark. The second mark is given for expanding on some details of the water use from your own knowledge, e.g. each of the following statements would get a mark:
Everything needs water to be made.
It takes more water to make 1kg of apples than 1kg of beef.
700 litres of water are needed for apples and 15,500 for beef.
A vegetarian diet uses less water than a carnivorous diet.

2 Explain why water demand has grown in the UK in the last 100 years. [4]

3 Use Source B and your own knowledge to explain how urbanisation can increase the risk of a river flood. [6]

4 'River floods will always cause more damage in poor countries (LEDCs) than in their richer counterparts (MEDCs).' How far do you agree with this statement? [8]

2 The key word in this question is *explain*. The question wants you to show that you understand the factors that have led to increases in demand for water in the UK. Giving four reasons will *not* get you all 4 marks, without some explanation of how each reason has led to increases in water use, e.g:
Population has grown; more people require more water. Our expectations and demands on water supply have increased as our incomes rise and prices fall. We collect more material possessions; our homes have machines which require more water, such as washing machines or lawn sprinklers. Increases in free time and changing lifestyles such as daily baths and showers, going swimming, washing our cars, etc.

3 This type of question gives you a source to help in your answer, but information taken directly from the source will only allow you to access low-level marks, as will your own knowledge with no reference to the source at all. You must use your own knowledge to expand on information from the source and to give ideas not shown in the source for top marks, e.g:
Tarmac roads are impermeable so water stays on the surface and travels to rivers quickly by surface runoff. The river can't cope with the sudden increase and it floods. Trees have been cut down so evapotranspiration isn't using up any water and drains quickly transport all the water into the rivers.

4 For top marks in this type of question you must look at both sides of the argument. Give reasons why you could argue more damage *is* found in LEDCs, such as fewer flood defences, less well-equipped rescue services and medical facilities and less money for aid such as food, shelter, etc. but *also* suggest why MEDCs might suffer more through flood defences failing, causing quick devastation, more infrastructure to be destroyed, etc. Finish by giving your own opinion backed up by both sides of your argument.

Exam practice

1 Describe two ways rainwater can enter a river. [2]
2 What are the main causes of river pollution in the UK today? [4]
3 How can the effects of a flood differ between MEDC and LEDC countries? [6]
4 Why do areas such as Inverness-shire in Western Scotland rarely have hosepipe bans? [6]

5 'Soft flood defences are the best way to reduce the effects of a flood.' How far do you agree with this statement?
Give arguments for and against this statement by:
● *describing the advantages of soft flood defences*
● *explaining why some people feel hard defences are better at protecting areas from flooding*
● *conclude by saying how far you agree with the statement.* [8]

How has the tropical rainforest ecosystem evolved?

Where are tropical rainforest areas located?

An ecosystem is an area that contains particular plants and animals, all depending on each other to survive. They are made from both living and non-living things, such as air, soil and water. One small change in one part of an ecosystem can have huge effects on the ecosystem as a whole because of this dependence. Ecosystems range in size from a single drop of water right up to huge **biomes** such as tropical rainforests. Figure 13 shows the location of the main tropical rainforest biomes.

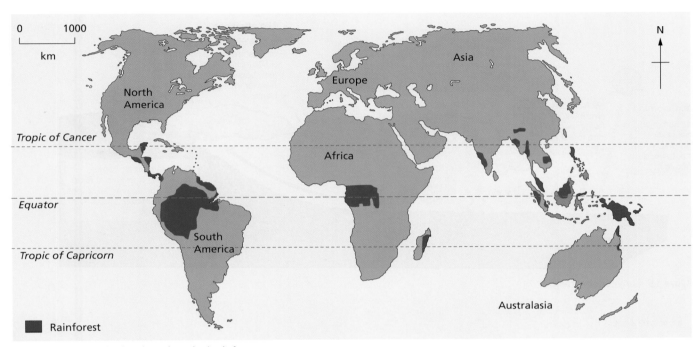

Figure 13 Global distribution of tropical rainforests

The equatorial climate is characterised by its consistency. In other parts of the world, seasons play a large part in a climate, but the equatorial climate tends to be hot and wet all year round. Although some areas may experience slightly lower or higher rainfall for a few months, they could hardly be called wet and dry seasons.

At the equator it is hot because the sun is directly overhead for much of the year. The sun's rays are therefore concentrated on a smaller area and so are stronger. As you move further from the equator, the sun is lower in the sky (consider the UK: even in the height of summer the sun is never directly overhead, and in the winter it is very low even in the middle of the day) so the sun's rays hit the earth at more of an angle, which means they are spread over a wider area and therefore weaker. We can demonstrate this by using a torch to represent the sun's rays as in Figure 14.

If the sun's rays are hitting the earth at an angle it means they have to travel further through the atmosphere, which

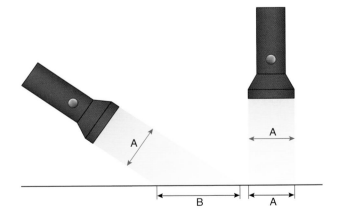

Figure 14 Torch experiment showing how the angle of the sun determines the area covered. A shows concentrated light hitting at the equator; B shows how the angle causes light to be spread over a wider area.

means more of their energy is absorbed or scattered back into space, further weakening them.

Hot temperatures all year round in tropical rainforests cause warm moist air to rise. As the air rises it cools and the water vapour condenses to form huge rain clouds. The rain produced is known as **convectional rainfall**. The rising air pulls in moist air from the surrounding oceans, and so the process continues.

The huge amounts of vegetation in tropical rainforests release lots of water vapour into the air, which can often be seen as a white mist. This water vapour rises, cools and condenses to form even more clouds and even more rain.

Rainforest vegetation is adapted specifically to this unique climate and so is only found where these climatic conditions occur, but it is this very vegetation which contributes to the climatic conditions by releasing huge amounts of moisture back into the air through transpiration. Such interdependence is a strong feature of the whole equatorial biome. A classic chicken–egg scenario!

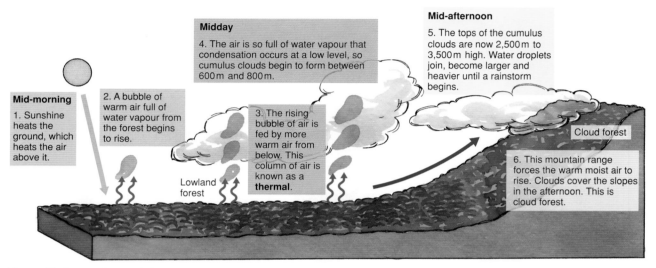

Figure 15 Convectional rainfall

Activity

1 Use Figure 13 (on page 15) and your own knowledge to describe the location of tropical rainforest biomes.

2 You are on holiday in the tropical rainforests of Indonesia. Write a text message or postcard to your ten-year-old brother describing the weather there.

3 Use Figure 14 (on page 15) to help explain why it gets warmer as you move closer to the equator.

4 Use Figure 15 to explain why you would expect more rainfall in the afternoon than in the morning in tropical rainforests.

What are the main features of the tropical rainforest?

Tropical rainforests are characterised by a distinctive forest structure consisting of various separate layers, as can be seen in Figure 16. Each layer has its own unique set of environmental conditions which both plants and animals are adapted to. Some species of animal may never move from their particular layer.

The tallest trees, known as **emergents** as they 'emerge' out of the top of the canopy, can reach 60 metres in height. That's as high as twelve double-decker buses.

Thick **buttress roots** stop these relatively thin giants from toppling over.

The canopy itself contains the densest vegetation and is where most of the wildlife can be found. Due to the density, little sunlight manages to pass through and lower levels are shaded and therefore contain less vegetation. Thick vines called **lianas** use trees as climbing frames to reach up to the sunlight rather than expending energy growing solid trunks, whilst **epiphytes** 'piggy back' on growing trees to reach sunlight. They are adapted so as not to need nutrients from the soil and get all their needs from rainwater and sunlight. This has led to them being commonly referred to as 'air plants'. In other ecosystems, trees have developed thick bark to protect them from cold or moisture loss. As this is not a problem in tropical rainforests, trees tend to have thin, smooth bark which may help stop lianas climbing up them.

Heavy rain is a problem, however, and many leaves are smooth and have **drip tips** which help them get rid of water so it doesn't collect on their surface, weigh them down and snap them off their branch.

Looking at the size and amount of plants in tropical rainforests you would be forgiven for thinking that they have the most fertile soil in the world. In truth, rainforest soil is surprisingly poor. Virtually all the nutrients come from leaf litter falling from the trees above, which rots quickly in the hot, humid climate and releases nutrients. These are quickly absorbed by plant roots and used to grow new leaves, which start the cycle all over again.

Figure 17 Rainforest tree

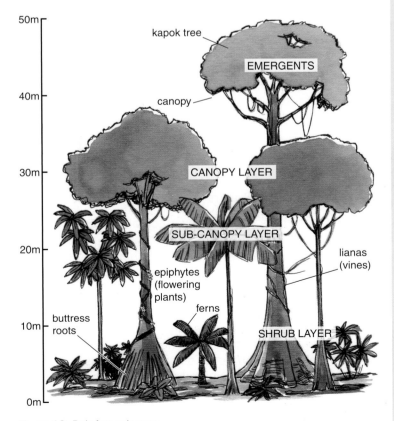

Figure 16 Rainforest layers

Activity

5 Sketch a copy of Figure 16, label each layer and describe what happens to the amount of vegetation and amount of sunlight as you move down through the layers. Why do you think tropical rainforest trees grow so tall?

6 Sketch a copy of Figure 17 and add as many labels to it as you can to show its unique features. Explain how each feature is a result of its adaption to its environment. Include any features you can't see but have learned of in the text.

7 In what way can the plants of tropical rainforests be said to be living off themselves?

8 Tropical rainforests contain a large number of animals. Imagine you have been asked to create a new exhibit in a local safari park that contains five animals from tropical rainforests. Plan how you will house them and show them and what information you will share with the public about them.

How do people exploit the tropical rainforest ecosystem?

How did native people traditionally use the rainforests?

Tropical rainforests have been home to indigenous people for thousands of years. Great civilisations like the Incas and Aztecs have grown and fallen under the shelter of its branches. These people understood the importance of living in harmony with the forest rather than trying to control it, and today their ancestors still benefit greatly from the countless renewable resources the forest can provide.

There are fewer and fewer tribes that now live in the traditional way. Many have been forced from their lands by developers and can no longer survive in the same way as their ancestors because they can no longer use the rainforests' resources.

Those still living in the rainforests often do many of the same things you do. They may not watch TV or use iPods but they do play with friends and help their family, and whilst you might go shopping or bowling, they would go fishing, hunting and swimming.

Native tribespeople obtain food through hunting and harvesting the natural resources around them. Farming is small scale and **subsistence** (they grow the food to eat themselves) and they use a system called **shifting cultivation** where a small area of rainforest is cleared by cutting down smaller vegetation but leaving the large trees. The cut vegetation is then burnt and the ash scattered over the soil to give it a final boost of nutrients. A variety of crops are planted by hand so the nutrients taken out of the soil are balanced and the fragile soil structure is not destroyed. After a few years, due to the rainforests' poor soils, the crop yield begins to fall. The area is then left to recover and another area cleared. With an intact soil structure and the main trees still in place, the area could take as little as twenty years to recover and soil nutrients to be replaced. Tribes such as the Yanomami can then return and grow crops in the area again in a perfectly **sustainable** and balanced use of the rainforest resources. Each tribe produces the bare minimum of food and needs large areas of rainforest to supply even a small tribe. Whilst some see this type of farming as highly destructive, wasteful and environmentally damaging, done properly it can be a sustainable way of using the rainforest for farming.

The Huli

The Huli are one of the many tribes that live in the remote highland forests of Papua New Guinea. They live by hunting, gathering plants and growing crops. Men and women live separately, in large group houses. The men decorate their bodies with coloured clay and wear elaborate headdresses for ceremonies.

The Yanomami

One of the largest groups of Amerindian people in South America is the Yanomami. Their village life is centred around the **yano**, or communal house. The yano is a large, circular building constructed of vine and leaf thatch, which has a living space in the middle. The whole tribe live in close proximity to each other.

Activity

1 Choose a tribe such as the Huli or Yanomami and describe a 'day in the life' of a teenager in such a tribe.

2 Draw a flow diagram to show how shifting cultivation works and how different stages follow on from each other before returning back to the start.

3 What do you think would happen if a village that used shifting cultivation had a large population increase?

4 Describe what might happen if each step of traditional shifting cultivation is not followed.

What is destroying the rainforests?

Although there is debate over actual figures, it is estimated that at least 32,000 hectares of tropical rainforest is destroyed every day. That's an area the size of Wales destroyed every week. Increased farming is blamed for a great deal of this destruction.

As we have seen, shifting cultivation only works on small scales and by using large areas of land surrounding each tribe, who have skilled and knowledgeable farmers. Today's situation is very far from this. The only similarity is that farmers still clear the land and burn it, which is why it is often called slash and burn.

Poor farmers from the cities have moved into the rainforests searching for a better life or have been forced out of cities by increasing population pressures. In Guatemala, indigenous people were forced off their own land by big corporations who used it for large plantations. The indigenous people had no choice but to farm the rainforest as it was the only land available to them. In Brazil, the government actively encouraged people to move into the rainforest. They even had a slogan, 'Land without men for men without land'. Often these people don't have the knowledge required to keep the soil undamaged and the true rainforest needed to replenish the soils does not grow back when the 'farmers' move on. There are many more farmers using the rainforests and the land is not left long enough between harvests, causing the soil to be damaged beyond repair. This results in huge areas of rainforest left destroyed. With no vegetation for protection, the already damaged soil is soon washed away by the daily rainfall.

Commercial farming and cattle ranching clear vast areas of forest, leaving no chance for the surrounding rainforest to re-colonise the area. Nothing larger than shrubs is ever likely to grow there and so the soil will never regain its nutrients. Single crops like soya or palm oil are grown, which take out the same nutrients from the soil, which can often only support a single harvest before farmers are forced to move on and cut down new areas. Increasing demand for produce such as palm oil and beef is speeding up rainforest destruction.

Governments in developing countries are under increasing pressure to improve the economy and therefore the lives of the citizens of their country by using the vast natural resources the rainforests have to offer.

The most obvious resource rainforests have is of course timber. Hardwoods like mahogany are in great demand in the developed world but are often dispersed widely amongst other trees and so large areas of forest are destroyed just to get to them. Logging roads built to get to these trees encourage further settlement in previously inaccessible areas by poor farmers, which greatly increases the rates of rainforest destruction.

Mining not only destroys rainforest to make way for the mine, road and rail systems and miners' housing, but it also pollutes local waterways with poisons such as mercury and cyanide (used to extract precious metals).

Native tribes are often 'encouraged' to move from their traditional homes by developers, who also bring

Figure 18 Effects of unsustainable rainforest development

diseases like measles which the tribespeople have little resistance to. Direct conflict may not be needed as many lose their homes and culture by having their land destroyed, their rivers polluted and their food supply scared off, leaving them with no choice but to move. Moving often means leaving behind their way of life and livelihood as their traditional industries, such as rubber-tapping, require the trees in the rainforest they are forced away from.

Activity

5   What are the different modern-day developments that are causing rainforest destruction?

6   Research for yourself how much rainforest is being destroyed. Why do you think you encounter different figures?

7   Use your figures to make up your own comparisons to the size of area being destroyed (for example, I used the size of Wales every week in the first paragraph of this page).

8   'Building roads into the rainforest is the number one cause of its destruction.' To what extent do you agree with this statement?

Is sustainable development of tropical rainforests possible?

Why is the tropical rainforest such an important ecosystem?

It would be wrong to suggest the rainforest produces large amounts of oxygen. Rainforests use about as much as they produce, but they absorb huge amounts of carbon dioxide from the atmosphere and store it as wood, etc. as they grow. Destroying these trees releases all the carbon stored in the trees back into the atmosphere and so increases greenhouse gases in the atmosphere. Figures suggest that the burning of tropical rainforests creates more CO_2 emissions than all the planes, trains and cars on the planet.

Global warming changes global weather patterns. Some areas get hotter, others colder. Some areas get wetter, others drier. Ecosystems cannot adapt to changes in such a short timeframe and so are destroyed.

Without trees transpiring water into the atmosphere, less rain cloud forms above the now destroyed forest and less rain will fall. Areas suffer droughts and even more vegetation dies. Rain that does fall quickly washes away the now unprotected soil and arrives in rivers more quickly, increasing flash-flood risks.

One single tree in Peru was found to harbour 43 different species of ants – about the same number of species found in the whole of the British Isles.

The number of species of fish in the Amazon exceeds the number found in the entire Atlantic Ocean.

80% of the food we eat originated in tropical rainforests. We only eat 200 of the 3,000 fruits found in tropical forests; local Indians eat 2,000 of them.

25% of our medicines originate from tropical forests and yet we have tested less than 1% of all the plants found there.

Figure 19 Rainforest treasures

Forests act a bit like a sponge. They hold rainwater released by tropical storms and release it slowly, so reducing the chance of both floods and droughts.

Tropical rainforests have been around for a very long time and have had literally millions of years to change and evolve, to the extent that of the 250,000 species of plants in the world known to us, 170,000 can be found in the rainforests.

The number and types of organisms in an area is known as **biodiversity**. Tropical rainforests have the greatest biodiversity on the planet.

Activity

1 What is biodiversity?

2 How might the biodiversity of the rainforests help to develop new medicines?

3 Describe the effect of cutting down tropical rainforests on both the local climate and on a global scale.

4 Using your own research, make a list of five things we use the rainforest for. Rank them in order of importance.

The US National Cancer Institute has identified 3,000 plants that are active against cancer cells. 70% of these plants are found in the rainforests.

Vincristine, extracted from the rainforest plant called the **periwinkle**, is one of the world's most powerful anticancer drugs. It has dramatically increased the survival rate for acute childhood leukaemia since its discovery.

Scientists estimate that we are losing more than 137 species of plants and animals every single day because of rainforest deforestation. Any one of these could contain the breakthrough we are looking for in the battle against cancer, AIDS, even the common cold.

How can we protect the rainforests?

At present rates of deforestation, our tropical rainforests will be all but destroyed in 30 years. Once gone, they will never grow back. None of the valuable resources will be available to us.

But what business is it of ours what countries like Brazil do with their rainforest? There was a time when the UK was covered in forest. We cut the trees down to make way for agriculture and industry for very much the same reasons the people of Brazil are cutting theirs down today. If countries like the UK wish to save the rainforests, shouldn't they compensate countries like Brazil or show them sustainable ways of exploiting the rainforests' resources?

Particular trees in demand for their wood can be grown together on plantations. The area is managed so the soil isn't destroyed and new trees are grown to replace those cut down. These trees can be harvested easily without having to destroy the surrounding rainforest. Timber exported to other countries can be stamped so people know it comes from a sustainable source and it can be taxed, with the money earned being used to police illegal deforestation. Timber without this stamp cannot be sold so will not be cut down in the first place as there is no money in it for the illegal loggers.

Scientists looking for the next big cure amongst the rainforests' plants and animals stand to make a fortune if they find what they're looking for. At present, permission to research in rainforests is free, but there are plans to charge for this. Money earned can be used to restore rainforest ecosystems that have been destroyed, by planting trees, etc.

MEDCs like Norway have promised millions of pounds to countries such as Brazil, providing the destruction of the rainforests continues to fall every year.

Ecotourism and National Parks are big business in many tropical rainforests. The tourist pays to experience the natural beauty of the forest and the money made by the local economy encourages locals to preserve it because, ultimately, the fate of these rainforests lies in the hands of the locals.

Rwanda's gorillas have ecotourism to thank for their continued survival. Threatened by poachers and farmers who cleared the gorillas' natural habitat for crops, the Parc des Volcans was set up as a wildlife preserve for the gorillas. The Parc des Volcans is now the third largest source of foreign revenue in the country and has allowed the government to create

Figure 20 Ecotourism in a rainforest; other activities include boat trips, jungle treks and animal-watching

anti-poaching patrols and employ local farmers as park guides and guards.

All schemes rely on the locals to succeed and so they must be shown that it is in their material interest to conserve the rainforests.

Companies who have a policy to conserve rainforests have begun to 'advertise' this fact, much like **Fair Trade** products. Customers are prepared to pay slightly more for these products. An example of this would be the Rainforest Alliance.

Over half of all rainforest destruction is caused by slash-and-burn farmers. By giving ownership of land to these farmers you encourage them to look after it. Such land reform may involve taking land from rich land owners and giving it to the farmers. Farming techniques such as **permaculture, polycultural planting** and rotation preserve the soil and allow farming to continue on the same piece of land year after year.

Activity

1 What does sustainable development mean? List all the different ways the rainforest resources can be used sustainably. Which do you think would be the most successful?

2 Imagine you want to set up an ecotourism business in the tropical rainforest. What kind of activities would you offer? Who would you get to work for you? Use your ideas to produce a holiday brochure.

3 Design an emblem to go on products produced sustainably in tropical rainforests.

4 'Without the support of the local population, *all* sustainable development schemes are doomed to fail.' How far do you agree with this statement?

Examiner's Tips

To help with your preparation of the exam, make sure that you know:

● where tropical rainforests are located, the climate they grow in and how they are perfectly adapted to their climate and environment
● about traditional and modern uses of the rainforests and their effects on both the people and the environment of the rainforest and the wider world

● the value of tropical rainforests and what people can do to protect them.

Wherever you can, always try to use actual examples to support your answers. Use the case studies given in this chapter or other examples that you have covered in class.

Sample question

Source A A Yanomami yano in Brazil

Source B An example of deforestation in Madagascar

1 Use Source A and your own knowledge to describe how some tribes live in tropical rainforests. [2]

What the examiner has to say!

1 The source is deliberately basic. You should only be looking for one piece of information from it, such as: *they all live together* or *houses are made from local materials*. Your second mark can come from elaboration using your own knowledge, such as: *they have strong tribal bonds to each other rather than family bonds* or *they live sustainably, using what the forest provides*.

2 Why are tropical rainforests being destroyed? [4]

2 A list of four different causes of rainforest destruction will *not* get you all 4 marks on this question without some development of your ideas. The question is asking *why*, so you should give reasons for the destruction. You could say that logging and slash-and-burn farming are two causes of destruction for 2 marks, but to get any more you would need to elaborate on each:
Logging: *Demand for hardwoods from foreign countries making trees such as mahogany desirable* or *each tree cut down destroys many more as it falls and is dragged out of the forest.*
Slash-and-burn farming: *Poor migrants from the cities move to the forest to try to make a better life for themselves but they don't know how to use the land properly, so destroy it and are soon forced to move on to another piece of land.*

3 Use Source B and your own knowledge to describe deforestation and explain the effects on the rainforest ecosystem. [6]

3 The source is really only a prompt, although it does illustrate areas of land that have been cleared. You should always include some reference to the source in your answer. As with question 2, a list of six brief descriptions will not get full marks. You have to explain how the area is affected.
More vegetation has died – how might that lead to droughts and/or floods?

4 'Tropical rainforests belong to the whole world and countries like Brazil have no right to destroy them for their own gain.' How far do you agree with this statement? [8]

4 For top marks, both sides need to be discussed, weighed against each other and a conclusion made.

Why shouldn't the rainforests be destroyed? What damaging effects could the destruction have on a global scale that we should be concerned about? Answering these questions would give the argument for us having a right to tell these countries not to destroy their rainforests.

How could we *help* them use the forests' resources in a sustainable way so they can benefit just as other countries benefit from the resources they have? This would give another side to the argument, where development of the rainforests is possible.

You would finally come to a judgement on the best way forward for rainforest development.

Exam practice

1 Give two causes of tropical rainforest destruction today. [2]

2 Explain how two main features of the tropical rainforest vegetation have been adapted to suit their environment. [4]

3 To what extent can the tropical rainforest climate be said to have only one season? [6]

4 How can logging in tropical rainforests be made more sustainable? [6]

5 'The tropical rainforests are one of the most important ecosystems on the planet and must be protected at all costs.' How far do you agree with this statement?
Give arguments for and against this statement by:
● *describing why the tropical rainforests are such an important ecosystem*
● *explaining the advantages of developing the tropical rainforests*
● *conclude by saying how far you agree with the statement.* [8]

How does farming affect the landscape and environment of the United Kingdom?

How has farming in the UK changed since the end of the Second World War?

Winston Churchill once wrote that '... the only thing that ever really frightened me during the war was the U-boat peril'. German submarines threatened to cut our Atlantic lifeline, which we were dependent on for supplies, food amongst them. Had we lost the Battle of the Atlantic, Britain could easily have been starved into submission.

After the Second World War, politicians were determined that the UK would become self-sufficient in food production so that no such situation could happen again. Unfortunately, farming in the UK was in a mess, using medieval techniques that, despite employing over a million workers, produced so little food that most had to be imported from abroad.

The solution? Money was poured into UK agriculture. Farmers were given grants to improve infrastructure such as buildings and machinery, and fixed prices were paid for crops to ensure that farmers could plan ahead and improve efficiency and use of resources. These changes had five main effects:

Agribusiness

Farming has become large scale and **capital intensive**, now often run by large companies rather than owned by individual farmers. These agribusiness companies use high technology and agrochemicals to maximise yields and profits.

Field size and mechanisation

Hedgerows have been removed to increase field size to increase production and also to enable machinery such as tractors, combine harvesters, etc. to be used more efficiently.

Land reclamation

Land previously not used for agricultural production has been reclaimed in order to provide more opportunities for agricultural land use. This has involved clearing woodlands, draining marshlands and fertilising sandy soils.

Improved buildings

Specialised buildings are now constructed, including temperature-controlled storage sheds for drying grain and keeping harvested crops at optimum temperatures.

Chemicals

There has been an increasing use of fertilisers to support new hybrid seeds and to increase yields, by allowing crops to continually be grown in the same fields without the need for crop rotation. There has also been an increase in the use of pesticides and herbicides.

Impact of the EU

In an attempt to achieve food self-sufficiency and stabilise the agricultural markets of Europe after the war, the Common Agricultural Policy (CAP) was created to support European farmers and protect them from cheap imports. In 1973, the UK joined the European Union and so UK farmers joined the CAP. The three main policies of the CAP were:

Subsidies and grants	**Tariffs (import taxes)**	**Guaranteed prices**
Money was given to support farmers by supplementing their income, in the form of subsidies. Grants were also given to enable farmers to fund schemes to increase production.	Import taxes were used to restrict imports and therefore stimulate the market for products from the EU, further encouraging increased production.	Regardless of world market prices, the **Common Agricultural Policy (CAP)** ensured that farmers were guaranteed a fixed price for what they produced.

By the mid-1980s, the Common Agricultural Policy had been so successful that over-production had become a problem, with large surpluses of produce resulting in 'grain mountains'. Excess food was often sold cheaply to LEDCs, undercutting local farmers there and making it difficult for them to sell their produce. The CAP was being blamed for encouraging environmentally damaging farming techniques. A number of changes were made to the CAP to try and control the problem of over-production, as summarised in Figure 21.

Quotas	These involved setting amounts for how much milk or crops could be produced. If farms exceeded these amounts then they were fined.
Set-aside	The European Union funded set-aside in order to reduce the problems of surplus. This is where farmers were paid not to farm some of their land, which would, for example, be left fallow or used for non-agricultural purposes. In 1995, due to the EU shortage of vegetable oil, farmers were paid a high subsidy of £445 per hectare for planting oilseed rape.
Diversification	Farmers were encouraged to move into other areas of business to make money. This included PYO (Pick Your Own), farm shops, bed and breakfast, camp sites.

Figure 21 The changes implemented by the CAP to control the problem of over-production

Set-aside has now been suspended and quotas will disappear by 2015. The CAP is moving away from a production-oriented policy where farmers are 'rewarded' for the quantity they produce and becoming more influenced by environmental and welfare concerns. Farmers now get a single payment, provided they can show they are managing their land carefully and fulfilling a variety of land stewardship requirements, with more emphasis on caring for the environment rather than increasing production.

Figure 22 Locally-sourced vegetables being sold in a store

The impact of supermarkets

The impact of the rise of supermarkets has had a huge effect on UK farmers. Supermarkets sell us three-quarters of our food and in order to satisfy our demand for ever-cheaper food, many farmers believe supermarkets have been forcing down prices paid to farmers for their produce. Many farmers believe that if they do not accept the prices offered by supermarkets they will have no one else to sell to.

The supermarkets' enormous influence over the food industry and their ability to buy and sell cheaply due to economies of scale makes it harder for small shops and small-scale producers to survive.

Supermarkets have recently begun to source locally but still sell many imported goods that have travelled huge distances and increase the problems associated with transport, such as pollution.

Activity

1 How have farms changed in the UK since 1950 and how have each of these changes increased production?

2 What are the advantages and disadvantages of buying locally produced food?

3 What do you think land stewardship means? What kind of activities do you think farmers might perform?

4 Many would say that the Common Agricultural Policy was too successful and resulted in huge surpluses. What was done to try to reduce these surpluses?

5 Imagine you are a small-scale farmer who feels they can no longer profit from farming and are thinking of accepting an EU subsidy to diversify into another business. What would you use your farm for? Produce a plan showing your 'new look' farm and a leaflet to place in the local information centre to attract visitors/customers.

How have recent farming changes affected the UK environment?

Hedgerows

Almost half of the UK's hedgerows were removed between 1945 and 1990, resulting in the destruction of important habitats, causing a decline in animal populations and reducing the biodiversity of the area. Some farmers see this as an advantage as these animals eat some of the farmers' crops, but most see it as a negative effect on the environment. Removal of the hedgerows has also resulted in increased soil erosion, particularly in areas such as East Anglia, as the hedges used to act as windbreaks and reduced wind speed.

Pesticides, herbicides and GM crops

The increased use of pesticides and herbicides has increased water pollution as more chemicals are washed into local waterways. This has led to the eutrophication of surrounding water courses where algae grows, uses up all the oxygen in the water and so kills off all other life.

At present there are no **genetically modified (GM) crops** grown commercially in the UK. However, they are grown around the world in many countries including America. GM crops are focused mainly on improving resistance, so either fewer pesticides need to be used because crops have built in resistance, or stronger ones can be used without destroying the crop. Future uses of GM crops, however, is much more exciting. Scientists envision bananas with vaccines for diseases, low fat oils, and nutrients like vitamin A added into foods (vitamin A deficiency kills two million children a year worldwide).

At present, the main environmental arguments against GM crops being grown in the UK are the risk of cross-pollination, leading to organic crops that are advertised as being GM-free becoming contaminated, or the gene used to modify the crops escaping into wild plants, creating 'super weeds' with pesticide immunity.

Organic farming

Organic farming does not use chemical fertilisers, pesticides or livestock hormone injections. Instead, they rely on techniques such as crop rotation, compost, natural pest control and animal husbandry to maintain soil productivity and combat pests and diseases. These techniques mean the cost of production is high and so organic food tends to be more expensive.

As harmful pesticides are not used, they are not found on the final product nor are they washed into local waterways. Fertilisers do not contaminate these waterways and so there is a lower chance of eutrophication.

The jury is still out on whether organic food contains more nutrients or tastes better. Taste is a very personal judgement, and the amount of nutrients in food is determined far more by how fresh the food is rather than how it was grown.

There is no such thing as a 'natural' environment in the UK anymore and virtually all of our land has been affected in some way by human action. Much of what we think of as countryside is in fact farmland – and so who better to look after our 'countryside' than the farmers themselves? Many feel that we can no longer expect farmers to look after the countryside for everyone while earning no money for doing it.

There is growing support for farming subsidies to be given for maintaining a traditional landscape, with money available to farmers prepared to graze sheep on hillsides, build dry-stone walls, plant hedges and switch to organic or less **intensive farming** methods, rather than to produce cheap food no matter the cost to the environment.

Activity

6 What are the advantages and disadvantages of GM crops?

7 Why is organic farming sometimes called 'rich-man's farming'?

8 Are there any advantages to buying organic food or are we simply paying for a lifestyle choice?

9 How has hedgerow destruction and increased use of chemicals in farming affected the local environment?

What challenges face farmers in LEDCs?

How do people traditionally farm in LEDCs?

Farming is the number one industry in LEDCs, although the type of farming differs immensely. Traditional farmers in LEDCs primarily grow food to feed their families, although a very small percentage may be used to trade for the odd luxury, or for other crops to vary their diet. This is known as **subsistence farming**. Commercial farming is when crops and animals are grown for profit. They may be called cash cropping or plantation farming in LEDCs and usually involve a great deal of investment from a wealthy MEDC company. Commercial cash crops are **monocultures** in that they grow a single crop such as bananas, coffee or sugar cane in large fields using modern machinery, fertilisers, pesticides and techniques to ensure the greatest possible yield or harvest in order to maximise profits.

Advantages	Disadvantages
Workers are trained in using modern machinery and farming techniques that increase yields.	Monoculture destroys the natural vegetation and reduces the biodiversity of the area.
Crops provide employment for the local population.	Workers are low paid and have little control over their working conditions.
Crops are sold abroad and provide the country with much-needed foreign currency from exports.	Most of the profit goes to the owners who are usually rich multinational companies.
Investment is sometimes made in the local infrastructure, such as roads.	Reliance on a single crop means that if world prices fall you get very little money, and you are vulnerable to diseases and pests that can destroy your whole crop.

Figure 23 Commercial cash crop production has both advantages and disadvantages in LEDCs

High-input farming is known as intensive farming and is where farmers try to get the highest yields possible from relatively small areas of land. Subsistence farming can also be intensive; indeed it is the most common type of farming found in LEDCs, although they tend to rely on large inputs of labour rather than modern technology. The opposite of intensive farming is **extensive farming**, where large areas of land are used so whilst yields per hectare are low, a much larger area is farmed to make enough produce.

Activity

1 What different types of farming are there? What are the differences between them?

2 Use Figure 24 and your own knowledge to describe the features of an intensive rice farm.

3 Imagine you are a businessperson from the UK trying to develop a banana plantation in an LEDC. You have to persuade the government of the LEDC to let you develop your plantation. What would you say to them?

4 Who might be against the development of the banana plantation? What arguments would they use to persuade the government to say no to the development?

Case Study

Intensive rice farming in India

India has a monsoon climate, warm and wet, ideal for growing rice all year round. Rice is the staple food of over half of the population of India and forms 90 per cent of the total diet. Soils are very fertile thanks to the silt deposited from river floods, and the flat land means the water doesn't flow away downhill. India's high population provides a large labour force, with around 70 per cent of the working population finding employment in the rice-farming industry.

In India, many rice farms are very small, perhaps as small as one hectare (the size of a football pitch) and many farmers do not actually own the land they work on but 'rent' it from landowners. The small size means that machinery can't be used easily and most farmers couldn't afford it anyway. Farming is very labour intensive, with planting, weeding, harvesting, etc. all being done by hand or with the help of water buffalo, whose manure helps fertilise the fields. Crops are used to provide seeds for the following year's crop and to feed the

Figure 24 An intensive rice farm in Asia

farmer, his family and workers. Any surplus is used to pay the land owner rent or can be used to trade for other things they are not able to grow or make themselves.

Has the Green Revolution been a success?

The changes that occurred in large parts of the developing world from the 1950s onwards came to be known as the Green Revolution. It introduced technologies such as mechanisation, irrigation, chemical pesticides and fertilisers and new strains of **high-yield crops** that had previously only been seen in developed, industrialised nations.

In countries like Mexico and India, the Green Revolution certainly appeared to be a success in the short term, with cereal production more than doubling. In Africa there was less success due to a lack of infrastructure and uninterested governments as well as the lack of availability of water for irrigation.

With higher yields of basic crops such as rice, farmers could diversify into other types of crops which allowed for a more varied diet and more crops to sell, which, despite the decline in food prices, gave farmers more money and a better standard of living. The overall decline in poverty in countries like India has partly been attributed to this agricultural growth and associated decline in food prices.

However, to get these huge increases in output, much more had to be put in. Pesticides to protect the crops, fertilisers to feed them, irrigation schemes to water them and machinery to plant and harvest them are expensive, and many small, poor farmers either cannot afford them or are crippled by huge loans. Often an area with hundreds of small farms turns into one with only a handful of much larger farms as the smaller farmers are bought out by the larger. Add increasing use of machinery and you get high levels of unemployment, and with no other jobs available many migrate into the already densely populated cities.

Chemical pesticides and fertilisers are washed into nearby streams and rivers, poisoning fish, contaminating drinking water and causing eutrophication. Irrigation schemes to supply the highly water-intensive farms are putting a strain on already low water supplies. Concentration on one type of crop (monoculture) in order to achieve the highest possible yields reduces the biodiversity of the area.

Intermediate or **appropriate technology** is seen by many as a middle way to help farmers in LEDCs. Whilst they agree technology is needed, they say it should be appropriate and suited to the needs, skills, knowledge and wealth of the people using it. Large, expensive irrigation projects and dams have too many disadvantages to be built in most LEDCs, particularly when a simple well dug in each farm, a basic easy-to-maintain pump and channels to move the water to the field would do just as well.

Figure 25 Crop-irrigation system in Kenya

High-tech machines needing expensive fuel, spare parts and skilled maintenance should be replaced in favour of local labour, of which there is a large supply, and basic tools. Energy should come from **renewable sources** such as wind and solar power, which are easy to maintain.

It is hoped that **land reform** will address the problem of smaller farmers being taken over by larger ones by increasing the farm size of smaller landowners so they can make more money from their farm, by setting a limit on how much land any one landowner can own and giving this extra farmland to landless farm labourers. The Landless Workers Movement of Brazil continues to campaign for such reform – a battle that has been fought since the 1930s.

Activity

1 What advantages has the Green Revolution brought to LEDCs such as India?

2 How can the Green Revolution be said to have contributed to the growth of cities in LEDCs?

3 What problems may be caused by irrigation schemes in LEDCs, such as that shown in Figure 25?

4 How have some of the problems associated with the Green Revolution, such as expensive machinery and small farms bought out by larger ones, attempted to be solved?

5 Research an example of appropriate technology at work in countries such as Kenya or Bangladesh.

How can people cope with the problems caused by desertification?

What are the causes of desertification?

Desertification is caused by soils becoming less and less fertile, until little can grow in them. Most areas at risk of desertification are already semi-arid and fragile and it only needs a little nudge from climate change or human over-exploitation of the land to turn them into deserts incapable of supporting life.

It is estimated that around one-third of the planet's land is made up of these semi-arid areas, with over a billion people relying on them for survival.

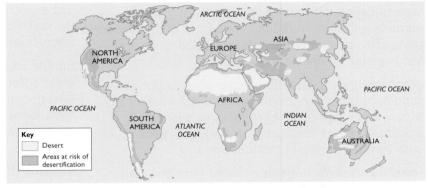

Figure 26 World map showing areas most at risk of desertification

World population continues to grow, particularly in LEDCs where many of the areas at risk of desertification can be found. The additional mouths to feed put increasing pressure on farmers to grow more crops and rear more animals, but the amount of land they have to do this remains the same. This can lead to over-cultivation, over-grazing and deforestation, which in turn leads to desertification and loss of farmland, causing more pressure to be put on the farmland that still remains. Conflict occurs as people fight for the remaining resources, and some are forced to move, creating even more population problems in other areas.

Desertification is not a problem found solely in LEDCs. Figure 26 shows that many richer countries such as the USA and Australia are also affected.

Over-cultivation	Too much pressure is put on the soil. Crops are grown constantly in order to satisfy the ever-increasing demand for food and the soil is given no time to rest and regain its nutrients. Soil structure is lost and the soil is blown away.
Over-grazing	Too many animals on the land mean the vegetation is grazed on so much that it can't recover, and it completely dies off. Without vegetation roots to bind the soil together and rotting vegetation to replenish soil nutrients, the soil becomes infertile and is blown or washed away.
Deforestation	Trees are cut down to clear land for farming to provide for increasing populations and to provide heat, light and warmth for them. Trees provide shelter to the soils from heavy rains. Roots bind the soil together and stop it being blown or washed away. Leaves fall, rot and replenish soil nutrients. Cut the trees down and replace them with crops which take from the soil rather than give and you increase the risk of soil erosion. Once the top soil disappears, the land becomes infertile and nothing will grow.
Monoculture	This is where we replace all the different types of plants and animals growing in an area with a single crop that is usually grown for profit. This reduces biodiversity and puts huge pressure on soils, because a single crop means every plant wants the same type of nutrients from the soil rather than many plants taking a more balanced range of nutrients. Soil structure is damaged and the soil is more susceptible to erosion.
Natural causes of desertification	Climate change increasing the number or duration of droughts can kill off vegetation, particularly bushes and shrubs with large root systems which protect the soil. Soils dry out and the likelihood of soil erosion increases. Rains may occur less often but be more severe, washing away topsoil and reducing soil fertility.

Figure 27 Problems leading to desertification

Activity

6 What is desertification and who does it directly affect?

7 Use Figure 26 and your own knowledge to describe the areas that are most at risk from desertification.

8 How is population growth linked to the main cause of desertification?

9 How are global warming and desertification linked?

What are the solutions to desertification?

One of the causes of desertification is an increase in the frequency and/or duration of droughts, which many think are caused by increases in temperatures and changing rainfall patterns due to global warming. It stands to reason then that one solution to desertification is to tackle the causes of global warming and work to reduce the output of greenhouse gases. This cannot be tackled on a local scale and needs global co-operation.

Other solutions include improving water supplies by building reservoirs or drilling deep wells in order to supply water during times of drought, planting drought-resistant seeds and controlling rainwater runoff with terracing or contour bunding.

Terracing involves flattening sloped farmland into steps so that rain falling on the land will stay and sink into the ground rather than run off down the slope. Contour bunding involves building small barriers from stones, etc. which prevent rainwater flowing down slopes and give it time to soak into the soil, so that plants can use it and it doesn't wash away valuable topsoil.

Figure 28 Contour bunding to trap surface water

Using slow-release drip irrigation will ensure water is not evaporated away and lost before being absorbed by the soil and is available to plants, and so save valuable water.

Planting fast-growing plants called cover crops in between rows of 'normal' crops protects the soil from erosion, particularly when the soil is bare, and provides organic material and nutrients for the soil.

As deforestation can cause desertification, so reforestation can prevent it. Trees provide barriers to soil erosion caused by wind and rain and so protect the soil, as well as adding much-needed nutrients through dropped leaf litter.

Simple changes to farming practices can make a great difference in the fight against desertification. Government incentives and/or simple campaigns to show farmers the advantages of using these practices can be used to promote changes.

Changes might include:
- using the manure from animals to fertilise the soil or to be dried and burnt for fuel to reduce the demand for wood
- promoting crop rotation so that different nutrients are taken from the soil and it has time to recover between plantings
- fencing off newly planted trees and cover crops to prevent grazing by animals.

Government help to promote alternative livelihoods to farming in these areas and offering grants to explore new techniques to improve yields sustainably would also reduce the pressure on farmland and so reduce the risks of desertification.

Activity

1   Use Figure 28 and the text to describe how terracing and contour bunding can help combat desertification.

2   List all the solutions to desertification suggested in this chapter. Divide them into which you feel would be the most effective and which you think would be easiest to put into practice. Order the lists into most to least effective and easiest to hardest.

3   From the lists in question 2, give your top three tips for reducing the risks of desertification and explain why you think they would work.

4   What role can governments and other agencies play in reducing the effects of desertification?

Examiner's Tips

To help with your preparation for the exam, make sure that you know:

- how farming has changed in the UK since 1950 and what has caused these changes
- how these farming changes have affected the environment
- the different kinds of farming found in LEDCs and how the Green Revolution has affected the way farming takes place today

- where desertification is taking place and those most at risk
- the causes and solutions to desertification.

Wherever you can, always try to use actual examples to support your answers. Use the case studies given in this chapter or other examples that you have covered in class.

Sample question

Source A Tea plantation farm in Kenya

Source B A modern farm scene in the UK today

1 Use Source A and your own knowledge to describe plantation farms in LEDCs. [2]

2 Explain why LEDC governments might grant licences for an MEDC company to set up a plantation farm in their country. [4]

What the examiner has to say!

1 The source clearly shows monoculture and an intensive farming technique. You could add your own knowledge as to what intensive farming is all about or give your opinion as to the story behind the greenhouses seen in the background or the workers houses.

2 This is a simple enough question, asking for the advantages of a foreign plantation farm to the 'host' country. Top marks will require you to explain why each point is good for the country – so don't just say it provides jobs, talk about high levels of unemployment or that the workers will be trained in modern farming techniques, which they can take with them when they move to other jobs. Don't just say it makes money for the country, talk about how foreign currency from exports strengthens the country's economy, or that investment in local roads to help move the crops can also benefit locals and local businesses.

3 Use Source B and your own knowledge to explain why the average yield of a UK farm has risen since the end of the Second World War. [6]

3 Although the question gives a source, full marks will require you to give evidence both from the source *and* your own knowledge on how farming changes have increased yields. Make sure that every farming change you give is matched with a sentence explaining how it allowed yields to increase. Three changes should be enough to secure all 6 marks. One change should be evident in the source.

4 'Population growth is the underlying cause of all causes of desertification.' To what extent do you agree with this statement? [8]

4 What causes desertification? Climate change and human influences. Both need to be discussed to show you understand each side of the argument. Often statements like this are used because they are so one-sided and almost impossible to agree and/or disagree with. This one, you can't agree with, but you should be saying that population growth *is one* of the reasons for desertification, and indeed it is probably the most powerful cause of desertification due to increases in deforestation, over-grazing, over-cultivation, forced migration into fragile ecosystems, etc.

Exam practice

1 Describe two human causes of desertification. [2]
2 What are the advantages and disadvantages of farmers supplying to supermarkets? [4]
3 Describe two responsibilities put on UK farmers as custodians of the countryside. [4]
4 Explain how desertification is being combated in countries around the world. [6]
5 'The Green Revolution was a resounding success and the benefits far outweighed the problems for farmers in LEDCs.' To what extent do you agree with this statement?
Give arguments for and against this statement by:
- *describing the advantages of the Green Revolution to LEDC farmers*
- *explaining the problems faced by some small farmers*
- *conclude by saying how far you agree with this statement.* [8]

How can the distribution and growth of the world's population be explained?

Where do people live?

Population is not evenly distributed throughout the world. In some places, for example in Western Europe, **population density** is very high but there are many parts of the world where very few people live. Figure 1 shows the distribution of the world's population.

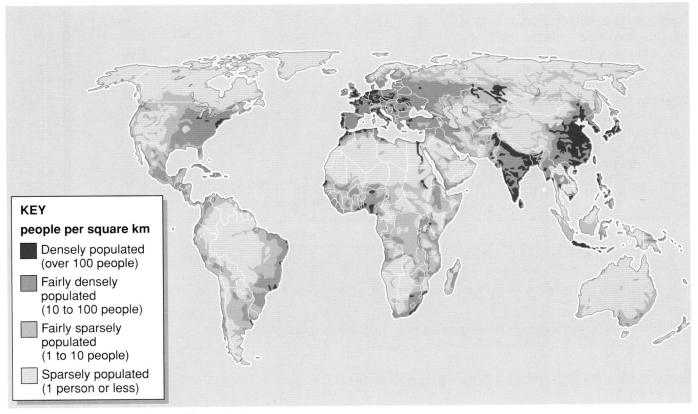

KEY

people per square km

- Densely populated (over 100 people)
- Fairly densely populated (10 to 100 people)
- Fairly sparsely populated (1 to 10 people)
- Sparsely populated (1 person or less)

Figure 1 The distribution of the world's population

Areas with high population density can be found around the large industrial cities in MEDCs (More Economically Developed Countries), such as north-west Europe and eastern USA. High population densities are also found in many LEDCs (Less Economically Developed Countries) where many people live as subsistence farmers growing crops on fertile soils deposited by rivers or formed from volcanic rocks, for example, northern India, Bangladesh and south-east Asia.

Figure 1 also shows large parts of the world where there is very low population density. Low population densities are often the result of physical factors such as climate, landscape or the natural vegetation that make life difficult for people.

Activity

1 What does Figure 1 tell you about the distribution of the world's population?

Case Study

Low population density in the Himalayan mountains

The Himalayas are the world's highest mountains. They form a barrier between India and China that is over 2,400 kilometres long. It is an area of very low population density. The high mountains and deep valleys make transport and communications difficult and the extreme climate at such high altitudes adds to the problems.

Ladakh in northern India is a typical Himalayan region: 300,000 people live in the region but population density is less than one person per km².

In winter the temperatures drop to -45°C and farming is only possible from April to August. Most people are peasant farmers, scratching a living from the infertile soils by growing barley, wheat and potatoes and keeping a few animals. There is often a shortage of food and many people rely on subsidised food from the government. Many young people are moving out of the region or trying to get jobs in the tourist industry, supporting the visitors who come to trek in the mountains.

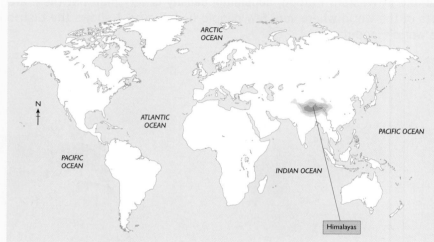

Figure 2 The location of the Himalaya mountains

Activity

1 Label and name areas of high and low population density on a blank map of the world.

2 Explain why the areas you have named have high/low population density.

How and why has world population changed?

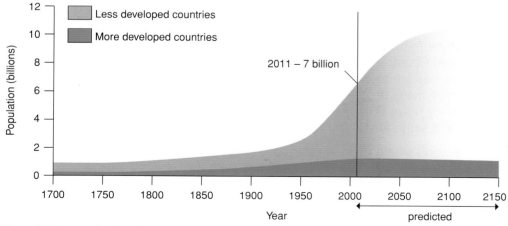

Figure 3 The growth of world population

Figure 3 shows how world population has changed since 1750. The world population grew rapidly during the mid twentieth century, especially between 1950 and 1990. World population increases by three every second, and by 2050 the United Nations estimates that the world's population will be between 7.7 billion and 11.2 billion.

There are signs that world population growth is beginning to slow down and the graph should begin to level off in the next 100 years. Different parts of the world show different growth rates. In most LEDCs the rate of population increase is slowing down. However, according to United Nations statistics, most LEDCs still have higher population growth rates than MEDCs. The population of Africa is expected to double by 2025 and Asia's population could increase by 40 per cent.

Population change is caused by changes to birth and death rates. This can be explained using the **bathtub principle** (see Figure 4).

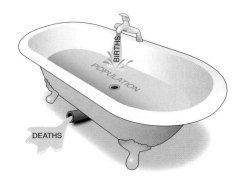

Figure 4 The bathtub principle

Many people think that the growing world population is caused by an increase in the birth rate – people having more children. This is not so. The world's population is increasing because of a decline in the death rate – people are living longer.

Changes to birth and death rates in most parts of the world follow a similar pattern and go through a number of stages. This is called the **population cycle**. The stages happen at different times in different countries and are linked to the economic and social development of a country. The stages of the population cycle are shown in Figure 5.

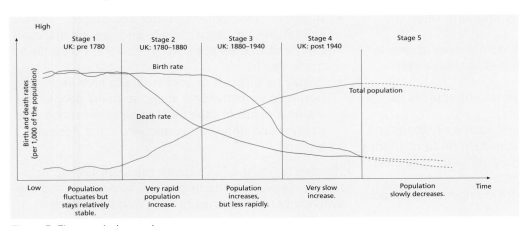

Figure 5 The population cycle

Some experts think that the population cycle is too simple to explain something as complex as population dynamics. However, many countries do follow the general pattern and those with the highest growth rates (for example, in Africa) are the least developed.

Activity

3 Describe the growth of world population shown in Figure 3.

4 Use the bathtub principle in Figure 4 to explain how changes in birth and death rates will cause total population to change.

5 Describe how birth and death rates and total population change in each stage of the population cycle.

What is population structure?

Population structure is the make-up or composition of the population. It is shown using a **population pyramid** or an age–sex graph.

Different birth and death rates cause differences in the shape of a country's population pyramid. For example, the population pyramid in Figure 6 shows a high birth and death rate. A high birth rate means lots of young children – so the pyramid has a wide base. The high death rate means that many people die before they reach old age – so the pyramid gets smaller with each age group.

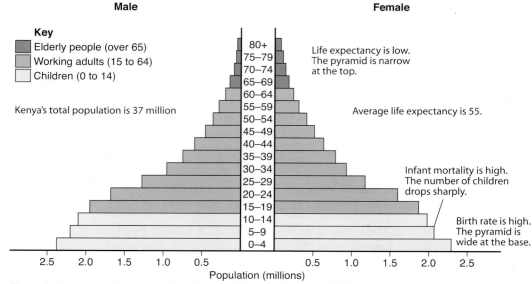

Figure 6 The population pyramid for Kenya, Africa, for the year 2000

There are a number of reasons why birth rates are often high in LEDCs:
- In many rural areas people do not have access to family planning services and education about contraception is poor.
- Some religions and cultures do not approve of using contraceptives.
- Children are often a valuable source of labour and income for a family. They can help on family farms from a young age and as they get older they can earn money from other jobs.
- Children can help to care for younger children and elderly family members.
- High rates of infant mortality mean that families need to have many children in order to ensure that some survive through to adulthood.
- It may be traditionally important for people to have a large family.

Death rates are much more complex and it is more difficult to see patterns in different parts of the world. In the least developed countries of the world death rates are still high:
- Lack of food and famine cause many early deaths due to malnutrition or deficiency diseases such as Kwashiorkor.
- A lack of clean drinking water and proper sanitation (e.g. proper toilets and sewage disposal) may lead to diseases such as cholera, which cause many deaths.
- It may be difficult to access health care and hospitals in many rural areas, so many people can die as a result of infections or sickness which lead to fever and dehydration and would not normally be fatal.

However in most LEDCs death rates are falling rapidly. Improvements in medical technology and the availability of medicines provide cures for many illnesses, more people are gaining access to clean drinking water and changes in farming or employment patterns mean that people have more food and better diets than in the past. All of these factors mean that fewer children die from diseases that can be easily prevented or treated.

Surprisingly, death rates are often higher in many MEDCs. This is largely because many MEDCs have ageing populations. With a greater proportion of older people, death rates are likely to rise. Other factors connected to lifestyle, e.g. deaths due to tobacco, alcohol and stress-related illnesses, are also important. Despite this, people in MEDCs generally have a longer life expectancy than people in LEDCs.

However, death rates are falling. Improvements in farming techniques mean that more food can be grown and so people's diets are better. Advances in medical technology and the availability of medicines provide cures for many illnesses, and more people are gaining access to clean drinking water.

The population pyramid for the United Kingdom (Figure 7) is a completely different shape. It has a narrow base because the birth rate is low and the square shape shows a low death rate and a much longer **life expectancy**. This shape is typical of many MEDCs.

Population pyramids can also show how the population of a country is likely to change. Figure 8 shows the population pyramid for the UK in 2025. It shows that there will be more people over the age of 65 and fewer people of working age. This may cause problems as the government will need to spend more money on healthcare and pensions, but will be getting less money from taxes.

Internet Research Activity

www.ons.gov.uk

Visit the Office for National Statistics website and investigate the population structure of the UK at different times between 1971 and 2083.

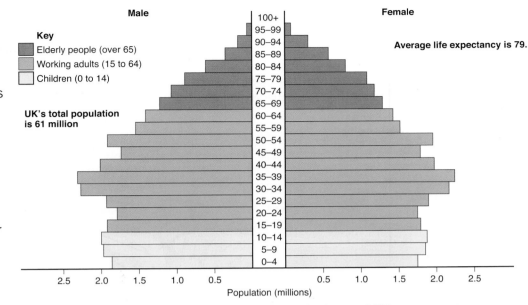

Figure 7 The population pyramid for the United Kingdom for the year 2000

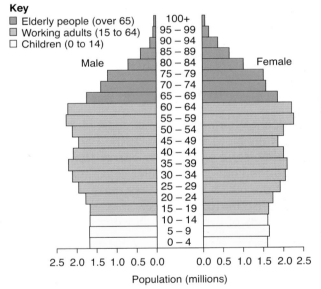

Figure 8 The population pyramid for the UK in 2025

Activity

1 Describe the differences between the population pyramids of Kenya and the UK (Figures 6 and 7).

2 Explain why an LEDC such as Kenya has high birth rates and high death rates.

3 Working in groups, imagine that you are advising the UK government on population issues. Using Figure 8, describe how the population of the UK will change by 2025. What problems will this cause? What could the government do about it?

How do extreme climatic events affect people?

What are hurricanes?

Hurricanes are huge rotating storms that occur in tropical regions of the Atlantic Ocean. In the Pacific Ocean they are called **typhoons** and in the Indian Ocean they are **cyclones**.

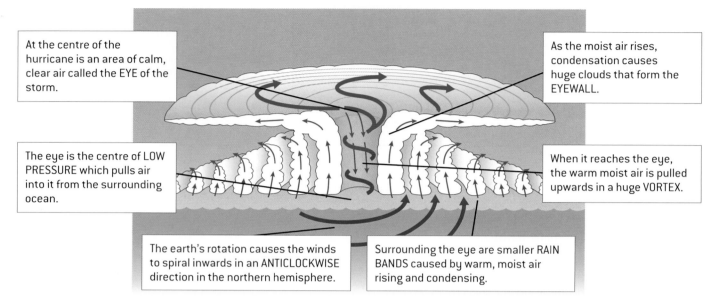

At the centre of the hurricane is an area of calm, clear air called the EYE of the storm.

As the moist air rises, condensation causes huge clouds that form the EYEWALL.

The eye is the centre of LOW PRESSURE which pulls air into it from the surrounding ocean.

When it reaches the eye, the warm moist air is pulled upwards in a huge VORTEX.

The earth's rotation causes the winds to spiral inwards in an ANTICLOCKWISE direction in the northern hemisphere.

Surrounding the eye are smaller RAIN BANDS caused by warm, moist air rising and condensing.

Figure 9 The main features of a hurricane

Most hurricanes form off the west coast of Africa between June and October. As they grow, they move west towards the Caribbean Islands and the Gulf of Mexico, picking up moisture and gaining energy from the warm, tropical ocean. Once they move on to the land or over cooler seas, hurricanes quickly lose their source of energy and die out, but where they make landfall on islands or the coast of the USA they cause terrible damage:

- Strong winds of over 100 mph will damage buildings. People will be at risk from flying debris.
- Heavy rainfall causes flash-floods and landslides.
- The winds cause huge waves which crash on to the land.
- Coastal areas will also be affected by a storm surge. The strong winds and low pressure cause sea level to rise up to 7 metres higher than normal. This may cause severe flooding and destroy property near the coast.

Activity

1 Make a copy of Figure 9 and add labels to show the main features of a hurricane.

2 Imagine you are on holiday on the coast of the USA when it is hit by a hurricane. Write a letter home describing what it was like during the storm.

Internet Research Activity

www.nhc.noaa.gov/index.shtml

Visit the National Hurricane Center website. Research active storms, look at past hurricane seasons and learn about how to prepare for a hurricane.

How do people deal with the threat from hurricanes?

Because hurricanes are so destructive, the USA has developed a hurricane warning system. The National Hurricane Center in Florida identifies and tracks hurricanes using satellites, weather radar and special aircraft which fly through a hurricane taking measurements. Once it is clear that a hurricane will make landfall, warnings are issued on the internet, television and radio and through a system of flags. People are encouraged to protect their property or to evacuate the area to hurricane centres or places further inland.

Because of these measures, the death toll from hurricanes in the USA is usually quite low although the cost of the damage can be enormous. However, for many of the small island nations of the Caribbean the effects can be much worse. In 2004 Hurricane Ivan hit the island of Grenada, devastating its agriculture and tourist industries, killing 39 people and destroying 90 per cent of the country's 28,000 homes.

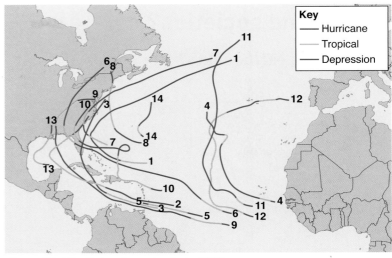

Figure 10 Atlantic hurricane tracks in 2004

Case Study

Hurricane Katrina, New Orleans, USA, 2005

Hurricane Katrina was the sixth strongest storm to hit the USA and the costliest ever recorded. At least 1,500 people were killed and around $300 billion worth of damage was done.

Katrina made landfall near the city of New Orleans. Although warnings were issued urging people to evacuate, many of the poorest people could not or would not leave their homes.

As with most hurricanes, it was the storm surge that did the most damage and caused the most deaths. Much of the city lies below sea level and is protected by defences called levees. Many collapsed and a wall of water rushed in, flooding 80 per cent of the city to depths of up to 6 metres.

It took many weeks for enough supplies of food and water to be airlifted into the city and for engineers to begin the task of repairing the levees. The flood water in the streets of New Orleans took several months to drain away.

Activity

3 Use Figure 10 to write a report about the 2004 hurricane season. (You could mention the number of storms, their dates and tracks and the areas/countries affected.)

4 Study the track of Hurricane Jeanne in 2004 (storm 10 in Figure 10). Why was it difficult for forecasters to issue warnings about this storm?

5 In small groups either imagine you are an ordinary family living on the island of Grenada (an LEDC in the Caribbean), or in a city in the USA. You have heard on the TV that a hurricane is approaching. What action could you take to protect yourself and your property? Discuss the different responses and why the effects might be more serious for the family on Grenada.

What impact do natural disasters have on people and societies?

What causes earthquakes?

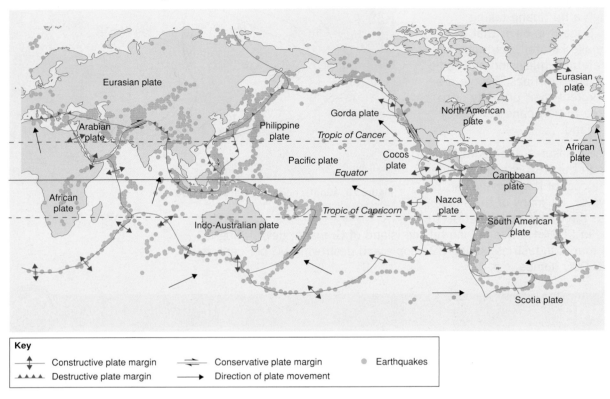

Key

↕ Constructive plate margin ⇌ Conservative plate margin ● Earthquakes

▲▲▲ Destructive plate margin → Direction of plate movement

Figure 11 Global distribution of tectonic activity

Earthquakes are not random events. Figure 11 shows that earthquakes often occur in narrow zones along the edge of continents and oceans. This is because earthquakes are caused by **tectonic activity** – movement in the rocks of the earth's crust.

The earth's crust is made up of a number of plates like the panels on a football. These plates are constantly moving around, driven by currents in the molten rocks deep beneath the crust. Earthquake zones are usually found at **plate boundaries**, where two or more plates come into contact with each other. The different types of plate boundary all cause earthquakes (Figure 12).

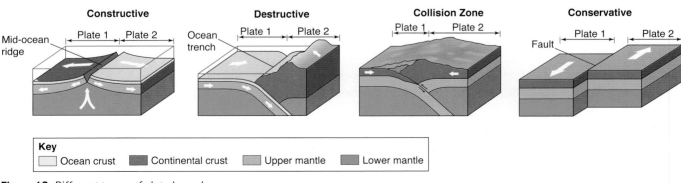

Key
▢ Ocean crust ▧ Continental crust ▢ Upper mantle ▨ Lower mantle

Figure 12 Different types of plate boundary

Often, the boundary between two plates is hidden beneath the surface, but in California, the Pacific Ocean plate and the North American plate are moving in opposite directions along the **San Andreas Fault**.

Movement of the plates is usually slow, on average about 2 centimetres per year. If this movement is smooth and continuous the effects may be hardly noticeable – inconvenient rather than dangerous (see Figure 13).

Figure 13 Gradual movement along the San Andreas Fault has caused the sides of this drainage channel to crack and move

Sometimes the two plates stick. The strain gradually increases until the rocks give way in a sudden movement. This sends out shockwaves which cause an earthquake. The point where the break occurs is called the **focus** of the earthquake and may be deep underground. The shock waves spread out from this point and so the worst effects are felt at the **epicentre** – the point on the surface directly above the focus.

The strength or magnitude of earthquakes is measured on a nine-point scale called the **Richter Scale**. The worst earthquakes occur when there has been a build-up of stress over a long time and where the focus of the earthquake is close to the surface.

Activity

1 Use Figure 11 to describe the global distribution of earthquakes.

2 Explain what is happening at each of the different types of plate boundary shown in Figure 12.

3 Research the effect of earthquakes at each point on the Richter Scale. Produce an illustrated poster to show drawings of the likely damage for each point on the scale.

What are the effects of earthquakes?

The most obvious or **primary effect** of an earthquake is the shaking of the ground. Buildings may collapse or partially collapse, landslides are triggered and roads and bridges become impassable. In an area of low population a large earthquake might not cause many casualties, but in a big city even a relatively small earthquake could kill thousands. People become trapped inside collapsed buildings. In the streets, broken glass, masonry and other objects falling from buildings may cause death and serious injury.

Although the primary effects are dangerous, the **secondary effects** can be much worse if help does not arrive in the area quickly. Gas pipes break and fires break out. These may be difficult to control as water mains will also be broken. Hospitals may have been damaged and the injured may be unable to get medical attention, leading to more deaths from infection. Many thousands of people may be homeless and have only basic shelter to protect them from the weather or the effects of **aftershocks**. The lack of clean water, food or medical supplies, and buried dead bodies slowly decaying beneath the rubble of buildings, may lead to disease such as cholera spreading amongst the survivors. These secondary effects may last long after the initial earthquake.

Figure 14 Primary effects of earthquakes – collapsed buildings, Japan, 2011

One of the most frightening secondary effects is a **tsunami**. An earthquake under the sea may cause a wave of water to spread out in all directions. This wave can travel for thousands of miles. It may be unnoticeable in deep water but as it nears the coast it builds in size before rushing inland and destroying everything in its path. On Boxing Day 2004, a large earthquake occurred in the Indian Ocean. Although there were no deaths caused by the earthquake itself, the resulting tsunami killed 230,000 people in fourteen different countries. And in March 2011, Japan's most powerful earthquake since records began struck its north-east coast, triggering a massive tsunami that killed over 20,000 people.

Activity

1 Explain the difference between primary and secondary effects.

2 Work in groups and discuss how each of the following factors may cause the effects of an earthquake to vary: *earthquake strength; position of epicentre; population density; type of land; time of day; time of year/weather.*

Case Study

Haiti Earthquake 2010

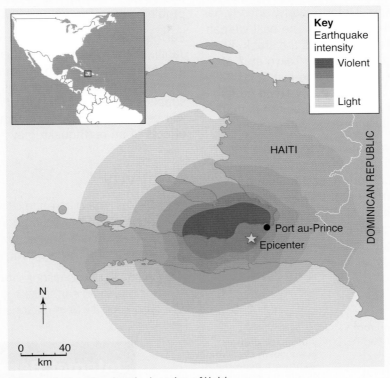

Key
Earthquake intensity

Violent

Light

HAITI

DOMINICAN REPUBLIC

● Port au-Prince

★ Epicenter

N

0   40
    km

Figure 15 Map showing the location of Haiti

Haiti is an island nation in the Caribbean Sea on top of the plate boundary between the Caribbean and North American plates. On 12 January 2010, a magnitude 7 earthquake struck the island. The epicentre was close to the capital city, Port-au-Prince.

The primary effects of the earthquake and the aftershocks were devastating:

- 222,000 people killed
- 300,000 injured
- 1.5 million made homeless
- 250,000 homes and 30,000 commercial buildings collapsed or severely damaged.

There are a number of reasons why the death toll was so high:

- The earthquake occurred at shallow depth.
- It struck the most densely populated area of the country.
- Haiti is a very poor country and many of the buildings were not earthquake resistant.

The earthquake damaged the only airport on the island and the port area so water, food and other equipment for the aid effort took up to 48 hours to arrive. Local people had to use their bare hands to try and dig people out of the rubble, and a severe shortage of doctors and medicines meant that many people died of their injuries that became infected.

In the months after the earthquake, thousands were forced to live in crowded tent cities without water or sanitation. In October the disaster was made worse by an outbreak of cholera on the island. By December almost 100,000 people had contracted the disease, causing more deaths.

How do people respond to the threat of earthquakes?

It is impossible to prevent earthquakes. Instead, scientists try to find ways of predicting an earthquake by looking for warning signs. Unfortunately, nobody has successfully predicted an earthquake. The best we can do is to identify areas where the plates are stuck. For example, earthquakes regularly hit the Tokyo area of Japan – on average every 72 years. The last Tokyo earthquake was in 1923 and so the city could suffer another earthquake at any time. The problem is that nobody can predict exactly when that will happen.

Instead, many earthquake zones try to prepare for earthquakes by having disaster plans and well-drilled emergency services. In California, earthquake drills are part of the school curriculum. People are advised to keep basic earthquake survival kits easily accessible in their homes. In Tokyo the public take part in a practice day once a year which involves local people and the emergency services.

Cities in earthquake zones in MEDCs have strict building regulations and modern buildings are designed to withstand a major earthquake. However, older buildings may not reach modern-day safety standards and as each earthquake is different this can cause problems even for buildings which should be safe.

Earthquake preparation is much easier in MEDCs like Japan or the USA because they have the technology and money to spend on building regulations and emergency plans. Extra equipment and medical supplies can be sent to the affected area quickly and it will be easier to pay for the cost of rebuilding. The effects of an earthquake may be much worse in LEDCs.

Activity

1 Explain the difference between earthquake prevention, prediction and preparedness. How successful are each of these in lessening the impact of a major earthquake?

2 In small groups discuss the items you would include in an earthquake survival kit. Where would you keep it? Give reasons for your choices.

Internet Research Activity

www.shakeout.org

Visit the website and explore how people in California are preparing for the next big earthquake. Play the interactive game 'Beat the Quake' (see bottom right of web page), which tests your knowledge of earthquake preparedness.

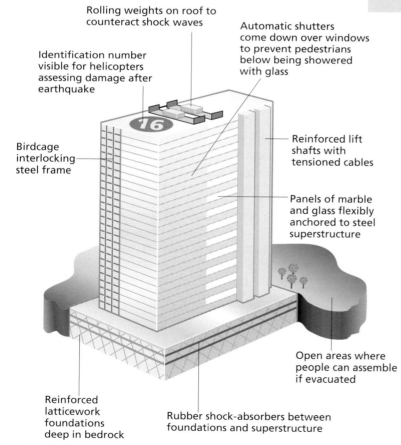

Rolling weights on roof to counteract shock waves

Identification number visible for helicopters assessing damage after earthquake

Automatic shutters come down over windows to prevent pedestrians below being showered with glass

Birdcage interlocking steel frame

Reinforced lift shafts with tensioned cables

Panels of marble and glass flexibly anchored to steel superstructure

Open areas where people can assemble if evacuated

Reinforced latticework foundations deep in bedrock

Rubber shock-absorbers between foundations and superstructure

Figure 16 Earthquake proofing for buildings

Examiner's Tips

To help with your preparation for the exam make sure that you know:

- where the world's main areas are of high and low population density, and that you understand why the density is high or low in these areas
- how changes to birth rates and death rates have led to population growth, and you can explain birth and death rate changes in both LEDCs and MEDCs
- the causes of hurricanes and earthquakes and the primary and secondary effects of these natural disasters on people
- how people can be protected from the worst effects of these events
- why the response to natural disasters will be different in LEDCs and MEDCs.

Wherever you can, always try to use actual examples to support your answers. Use the case studies given in this chapter or other examples that you have covered in class.

Sample question

Earthquake crisis overwhelms Pakistan

The earthquake, thought to have been the strongest in the region in a century, has killed more than 19,000 people.

With some towns and villages completely flattened, Pakistan needs 'massive cargo helicopter support' and international aid supplies because the worst hit areas are in remote regions of the Himalaya mountains.

Source A Newspaper report of an earthquake in Pakistan, 2005

1 Explain why birth rates are high in many less economically developed countries (LEDCs). [4]

2 Use Source A and your own knowledge to explain why the effects of a large earthquake are likely to be worse in a less economically developed country (LEDC) like Pakistan. [4]

3 Using an example that you have studied, describe the damage that may be caused by a hurricane. [6]

What the examiner has to say!

1 The key word is *explain*. You need to show that you *understand* the factors that lead to high birth rates. Don't just give a list of reasons and don't use bullet points. Always answer using full sentences.

To get high marks, try to give three or four reasons for high birth rates, e.g. 'Many children die at a young age', but then add something extra about each reason 'so parents have many children so that some will survive to become adults'.

2 This is a *source-based question* but it also asks you to use your own knowledge. Source A will help you but don't just copy statements from it in your answer. Make sure that you show that you understand why the effects of the earthquake were so bad.

To get full marks you must add something that the source doesn't tell you – this is why good revision is so important.

3 This question is asking you to describe the effects of hurricanes. The key phrase is *using an example you have studied*. You must base your answer on an actual example or case study.

You will get some marks for giving general statements but to get the highest marks you must link these to an actual event.

Exam practice

1 Use Figure 3 (on page 36) and your own knowledge to describe the growth of the world population since 1900. [4]
2 Describe what can be done to limit the effect of hurricanes. [6]
3 Explain the causes of earthquakes. [6]

What are the causes and effects of urbanisation?

Why does urbanisation vary around the world?

Urbanisation is the growth of urban population. Two hundred years ago only one person in ten lived in cities, but by 2010 it was more than one in two.

In 1950 there were 70 millionaire cities (cities with a population of over one million) around the world, but by 2000 there were nearly 300, mostly in LEDCs. There are also some mega-cities such as Sao Paulo in Brazil and Shanghai in China, which have populations as high as twenty million and which continue to grow.

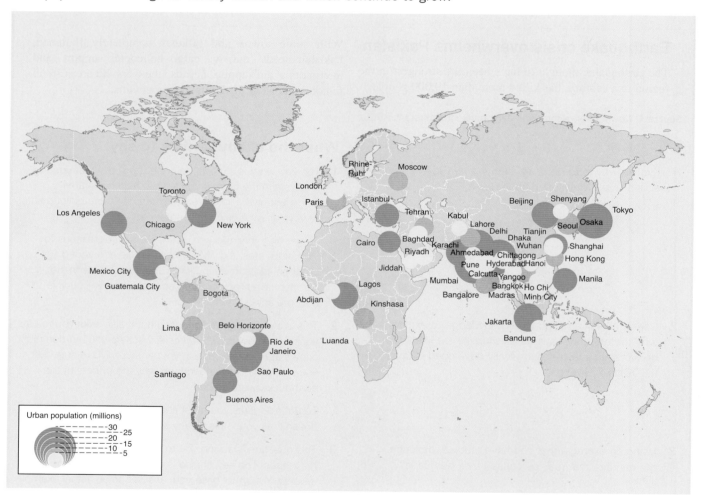

Figure 17 The world's mega-cities

Urbanisation on a global scale is very uneven. In MEDCs like the UK, rapid urbanisation occurred during the industrial revolution in the 1800s. Huge numbers of people moved from the countryside into the new industrial towns to find better-paid jobs in the factories. Today urbanisation has slowed down. In LEDCs, urbanisation is a much more recent process and the major cities are still growing very rapidly (Figure 18).

The main cause of urbanisation is **rural–urban migration** as people move into cities from rural areas in search of a better quality of life.

Case Study

Rural–urban migration in Brazil

Bahia state in North-East Brazil is one of the poorest parts of Brazil. Most people struggle to make a living from **subsistence agriculture**. Crops grow badly in the poor soils and the hot and dry climate. Irrigation is expensive and there are few rivers. **Infant mortality** is more than double the rate in the cities. Children die from malnutrition or because families do not have access to basic health care. Levels of education and **literacy** in the region are also very low. Such poor quality of life forces people to look for better conditions in the city.

Cities such as Sao Paulo offer jobs with regular pay and a better standard of living. So people migrate to the cities and set up home in one of the many slum areas called **favelas** on the edge of the cities. Life in the favelas is hard. They build shacks out of whatever materials they can find and there are few basic services. Regular work may be difficult to find and people have to work long hours for very low wages. Despite these conditions, many people are still better off than in the rural areas.

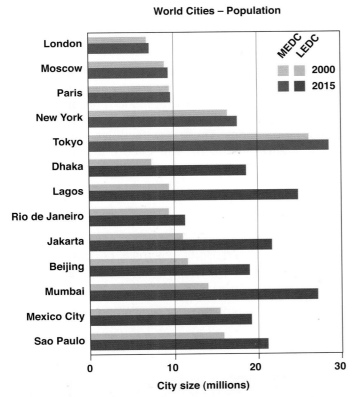

Figure 18 The growth of world cities 2000–2015

Activity

1 Use Figure 17 to describe the location of the world's largest cities.

2 What does Figure 18 tell you about the different rates of growth for cities in MEDCs and LEDCs?

What are the patterns of urbanisation in the UK?

In MEDCs like the UK, urbanisation has slowed down. Many people still move from rural to urban areas but there is also a lot of migration out of the cities. This is called **counter-urbanisation**.

Figure 19 shows population change in Britain between 1991 and 2008. Many large UK cities lost population. In contrast there has been rapid population growth in the rural areas of southern England. Even remote rural areas like central Wales grew by 6 per cent.

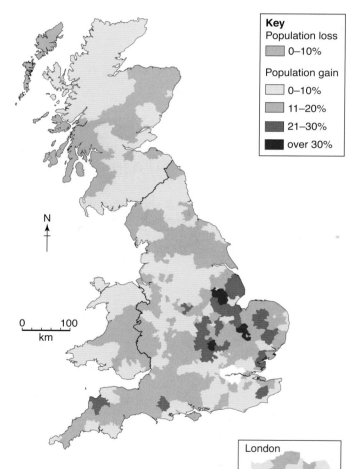

Key

Population loss

◻ 0–10%

Population gain

◻ 0–10%

◻ 11–20%

◼ 21–30%

■ over 30%

N

0 ___ 100
km

London

Figure 19 UK population change 1991–2008

People are choosing to live in rural areas for a variety of reasons:
- The cost of living is higher in cities. Houses in large cities are often smaller and more expensive than in rural areas.
- The quality of life may be better in small towns and villages. There is less traffic congestion, less noise and cleaner air.
- Crime rates are usually higher in urban areas.
- Increasing car ownership and better transport (fast train services, motorways, etc.) allow people to live in rural areas and commute to work in the city.
- Many retired people prefer the peace of the countryside or the coast.
- Many businesses have moved away from cities where space is limited and rents are expensive. Modern industrial estates on the edge of cities offer newer buildings and better transport links.

Counter-urbanisation can cause problems. The demand for housing raises prices above what many local people can afford and more building may change the character of rural villages. Commuting also increases traffic congestion on roads leading into cities.

However, there are signs that some people are moving back into the cities. Inner city areas have been improved and **regenerated** with modern housing and attractive offices replacing the slums and derelict industrial buildings. These new facilities attract young, highly paid people who choose to live in modern high-rise apartments close to the city-centre attractions.

Activity

1 Describe the reasons why many people prefer to live in rural areas of the UK rather than cities.

2 Explain how counter-urbanisation in the UK may cause problems for rural areas and the environment.

Internet Research Activity

www.un.org/esa/population

Visit the website for the population division of the United Nations. Explore and download some of the factsheets and data on urbanisation around the world.

What patterns can be seen in UK cities?

What different types of land-use can be seen in UK towns and cities?

Most urban areas show a similar pattern to the shape and structure of the land-use. A simple model of urban land-use reflects the history of towns and cities (Figure 20).

Figure 21 Inner city terraced houses

Further away from the centre are the **suburbs**. The inner suburbs have housing built in the 1920s and 30s. This is typically semi-detached housing with bay windows, gardens and garages.

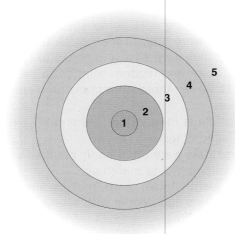

1	Central Business District
2	Zone of redevelopment
3	Inner-city housing
4	Inner suburbs
5	Outer suburbs

Figure 20 A simple model of urban land-use

The centre of a town or city is the historic core (a castle, church and older buildings) and the **Central Business District** (CBD) with shops and offices. Land values here are expensive and so buildings are often high rise.

Out from the CBD is a **zone of redevelopment**. Once an industrial area, the factories have closed down leaving the area derelict. Today, supermarkets and warehouse stores may locate here and some of the old industrial buildings get converted into luxury apartments.

Close by is the main area of **inner-city housing** dominated by Victorian terraced housing built to house the workers during the industrial revolution. Some of this old housing was replaced by high-rise flats during the 1950s and 60s but large areas of back-to-back terraced houses are still a feature of most inner cities.

Figure 22 1930s semi-detached housing

After the Second World War, large council estates were built in the 1950s and 60s often on the outskirts of the town as well. Since the 1970s, building has continued into the outer suburbs. Large private housing estates have been developed, filling in spaces and extending the city outwards.

Figure 23 Modern private housing

51

Since 1980, **out-of-town retail parks** and modern **industrial estates** have been built close to major roads on the edge of towns and cities. This continuous outward growth is called **urban sprawl**.

Activity

1 Draw your own diagram of the land-use model in Figure 20 (on page 51) and add labels to locate the different types of land-use found in each zone.

2 Draw a timeline to show the dates when the various types of buildings/land-use found in a typical UK town were built.

What has been done to improve the quality of life of people in UK towns and cities?

Quality of life depends on three main things:
- environmental quality, e.g. housing, air quality, open space
- economic factors – how much money you have
- social factors – access to shops and services.

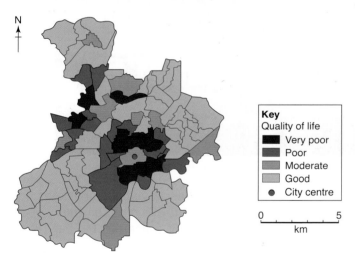

Figure 24 Quality of life in Nottingham

Figure 24 shows variations in the quality of life in Nottingham, and the pattern is typical of many urban areas of the UK. The lowest quality of life is found in the inner city, but there are also some poorer areas on the outskirts. The main problem in the inner city is housing quality and the decline of industry, which leads to unemployment and poverty. There have been many attempts to improve these areas.

In the 1950s and 60s many cities began a policy of **comprehensive redevelopment**. Bomb damage during the war and a **baby boom** meant that the country needed lots of new housing.

Areas of old housing were demolished and blocks of high-rise flats were built in their place (Figure 25). At that time they were easy and cheap to build and provided a quick and modern solution to the housing shortage. However, there were many problems with the schemes:
- Most residents missed the community spirit of the old terraced houses.
- High-rise flats were often badly planned and used poor-quality building materials.
- Lifts frequently broke down, making life difficult for pensioners and people with young children.
- Danger from fire.
- Problems of noise, vandalism and crime.
- Infestations of rats and insects.

Internet Research Activity

http://maps.google.co.uk

Visit Google maps and plan a route around your neighbourhood or nearby town. Use Street View to identify and locate the different types of housing and land-use mentioned on this page and page 51.

Figure 25 Comprehensive redevelopment, Bristol 1969

By the 1980s and 90s, many high-rise blocks were being pulled down.

By the 1980s the problems of inner city areas were getting worse. The government set up **urban regeneration schemes** to try to improve the worst affected areas. One of the first was London Docklands. Once the busiest port in the world, the area had become a wasteland with poor quality housing and high unemployment. Today the area has been transformed with luxury housing, businesses, shopping centres, leisure facilities and offices. However, the original residents could not afford the new housing and the new businesses often brought in workers from outside the area (Figure 26).

Figure 26 London Docklands before and after regeneration

Today, most improvement schemes are based on **urban renewal**. Housing is only demolished if it is absolutely necessary. Wherever possible the old housing is renovated to modern standards. Other aspects of the urban environment are also improved: trees and shrubs are planted, roads pedestrianised and street lighting upgraded (see Figure 27 and the Internet Research Activity).

Figure 27 Northmoor Home Zone, Manchester – an urban renewal scheme

Unfortunately, there is never enough money available to solve all the problems and there are still many areas with serious problems where the quality of life for people is very poor.

Activity

3 Make a list of the environmental, economic and social factors that may affect quality of life.

4 In groups, discuss the advantages and disadvantages of living in each of the areas shown in Figures 21–23 on page 51. Draw up a table to show your results.

5 Use an area of inner-city housing like the one shown in Figure 21 or choose an area of your own town. In groups discuss what you would do to improve the area under an urban renewal scheme.

Internet Research Activity

www.cardiffbay.co.uk

Visit the website for Cardiff Bay (a major urban regeneration scheme like London Docklands). Follow the links to 'Gallery' and use the photos of Cardiff Bay past and present to describe what Cardiff Bay was like and how the area has been improved.

How do social and environmental factors affect the lives of people living in cities?

What can be done about the problem of traffic congestion?

There has been a massive increase in road traffic. Between 1950 and 2010 the number of cars rose from 2.5 million to 31 million. Traffic congestion is a major problem in most towns and cities, particularly during the **rush hour**. The average speed of traffic in London is only 10 mph – the same as it was in 1900. Traffic also damages the environment, people are delayed getting to and from work and emergency services cannot get through.

In the past, solutions involved building bigger roads, urban motorways or by-passes such as the M25 London Orbital. It is now accepted that this only encourages more car use. It is also expensive, damages wildlife habitats, involves the demolition of buildings, creates even more noise and air pollution and makes life difficult for pedestrians. In recent years, urban areas have tried other ways to discourage people from using cars:

- Improving public transport – buses, urban railways and trams.
- Pedestrianising city centres and restricting access for private cars.
- Setting up **park and ride schemes** – parking is provided on the edge of the city with cheap and frequent bus services to transport people into the city centre using special bus lanes.
- Using cycle paths to make it easier and safer for cyclists.
- Multiple-occupancy car lanes that may only be used by cars carrying two or more people.

In London, a **congestion charge** has been introduced. Cars entering the centre of London at certain times of the day must pay a fee. This has cut down the amount of traffic and the money raised helps to pay for improvements to public transport.

Despite all these attempts, traffic congestion is still a major problem. People prefer the convenience of using cars. Using public transport can be expensive, difficult and time-consuming, particularly for elderly and disabled people and people with a lot of shopping or with young children.

Figure 28 Congestion charge sign, London

Activity

1   Solutions to the problem of traffic congestion usually involve penalising car drivers by making costs higher or providing incentives to encourage people to use public transport. Draw a table like the one below and list the penalties and types of encouragement that could be used.

Penalties	Incentives

Internet Research Activity

www.tfl.gov.uk/roadusers/congestioncharging

Visit the Congestion Charge section of the Transport for London website. Follow the links to 'Further information' (bottom right of page) and find out how congestion charging works and the benefits it brings.

How can the problem of shanty towns in LEDC cities be solved?

In the UK the best quality of life is usually found in the suburbs, with the poorest areas found in the inner cities. Cities in LEDCs show a different pattern. The wealthiest areas are often close to the centre and housing quality gets worse towards the edge of the city. The poorest areas are collections of shacks called **shanty towns** built by the huge numbers of migrants who move in from rural areas each day.

This type of housing is built on any unused land in the city but mostly it is found on the edge of the city, often up to 50 kilometres from the city centre.

The newcomers build their shacks out of any materials they can find – wood, corrugated iron, cardboard, etc. They are often very basic shelters and may have only one or two rooms for a large family. Much of the housing may lack basic amenities such as water, electricity, toilets and sewage disposal and the settlers usually have no legal rights to the land. These people have come to the city looking for a better life but it may be hard to find proper work. Instead they create their own employment – street-selling, shoe-shining, waste recycling, etc. Earnings are very low and most households only survive because children work as well as adults.

In the past, many cities tried to solve the problem of shanty towns by demolishing them. People were evicted and the area bulldozed. However, with nowhere else to go, the people just returned and rebuilt their shacks. Today it is recognised that a better solution is through **self-help schemes**. Land is divided up into plots connected to services such as water, electricity and proper drainage. People are then given help and materials to build their own houses (Figure 29).

Even without government help people gradually improve their houses. They connect to essential services, use more permanent building materials and add more luxury items as and when they can afford to. This can slowly turn shanty towns into better-quality suburbs. However, this can take 25–30 years and new migrants are arriving every day and adding to the problem.

Figure 29 Housing improvement through a self-help scheme, El Salvador, 2010

Figure 30 A shanty town in Jakarta, Indonesia

Internet Research Activity

- www.geography.learnontheinternet.co.uk/topics/urbanproblsledcs.html
- www.bbc.co.uk/learningzone/clips/shanty-town-growth-and-development-in-south-africa/1483.html

Find out more about the self-help schemes taking place in Brazil and South Africa.

Case Study

Kibera, Nairobi, Kenya

Nairobi is the capital city of Kenya, an LEDC in Africa. Like many cities in LEDCs the population has grown rapidly and overcrowding is a major problem: 45 per cent of the population live in shanty towns on just 6 per cent of the land area.

Kibera is one of the largest shanty towns, with 250,000 residents – the same as a city the size of Leicester. The shacks, made from mud, cardboard and tin sheeting, are packed so tightly that the average density is 110,000 people per square kilometre. There is no planning and the city provides no roads, sewage disposal, drainage, water or electricity. People must buy their water from tanks or kiosks at inflated prices. The only forms of sanitation are pit toilets shared by 50–500 people. It is not surprising that disease is common and death rates are high, particularly among children.

Activity

1 Describe the problems faced by people living in a typical shanty town.

2 Explain why people in shanty towns are often found on the outskirts of major cities.

Internet Research Activity

http://wn.com/kibera

Visit the World News website to view some of the video clips on Kibera. Using the video clips, make a list of the problems of Kibera and what is being done to help improve conditions.

Examiner's Tips

To help with your preparation for the exam, make sure that:

- you know that most cities in LEDCs are growing rapidly and that this is caused by rural–urban migration – people moving from country areas into cities
- you know that many cities in MEDCs are experiencing counter-urbanisation as people move away from the cities into more peaceful rural areas
- you can describe the different types of housing and land-use found in the different parts of a typical UK city
- you know the ways that governments have tried to improve the quality of life for people living in inner city areas using comprehensive redevelopment, urban regeneration projects and urban renewal schemes

- you know the benefits and problems of these schemes
- you know how city authorities are attempting to solve the problem of traffic congestion
- you know why so many people live in shanty towns in LEDC cities and what can be done to try to improve such areas.

Many of the topics in this section involve looking at issues where people have different views. Make sure that you understand the background to the issue and can explain why there are different views about it by giving the benefits and problems. For example: Why were high-rise flats built during the 1950s and 1960s? In what ways were high-rise flats better than the old terraced houses they replaced? What are the problems facing people who live in high-rise flats?

Examiner's Tips

Sample question

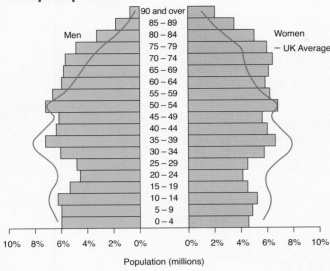

90 and over
85 – 89
80 – 84
75 – 79
70 – 74
65 – 69
60 – 64
55 – 59
50 – 54
45 – 49
40 – 44
35 – 39
30 – 34
25 – 29
20 – 24
15 – 19
10 – 14
5 – 9
0 – 4

Men

Women
— UK Average

10% 8% 6% 4% 2% 0%   0% 2% 4% 6% 8% 10%

Population (millions)

● The population of this town has been increasing in recent years due to counter-urbanisation.

● It is a small rural town in Sussex near the south coast of England about 70 miles from London.

● It takes just over an hour to travel into central London by train.

Source A A population pyramid for a south-coast town

1 Explain why high-rise flats were built in many inner cities in the UK during the 1950s and 60s.   [4]

2 Using Source A and your own knowledge, explain the population structure of this small town on the south coast of England.   [4]

3 Explain why it is so difficult to improve the quality of life of people living in poor-quality housing in cities in less economically developed countries (LEDCs).   [6]

Exam practice

1 Describe the type of housing you would expect to find in an inner city area of the UK.   [4]

2 Use Figure 18 (on page 49) and your own knowledge to explain the differences in growth of London (UK) and Mumbai (India).   [6]

3 Describe the measures that could be taken to reduce traffic congestion in a city in the UK.   [6]

What the examiner has to say!

1 To answer this question you must have done some revision. Don't just give a list of reasons and don't use bullet points. There are 4 marks so try to think of four reasons. Remember to elaborate (give something extra on each reason) and don't worry if you can't remember four reasons – just write in as much detail as you can about one or two.

2 This is another *source-based question* where you must also use your own knowledge. It is important to *look at the source very carefully* because it includes some important information. The main part of the source shows a population pyramid, but if you read the other information it tells you that the question is about counter-urbanisation. It's a tricky question!
To get full marks you should pick out the key features of the population pyramid and then try to explain these features. For example, there are a lot of old people in this town – why might this be?

3 The important thing here is that you read the question carefully. It asks you to write about housing in *LEDCs*. If you write about housing in the UK you will get no marks at all.

What factors are bringing about change to the world's climate?

What is the evidence for climate change?

The earth's climate has changed many times in the past. During the last million years there have been at least seven **ice ages** when the climate was colder and ice sheets spread across much of the earth's surface. The last ice age ended about 10,000 years ago.

Today, the term **climate change** is used to describe the more recent changes that have taken place over the last 100 years and which most scientists believe is caused by the actions of people.

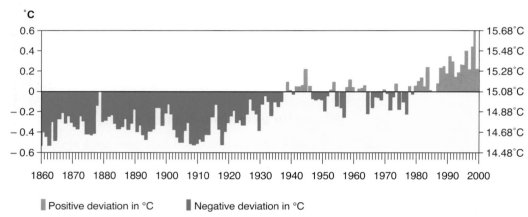

| Positive deviation in °C | Negative deviation in °C

Figure 31 Global temperatures 1860–2000

Figure 31 shows that temperatures have increased by an average of 0.6°C over the last 150 years and most of this global warming has happened during the past 20 years. In 2009, the UK's top ten warmest years (in order) were 2006, 2007, 2003, 2004, 2002, 2005, 1990, 1997, 1949 and 1999. Similar patterns can be seen around the world.

Even such a small rise in temperature is having an effect. The ice caps of Greenland and Antarctica are losing about 150 cubic kilometres of ice per year and mountain glaciers around the world are retreating. This melting is causing sea level to rise. In the last 100 years, sea level has risen by about 17 centimetres and most of this rise has taken place since 1998.

What causes climate change?

Most scientists believe that climate change is being caused by human activity. We are changing the way that the earth's atmosphere works and increasing a natural process called the **greenhouse effect**.

The sun sends out solar or short-wave radiation. Some of this solar radiation is reflected or absorbed by the atmosphere but the rest passes through and heats up the earth. At night, the earth gives off some of this heat as long-wave radiation. Some of the gases in the atmosphere can absorb long-wave radiation and this helps to keep the earth warm.

Most of the atmosphere is made up of nitrogen (78 per cent) and oxygen (21 per cent). These are vital for life but they do almost nothing to regulate the climate. The remaining 1 per cent is made up of trace gases such as water vapour, carbon dioxide and methane. These are called greenhouse gases because they stop the earth's heat from escaping back into space. Although the amount of these gases is relatively small they have a massive effect on our climate. This process is natural and very important. Without the greenhouse effect the earth would be about 30°C cooler.

However, the actions of people are increasing the amount of greenhouse gases in the atmosphere. This is increasing the greenhouse effect and causing the climate to warm up.

Carbon dioxide is released by deforestation and burning vegetation, but the main cause is when people burn **fossil fuels** such as coal, oil and natural gas. The more fuel and energy we use the more carbon dioxide is produced and the more the earth will warm up.

A few scientists disagree with the view that human activity is the cause of climate change. They believe that the changes we see are occurring naturally as they have done in the past. They argue that because the working of the atmosphere is so complicated, human actions will have virtually no impact. Instead they believe that changes in the sun's radiation or a slight shift in the earth's orbit are a much more likely explanation for climate change.

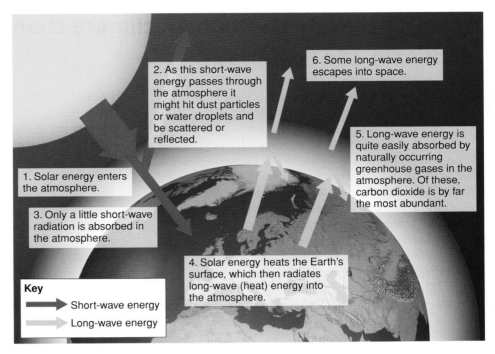

2. As this short-wave energy passes through the atmosphere it might hit dust particles or water droplets and be scattered or reflected.

6. Some long-wave energy escapes into space.

1. Solar energy enters the atmosphere.

5. Long-wave energy is quite easily absorbed by naturally occurring greenhouse gases in the atmosphere. Of these, carbon dioxide is by far the most abundant.

3. Only a little short-wave radiation is absorbed in the atmosphere.

4. Solar energy heats the Earth's surface, which then radiates long-wave (heat) energy into the atmosphere.

Key
➡ Short-wave energy
➡ Long-wave energy

Figure 32 The greenhouse effect

Activity

1 Use Figure 31 to describe recent changes in the earth's climate.

2 Make a copy of Figure 32 and add your own labels to show how the greenhouse effect works.

3 Draw up a diary for a typical day in your life. Alongside each entry put a tick if what you are doing is adding greenhouse gases to the atmosphere and add a sentence to explain how.

Internet Research Activity

● **http://globalwarming.com**
● **http://news.bbc.co.uk/cbbcnews/hi/find_out/guides/world/global_warming/newsid_1575000/1575441.stm**
● **http://epa.gov/climatechange/kids/index.html**

There are numerous websites which look at the issue of climate change and global warming. Visit one of the above to find out more about the greenhouse effect and how the actions of people are causing climate change.

What are the likely effects of climate change for people and societies?

What will be the impact of climate change?

The world's climate is changing. Scientists predict that global temperatures will rise by between 1°C and 3°C by the end of this century. This is already having effects that we can see. In the future, climate change may bring some benefits but also many problems.

- Rainfall patterns will change. In some parts of the world rainfall will increase and enable more food to be grown but in many of the poorest areas of the world rainfall will decrease. Severe drought may cause crop failure and starvation for millions of people.
- Extreme or unusual weather events will become more common and less predictable. In the UK, heavier summer storms may increase the risk of flash floods. Around the world, warmer sea temperatures could lead to more frequent and stronger hurricanes.
- Habitats for plants and animals will change – some species will move into new areas but many will not be able to adapt to the new conditions quickly enough and will die out. Up to 30 per cent of the world's plants and animals may risk extinction.
- Melting ice caps could increase sea level by up to half a metre over the next 100 years. This will increase the risk of flooding for millions of people who live in low-lying coastal areas – for example, Bangladesh.

Case Study

Polar bears

The species at greatest risk from climate change will be those that live in a very restricted range of environments. One of the best known is the polar bear. Polar bears live in Arctic regions and wander across the frozen sea ice hunting for seals – their main source of food. With climate change, the Arctic sea ice is melting more quickly. Polar bears are finding it more difficult to hunt for seals and are facing starvation. The number of polar bears is declining rapidly.

Figure 33 Polar bears – a species at risk from climate change

Activity

1 Complete a table like the one below, showing the likely effects of climate change.

Climate change effect	Impact on people/ environment	Example

2 Describe some of the impacts that a sea level rise of 1 metre would have on a country like the UK. What would the government have to do to protect the people?

3 Explain why people living in LEDCs are more likely to suffer the worst effects of climate change.

Could the effects of climate change get even worse?

Although most scientists agree on the likely effects of climate change, it is difficult to know exactly what will happen.

Weather is unpredictable and extreme events are not uncommon. The rainfall that caused flooding in many parts of the UK in July 2007 was 20 per cent higher than the previous record, but it is impossible to link this one event to climate change. In the same way, the record low temperatures in 2010 do not mean that global warming has stopped.

Most of the predictions give a range of effects. For example, a sea level rise of 30–50 centimetres by 2100 is thought to be most likely. However, computer models show that sea levels could rise by as little as 10 centimetres or as much as 1 metre.

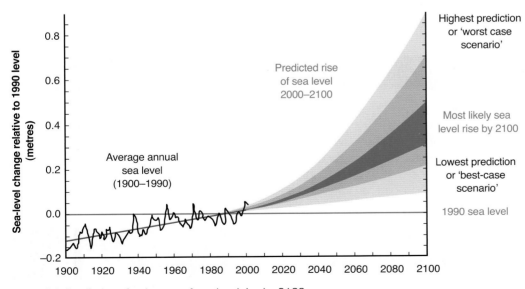

Figure 34 Predictions for the rate of sea-level rise by 2100

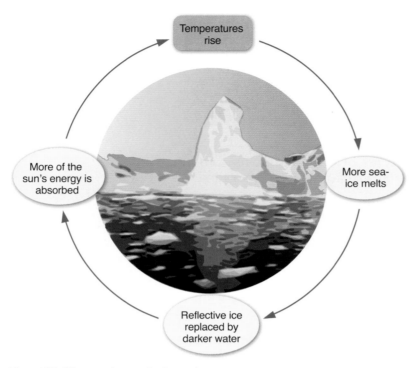

Figure 35 Climate-change tipping-point

Some scientists are concerned that the effects could be even worse. This is because of **tipping-points** which speed up the process. One possible tipping-point is the melting of ice. Ice-covered surfaces are white and reflect much of the sun's radiation back into space. When ice melts, it is replaced by darker rocks or water that absorb more radiation and heat up more quickly. This could speed up the process of warming, and so more ice melts, and so on.

Activity

1 Work in groups. Imagine that you are a group of scientists writing a report about the likely effect of climate change on sea levels.

a Use the graph in Figure 34 (on page 61) to describe how sea levels might change by 2100.

b Use Figure 35 to explain what is meant by a tipping point and why this could make sea levels rise even higher.

c Research some of the possible impacts of sea-level rise around the world. (You might consider: countries or regions that would be most affected; the impact on people; what could be done to reduce the effects.)

Case Study

The Greenland ice sheet

At the current rate of melting, the Greenland ice sheet would add about 1 metre to global sea levels over the next 1,000 years. However, there is evidence that the rate of melting is increasing. If the tipping-point is reached, it could cause the whole ice cap to melt within a few hundred years. This would raise sea levels by over 7 metres. It would cause a global catastrophe as virtually every major city in the world would be flooded and billions of people would be affected.

Internet Research Activity

www.tuvaluislands.com

Follow the links to the section on climate change.

http://media.adelaidenow.com.au/multimedia/2008/10/tuvalu/tuvalu-perthnow.html

This site has a good multi-media presentation exploring the problems facing the island.

How should people and society respond to climate change?

What can governments do to help reduce climate change?

Figure 36 shows the amount of greenhouse gas emissions around the world. There is huge variation between countries. This can make it difficult to get international agreement about tackling climate change.

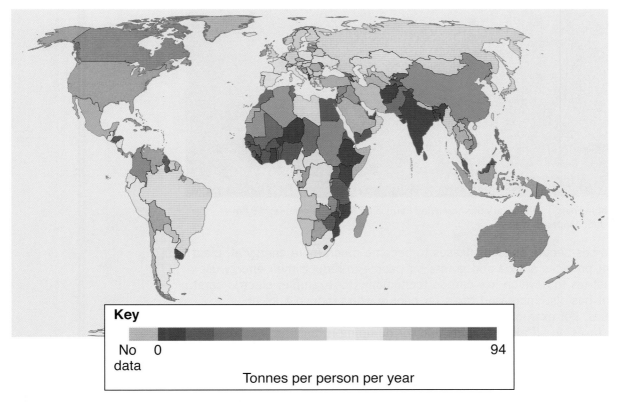

Key

No data   0   94

Tonnes per person per year

Figure 36 Global greenhouse gas emissions per person in 2000

MEDCs are responsible for about 75 per cent of the increased CO_2, but the worst effects of climate change will be felt in LEDCs. Newly-industrialising countries (NICs) like China or India feel that it is unfair to expect them to take action which might slow down their growth and development.

The first international conference on climate change was held in Brazil in 1992 when a UN agreement on tackling climate change was signed. In 1997 the **Kyoto Protocol** required MEDCs to reduce their emissions by 5 per cent by 2012. However, the USA, the biggest producer of CO_2, refused to sign the agreement because it would damage their economy. In 2009 a new agreement was signed in Copenhagen, but again not all countries signed up to it.

In the UK, the government passed the **Climate Change Act** in 2008 which aims to cut UK emissions by 80 per cent. By 2050, 40 per cent of all our electricity should come from renewable sources such as wind turbines and nuclear power. Both of these cause a lot of public concern. Some people think that giant wind farms are ugly and spoil the environment. Many people are against nuclear power because of the dangerous waste it produces and the risk of a major accident such as the one at Chernobyl in the Ukraine in 1986.

Figure 37 Renewable energy – Rhyl Flats Offshore Wind Farm is a 25-turbine wind farm 8 km north-east of Llandudno in North Wales

This act also forces people and businesses to become much more energy efficient. The government provides advice and grants for people to reduce their energy use and helps industries to develop low carbon technology (for example, electric cars). The government has also increased taxes for people who produce a lot of greenhouse gases. For example, road tax is higher for cars that use more fuel, and there are extra taxes on all airline flights and for dumping rubbish at landfill sites.

Activity

1 Use Figure 36 (page 63) to explain why it is so difficult to get international agreements on how to reduce greenhouse gas emissions.

2 Explain what is meant by renewable energy.

3 Work in groups to discuss the arguments for and against using nuclear power to generate electricity. What is your own view on this issue?

What can individuals do to help prevent climate change?

Most people today understand why we need to cut down on our use of energy and so reduce our **carbon footprint**. By reducing the tax on cars that use less fuel, the government hopes that people will buy more fuel-efficient cars. People are also being encouraged to use public transport more and cut down on unnecessary car journeys by walking or cycling.

The largest use of energy in the home is for heating and hot water. New buildings must be properly insulated but many older houses lose up to 60 per cent of their heat through the walls and roof. Government grants can help homeowners to install wall and roof insulation and to draught-proof doors and windows.

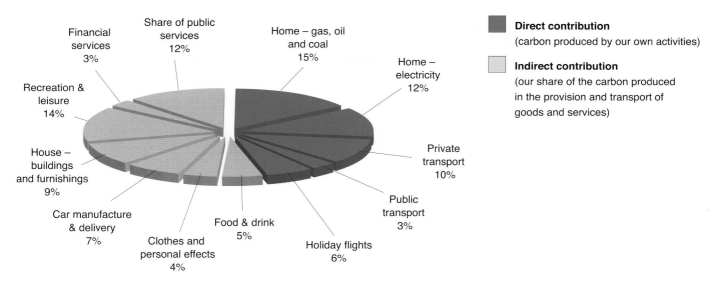

Figure 38 The average carbon footprint of a person living in the UK

There are many things we can do to save energy in the home but some are easier and cheaper than others:
- Install modern, more efficient central heating boilers or simply turn down the thermostat.
- Change light bulbs – by 2012 only low-energy bulbs will be on sale, but many people still use traditional bulbs which use 80 per cent more electricity.
- Turn off the lights as you go out of a room.
- Buy energy-efficient appliances such as washing machines, refrigerators, etc.
- Don't keep TVs and computers on stand-by – this can account for 10 per cent of household electricity use, and over the whole of the UK it is equivalent to the output from two medium-sized power stations.

We can also reduce our carbon footprint by making changes to our lifestyle.

The food and clothes we buy have often been transported huge distances. Choosing local produce reduces these **food miles** and global emissions. Households should also cut down on waste and recycle as much waste as possible. Recycling uses less energy than making materials from new and it saves the world's natural resources. Most household waste is dumped in land-fill sites and over time these give off methane which is a major greenhouse gas.

Activity

4   Consider your own household. How good are you at saving energy? What other measures could you take to try to reduce your carbon footprint?

5   Design and produce posters that could be used in your school to persuade students and staff to save energy.

Internet Research Activity

- http://actonco2.direct.gov.uk/home.html
- http://footprint.wwf.org.uk

Visit the government's website set up to encourage people to reduce their carbon footprint, and explore what the government is doing and what individuals can do to reduce carbon emissions.

You could also calculate your own carbon footprint at the WWF's site.

Examiner's Tips

Because learning outcome 3 (Exploring ways in which cultural, economic, environmental, moral and political factors interact through a study of issues connected with the world's climate) covers only one major issue – climate change – you will be expected to give greater detail in you answers.

In simple terms you need to understand the causes of climate change, the likely effects of climate change, and what can be done to try to solve the problem or make the effects less severe.

So to help with your preparation for the exam, make sure that you:

● know what the evidence is that the world's climate is changing
● can describe how the greenhouse effect works and can explain how the activities of people – e.g. burning fossil fuels – leads to global warming
● understand why some people feel that the problem is being exaggerated
● can explain the likely effects of climate change and the impacts these may have on people and animals
● understand why it is difficult to get international agreement about how to solve the problem of climate change
● understand why it is important for governments to pass laws to help reduce greenhouse gas emissions
● know what individuals should do to reduce their carbon footprint.

Sample questions

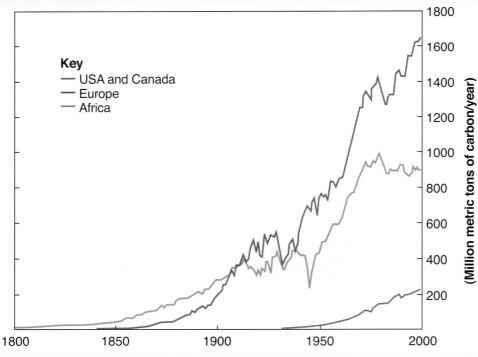

Source A Variations in annual carbon emissions 1800–2000

1 Use Source A and your own knowledge to explain why the amount of carbon emissions vary in different parts of the world. [4]

2 'There is very little that I can do to stop global warming and climate change. It is up to the government – they should be doing a lot more.' To what extent do you agree with this view? [8]
In your answer you should:
- *describe the ways individuals can reduce their carbon footprint*
- *consider what measures the UK government could take to cut down on carbon emissions*
- *say how far you agree with the statement.*

Exam practice

1 What does Figure 36 (on page 63) tell you about world greenhouse gas emissions? [2]
2 Explain how the actions of people are causing global warming. [6]
3 'Using more renewable energy such as wind farms is the best way of solving the problem of climate change.' To what extent do you agree with this statement? [8]

What the examiner has to say!

1 This question expects you to use the source *and your own knowledge* in your answer. You need to study the source and say what it tells you about variations in carbon emissions. Look at the differences in the amounts between the three areas but also look at the trends over time. However, if this is all you do the maximum you will get is 2 marks.
To get more marks you need to give reasons for the differences you have noted – say *why* the carbon emissions of the USA & Canada, Europe, and Africa vary.

2 This type of question asks you to make a *judgement* about a statement.
The statement will usually give a very one-sided view but there will often be arguments that you could use both for and against it. There are 8 marks available so it is important to do it well. The examiner will offer you advice (given in italics) about how to structure your answer. *You should always follow this advice.*
Write in proper sentences about each of the first two parts of the question and then finish up by giving your views on the issue. In the last part try to give a full *summary* – don't just repeat the points you have already made.

How can the lives of ordinary people be affected by the experience of war?

How can ordinary families be directly threatened by war?

The Second World War had a profound effect on the lives of the people of the UK. War was declared on Germany on 3 September 1939. Air raids were expected on UK cities, so everyone had to get ready for them.

The '**Blitz**' was the almost continuous bombing of the UK by the Luftwaffe, the German air force, between September 1940 and May 1941. One of the first places to be bombed was London, which would be attacked for 57 consecutive nights.

London was not the only city to be bombed. The Luftwaffe targeted other important centres, including military bases, industrial plots, ports, docks and civilian areas. Places such as Belfast, Birmingham, Bristol, Cardiff, Coventry, Glasgow, Hull, Sheffield, Swansea, Liverpool, Portsmouth and Southampton suffered very heavy air raids and large numbers of civilian casualties. High explosive and incendiary (fire-making) bombs were used.

Source A

These are memories from Alan Hartley who was 16 in November 1940 when Coventry was attacked. He served as an **ARP** warden during the night. Over 500 people were killed and more than 4,000 buildings destroyed in the raid. The source appeared in *The Guardian* newspaper in September 2010.

The bombs were coming straight at us. It's the most terrifying experience to stand there hearing the bombs from a distance and them getting louder and louder and louder, wondering how many they have got left and are you going to be next?

Figure 1 London during the Blitz

Source B

This source is taken from the memories of an ARP warden who worked in London during the Blitz in 1940. The memories were published in a book about the Blitz in 2002.

After a heavy air raid there was the task of piecing the bodies together in preparation for burial. The smell was the worst thing about it – that, and realising that these pieces of flesh had once been living, breathing people. It gave us grim satisfaction to put together a body, but there was always the odd limb which did not fit and legs left over.

Why did the Luftwaffe target these places?

Liverpool and Hull were important ports and necessary for the import of goods needed to fight a war. They were the most heavily bombed places after London. Birmingham and Coventry were attacked because they had factories which produced Spitfires and tanks.

Another reason for targeting different cities was to spread panic and despair among the civilian population with acts of terror bombing.

The effects of these sustained bombing campaigns were, in many places, devastating. Large numbers of civilians were killed or injured in the Blitz. By May 1941 over 43,000 civilians had been killed, over half of them in London. Hundreds of thousands of homes were destroyed and every week in September 1940, 50,000 people were made homeless. Industrial areas, factories and the railways were increasingly attacked and bombed. Coventry was almost totally destroyed, including its famous cathedral.

During the Second World War, the idea of targeting your enemy's civilian population was generally accepted as part of the way in which a war was fought. It was felt that by causing panic, breaking **morale** and disrupting the lives of ordinary people a country might lose the will to fight. That this never happened in the UK can perhaps be explained by the precautions taken by the government to protect the civilian population.

Activity

1 Read the reasons why the Luftwaffe bombed the UK. Put these reasons in order of importance. Give reasons for your choice.

2 How useful are Sources A and B to a historian studying air raids on the UK during the Second World War?

Figure 2 The remains of Coventry cathedral after the bombing raid in November 1940, in which over 500 people were killed

What methods were used to protect the civilian population?

To warn people of an air raid, sirens went off. Everyone was expected to stop what they were doing and take shelter. The government produced films and held civil defence practices to show people what to do in the event of an air raid.

Shelters

Anderson shelters were given to people living in areas expected to be bombed by the Luftwaffe. The shelters were made from curved corrugated steel sheets and could hold up to six people. They were half-buried in the ground with earth piled on top. Over three million Anderson shelters were issued, but people were reluctant to use them at night because they were dark and damp and sometimes they even flooded.

Many people living in the large industrial cities did not have gardens where Anderson shelters could be erected. Communal shelters were built in many towns which could hold up to 50 people. In March 1941 the government began issuing Morrison shelters. These were put in living rooms and provided shelter for two or three people.

The effectiveness of these shelters was questioned by the government, who realised that air-raid shelters on the surface did not offer protection from high explosive bombs. Deeper shelters were then used.

In London people used the Underground stations during the Blitz. The underground was popular because it was dry, warm and reasonably safe, though

not totally so – over 600 people were killed at Balham tube station in October 1940 during an air raid on London.

Blackouts and ARPs

To make things difficult for the German bombers, a **'blackout'** was established. People could be fined for showing a light at night during the blackout. Street lights were switched off, and Air Raid Wardens or the 'ARP' patrolled the streets looking out for any breaches of the blackout regulations. ARP wardens also helped rescue people from bombed-out buildings and recover dead bodies.

Gas masks

Millions of gas masks were issued because it was feared that the Germans would use poison gas bombs. It became an offence not to carry your gas mask at all times. Although the civilian population was never attacked using poison gas, they did need protection from the bombing of UK cities.

The Home Guard

The UK was organised to fight a total war. Women were conscripted in 1941 and many men too old to fight or considered unfit for military service joined the 'Local Defence Volunteers', which became the 'Home Guard', or more popularly known as 'Dad's Army'. They were given the tasks of defending the country in the event of a German invasion, protecting vital buildings such as factories and gas works, and looking out for German paratroopers and airmen who had been shot down. To begin with, the Home Guard did not have any uniforms or weapons because there was a great shortage of both. Eventually they were armed and provided a reassuring presence in towns and villages up and down the UK.

Figure 3 An Anderson shelter in a garden in London in 1940. They were very strong and could keep people safe even if a bomb landed quite close. Many people put flowers and vegetables on the top of the shelters.

Activity

1 Make a list of the methods used to keep the civilian population safe during the war. Which method do you think was the most successful? Give reasons for your choice.

2 Look at Figure 3 and read about air raid shelters. How effective do you think these were in protecting civilians from bombing in the Second World War?

3 How important was the London Underground in protecting civilians during the Blitz?

How can people's lives be influenced by government policy?

How can government policy affect people's lives during wartime?

One way in which the government attempted to keep up morale was to ensure that children were kept safe during the Second World War. The **evacuation** of children from the cities and major industrial areas to the countryside began in the UK on 30 August 1939, three days before war with Germany was officially declared. The experience of evacuation would affect many millions of children.

The UK was divided up into three zones or areas – neutral, evacuation and reception. Areas like North Wales and parts of South Wales, Devon, Cornwall and Scotland were designated reception areas for **evacuees** and received children evacuated from Liverpool, Birmingham and London. Evacuation was introduced to move children of school age, teachers, mothers with children under the age of five and disabled people out of the cities to the countryside where there was little risk of bombing raids.

Evacuation was voluntary, but the government expected more than three million people to take advantage of the scheme. A poster campaign was launched to persuade parents to send their children out of the threatened cities. As many as two million people, mostly mothers with children, made their own private arrangements to stay with relatives or friends. Some children were even sent abroad to places like Canada.

Children to be evacuated were assembled in their school playgrounds. They were given name tags and had to carry their gas masks. They were allowed to take with them only what they could carry. The evacuees usually travelled by train or coach to their destinations, where they were met by the people who were to house them. Host families were encouraged to volunteer to take in the evacuees by the government. Most of those evacuated had no idea where they were going, what their life as an evacuee would be like, when they would be able to return home, nor when or if they would ever see their parents again.

Figure 4 Children boarding trains ready to be evacuated to the countryside – this scene would be repeated in many cities all across the UK in 1939

What impact did evacuation have on society in the UK?

For many children, evacuation was a threatening and scary experience. Many had never been away from home or from their parents before, and now they were expected to live with total strangers. The government hoped that families and even whole schools might be kept together, but this was not always possible. Foster parents had to cope with problems such as homesickness and bed-wetting, brought on by their fears.

The children from the cities not only had to cope with a new family but a different culture. For some city children the way of life in the countryside seemed almost primitive (see Source A). For many others, life in the countryside turned out to be a very pleasant and enjoyable experience (see Source B).

Source A

Betty Taylor remembers her time as an evacuee from Bristol to the village of Bream in the Forest of Dean. Betty recounted her experiences 60 years after the war ended.

Having come from a modern house it was like going back in time. The toilet was half way up the garden. There was no running water. The house was sunless. I was just so homesick, you can't describe the feeling. Each time mum came to visit I thought she was going to take us home but she didn't.

Source B

June Fryer remembers her time as an evacuee from Bristol to Cornwall with her sister in 1939. June recounted her experiences 60 years after the war ended.

We were taken in by the harbourmaster and his wife but they had no children of their own. They lived in a luxurious bungalow overlooking the harbour. When we got there they bathed us and we had a huge bedroom just for me and my sister. To us it was pure luxury because when we were at home we had to be five in one bedroom. When we got up next morning we had two boiled eggs with toast soldiers for breakfast.

A number of Liverpool schools were evacuated to North Wales with their teachers. Local schools were forced to operate a 'shift' system where the local children were taught in the morning and evacuees in the afternoons. This caused resentment amongst local parents because their children now only got a half-day education. The fact that large numbers of these children from Liverpool were Catholic was an added complication in areas where most people attended Nonconformist chapels.

In many parts of South Wales there was also a language problem as many people there spoke Welsh as a first language and most of the evacuees came from England. Some host families were perhaps not as welcoming to the evacuees as might have been hoped (see Source C).

Some children fared better than others and their experience of life in the countryside was very beneficial – rosy red cheeks, sunshine, fresh country air and fresh food. The children from some of the inner city slums had often been ill and under-fed. Their appearance shocked many country people and helped convince them that once the war was over, free health care for all was needed.

Source C

From an article which appeared in a local newspaper in North Wales, written by the mother of a 'host' family who looked after two brothers from Birkenhead in 1940. The article was published in 1990.

Coming into our homes, dressed in rags, unclean, untidy with their shaved heads covered in purple dye. These children were wild. They had no manners. We had two toilets in our house and yet one child actually 'went' in the corner of the room. The ration allowance we were given was never enough to feed them and we had to share our own food rations with them. Were they grateful? – not a bit of it.

Activity

1 Describe the way in which evacuation was carried out.

2 Look at Sources A, B and C. Why did some children have very different experiences during evacuation?

How can whole populations be mobilised to fight a 'total' war?

How can the war effort be organised by governments?

Conscription

On 3 September 1939, parliament passed the National Service (Armed Forces) Act under which all men between the ages of 18 and 41 became liable for conscription. Conscription means that these men had to join the armed forces if called upon to do so and fight for their country. Conscription of men into the armed forces had begun in March 1939, when men between the ages of 20 and 21 were 'called up'. After the failure of appeasement, the UK government realised that war with Germany was inevitable and preparations for war began in earnest.

Women at war

The contribution made by women in the Second World War was far greater than it had been between 1914 and 1918. Women were at first encouraged to enlist in the armed services, the ATS, WAAF and the WRNS.

In December 1941, the National Service Act (Number 2) made the conscription of women legal. At first only single women aged 20 to 30 were 'called up'. By 1943, 90 per cent of single women and 80 per cent of married women were employed in essential war work. Day nurseries were set up by local authorities to enable married women to return to work.

Although women were not expected to fight, they provided valuable supporting roles, filling sandbags, packing parachutes and operating search lights and **AA guns**. The 93rd Searchlight Regiment was all female. Civilian and military hospitals relied overwhelmingly on female nurses and this became a highly regarded contribution made by women to the war effort.

Many industries, including factories and farming, suffered severe labour shortages when men were conscripted into the armed forces. Women were conscripted to work in factories producing all kinds of war materials. Women also worked on the railways, canals and buses. By the end of 1943, nearly 60 per cent of all workers in the UK were women.

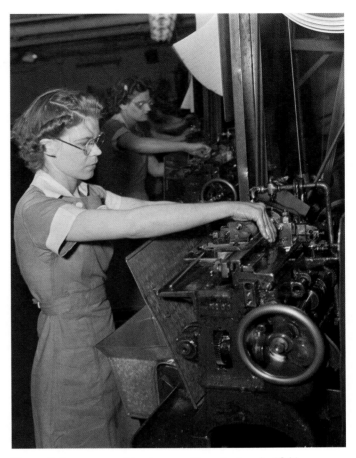

Figure 5 A woman working in a munitions factory in 1941

Source D

From the memories of Nellie Brook, who left a munitions factory because of poor health to work building Lancaster bombers. Her account was published in 2008.

I was told that my services were needed at A V Roe where they made Lancaster bombers. To get there we were taken out into the country. When you arrived you never thought there was a factory there; it was so well camouflaged, but once you went inside it was amazing. No windows, all these hundreds of people of both sexes all working away like ants. All doing different jobs to produce one of the UK's finest planes.

Activity

3 How useful is Source D to a historian studying the contribution made by women during the Second World War?

4 Describe the contribution made by women to the war effort.

The shortage of labour on the farms was met by the re-formation of the Women's Land Army in 1938. Women would be trained in agricultural work, tree-felling, rat-catching, horticulture and general farm work, leaving male farm-workers free to go to war. The Land Army helped double food production by 1943.

The Women's Voluntary Service (WVS) was formed in 1938. It coped with evacuees and orphans and helped set up rest centres and mobile canteens for troops. The WVS provided clothing exchanges and encouraged knitting to become a female obsession. Schemes gave advice on recycling and making clothes last longer; two of these were 'Make Do and Mend' and 'Sew and Save'.

This was not the end of women's contribution to the war effort. They were often expected to run the home alone, deal with **rationing** and food shortages, queue for hours for food, look after their children and go out to work.

Keeping up morale

It was essential that the government maintained a positive attitude to the war so that morale and people's spirits could be kept high. The Ministry of Information ran a poster campaign to help maintain morale. The press, cinema and radio were controlled or 'censored' by the government. Successes in the war such as the Battle of Britain and El Alamein were well publicised, as well as stories of heroism and courage during the Blitz. Failures and set-backs, such as the war in the Atlantic, received much less attention.

The 'war time spirit; never say die' attitude was personified by Winston Churchill. He became prime minister on 10 May 1940, and very soon became the symbol of defiance against Hitler. His frequent visits to the bombed areas of London and his famous 'V for Victory' gesture inspired ordinary people to keep fighting. Above all, it was his inspirational speeches broadcast on the radio which encouraged the 'Bulldog spirit'.

Government control extended over most aspects of people's lives during the war. There were strict penalties for spreading panic and alarm. Posters encouraged people not to engage in 'careless talk'. All sections of society were made to feel that they were 'doing their bit' for the war effort. Children were encouraged to collect scrap metal and take part in the 'Dig for Victory' campaign (see page 75).

Figure 6 One of the many **propaganda** posters encouraging women to help in the war effort in the home

Source A

Churchill's first speech as prime minister in May 1940.

I have nothing to offer but blood, toil, sweat and tears … You ask what is our aim? I can answer in one word: Victory – victory at all costs, victory in spite of all terror; victory, however long and hard the road may be.

How can the people be fed during wartime?

One way the government attempted to keep up morale was to make sure that the population was properly fed. A method had to be devised so that all people had a fair and equal share of the available food, as well as a healthy and balanced diet. In fact, war-time diets, with an absence of sugars and most fats, were far healthier than pre-war diets.

Rationing

Rationing was introduced in January 1940 and was run by the Ministry of Food. Ration books were distributed to the population and people soon became aware of how much food and other items they were allowed to buy for that week. Once an item had been bought, a mark was made in the ration book. 'Food Facts', which helped people make food that was always in short supply go further, as well as recipes for nutritional meals, were printed in newspapers and magazines. Potatoes, which were readily available, formed the basis of many recipes for sandwiches, cakes and puddings.

Two cartoon characters appeared – Dr Carrot and Potato Pete. 'Eat Us' was their message. 'Food Flashes' appeared on the radio, and people got used to making do with less food, and using substitutes like carrots in cake instead of sugar.

Dig for Victory

The 'Dig for Victory' campaign encouraged people to grow more food for themselves. Allotments became prized possessions; school fields and golf courses were dug up and planted with vegetables. Every available piece of land was used, including grass verges at the sides of roads.

The Black Market

Rationing was essential if the population of the UK was to fight the war effectively. Many goods other than food were strictly rationed. Petrol was rationed in September 1939, and by 1942 petrol was not available for private use. Clothes were rationed in 1941, and by 1942 coal was increasingly difficult to get. Most households still relied on coal fires for heating and coal-fired stoves for cooking and hot water.

Rationing was successful. Britain did become much more self-sufficient. Gardens and parks filled with vegetables. However for those people with money, many items in short supply might be available to buy on the '**Black Market**'. This was run by people who became known as 'spivs' and who could supply many items that were not available by more conventional

means – chocolate, razor blades, nylon stockings, food and petrol. There were severe penalties for people who were caught running the 'Black Market' but this did not deter people from trying to obtain items which had now become almost luxuries.

By the end of the war in 1945, Britain had been at war for one day short of six years. With the end of the war in sight, people were determined to create a better world for themselves and, especially, for their children – a 'New Jerusalem', almost – once the war was over. Indeed, planning for the post-war world had begun as early as 1942 with the publication of the **Beveridge** Report on welfare provision (see page 77).

Source B

This source is taken from the diary of Edna Davies, who lived in North Wales during the Second World War.

We're not too well off for food in this country right now … There's very little meat … but no cheese, not many eggs, only half a pound of bacon a week … some very unsatisfying sausages when you can get them. (23 January 1941)

We haven't had any green vegetable lately. All I could get was a lettuce and the price had doubled … We saw a soldier eat an orange … Did our mouths water. He made the most of it because he even ate the peel. (4 May 1941)

Source C

This source is taken from a GCSE history book written by a modern historian, about life in the UK in the twentieth century, published in 2003.

To say that the people of the UK went hungry during World War Two is a myth. It is true that basic foodstuffs were strictly rationed from January 1940, but the ration books enabled everyone to buy adequate amounts of food. The same amount of food was available to everyone. Rationing had the effect of actually improving the diets of many people.

Activity

1 Explain why Sources B and C have different views about rationing.

2 What was the 'Black Market' and why was it resented by ordinary people?

Examiner's Tips

Sample questions

1 Study the photograph of an Anderson shelter (Figure 3, page 70). How useful is the photo to a historian studying air-raid precautions used during the Second World War? [4]

2 Study Sources B and C (page 75). Why do Sources B and Source C give different views about the effects of rationing? [6]

3 'Evacuation was not a success. It caused far too many children and parents unnecessary stress.' How far do you agree with this statement? [8]

What the examiner has to say!

1 ● Study the source carefully. *Describe* clearly what the source shows you. Do not ignore the attribution of the source – this will tell you when the photograph was taken and, usually, where.

● *Remember your own knowledge* – how many Anderson shelters were distributed and where? Think about where the shelters were placed and how strong they were.

● A very important point to remember is that this is one source showing one example of air-raid precautions. Clearly, one source cannot tell you everything, but it is still very useful.

● To achieve 4 marks, you must suggest that the source is very useful to the historian but that it cannot tell the historian everything about air-raid precautions. Other evidence is needed – give some examples.

2 ● You must read both sources very carefully. In your answer you should consider the authorship and content of both sources. This is the clue to answering this question well.

– You should consider that the sources were written by different people at different times.

– The sources say different things about rationing – give examples of these differences.

– Source A was written by someone who lived in North Wales during the war and experienced rationing – consider the strengths of this.

– Source B is the view of a modern historian – consider the strengths of this; this historian has the benefit of hindsight and access to other evidence denied to the eyewitness.

– Remember your own knowledge about rationing – you have to consider *why* the sources are different, *not* who is right or wrong about rationing.

3 ● To answer this question you must think carefully about the experiences of the children who were evacuated, their mothers who were sometimes left behind in the cities or their fathers who might be away fighting in the armed forces.

● You must also consider the experiences of the 'host' families who volunteered to take in evacuated children, who sometimes already had children of their own.

● When you have considered all the different experiences you should be able to provide a balanced answer to a question about evacuation.

● To achieve level 3 (6 marks) you must consider *both* the positive and negative aspects of evacuation. Begin by writing about how and why evacuation was introduced.

● Consider the evidence for the positive experiences of evacuees and host families.

● Consider the evidence for the negative experiences of evacuees and host families.

● To achieve 7 or 8 marks you *must* make a judgement and justify it, e.g. 'evacuation was a success because…, however…'.

Exam practice

1 What does Figure 4 (on page 71) tell you about the way in which evacuation was carried out? [2]

2 How useful is Figure 3 (on page 70) to a historian studying methods used to protect civilians from bombing in the Second World War? [4]

3 What do Sources A and B (on page 68) tell you about the effects of bombing? [4]

4 Why do Sources B and C (on page 72) give different views about evacuation? [6]
(In your answer, you should consider both the content and the authors of the sources.)

5 'During World War Two evacuation provided children with the best experience of their lives.' How far do you agree with this statement? [8]
(In your answer you should consider how children's lives were affected, both positive and negative aspects; and whether or not you agree with this view.)

How can economic, political and social issues affect people's lives?

How can governments plan for peace after a major conflict?

The Beveridge Report

During the Second World War a committee was set up to plan for the rebuilding of the UK after the war had ended. The main aim was to improve welfare provision. A very important report was written by William Beveridge and published in 1942, when it was far from certain that the war would be won.

Beveridge identified five main problems facing the UK and its people. He referred to these problems as five 'Giants':
- want – a lack of food and the basics of life
- disease – avoiding illness
- idleness – unemployment
- ignorance – a lack of education
- **squalor** – living in poverty.

Beveridge said that each of these five 'Giants' would have to be overcome before a better society could be created in the UK.

The Report suggested ways in which the five 'Giants' could be overcome: the government should introduce more insurance schemes; build more houses; bring in child allowance; set up a National Health Service; create full employment; and provide free secondary education for all pupils up to the age of fifteen. The idea was that all people in the UK would be protected, in Beveridge's words, 'from the cradle to the grave'. Beveridge was clear that his welfare proposals should be universal – everybody in the UK would benefit, not just the poorest.

A new National Insurance scheme would be set up. Everybody would pay part of their wages to the government. In return, workers would receive money if they were sick or unemployed.

These benefits, Beveridge argued, would be available to everybody regardless of how much money they had. In this way a minimum standard of living would be established.

The 1944 Education Act

One of the first acts to be passed was the 1944 Education Act. Secondary education was now free from the age of eleven, so everybody could go to a secondary school. The school leaving age was raised to fifteen. Local Education Authorities would run all state primary and secondary schools.

In the last year of primary school, all pupils took the Eleven Plus examination to decide what sort of secondary school they would go to. Grammar schools selected the most able pupils who had passed the Eleven Plus. All pupils who failed the exam would go to Secondary Modern schools. Technical schools were for those pupils with good practical skills. Despite the fact that many people criticised the Eleven Plus exam as being unfair, secondary education was now freely available to all.

Activity

1 What were Beveridge's five 'Giants'?

2 What does the phrase 'the cradle to the grave' mean?

3 Describe three changes that took place in education after 1944.

Homes for all

By 1944, the UK was suffering a severe housing shortage. Beveridge had identified squalor as one of the five 'Giants' and a New Towns Act was passed in 1946 to tackle it. Whole new towns would be built in the countryside, properly planned with modern amenities. Many slums were demolished and houses were improved with indoor bathrooms and hot-water systems. Most of the new towns would be built near London to rehouse people from slum areas or areas destroyed by bombing raids. Basildon, Crawley, Corby, Glenrothes in Scotland and Cwmbran in Wales came into existence.

The Town and Country Planning Act of 1947 led to more council estates being built to provide cheaper housing for rental.

To meet the increasing demand for new homes, the government's solution was to manufacture houses in kit form. Factories turned out prefabricated houses or 'prefabs', one every four hours. These had an aluminium frame and asbestos sheets. They were expected to last ten years, but some 'prefabs' were still occupied 40 years after they were built.

Ernest Bevin, the Minister for Housing, promised that five million new homes would be built quickly; 800,000 were built between 1946 and 51, but there was a shortage of money, materials and workers so Bevin's promise was never kept. Some families were housed in disused army camps instead.

Source A

This source is taken from the memoirs of Renie Lester, who lived in a prefab in Lambeth, London in the 1940s. Her account was published in a book about memories of the past in 1998.

It was gorgeous. It had its own garden and was detached. You could have your windows open and hear the birds sing in the morning. Ours had two bedrooms, an indoor bathroom and toilet, cupboards and a stainless steel kitchen.

Figure 7 Building prefab homes

Activity

1. What was it like to live in a prefab?

2. 'The Labour government's housing policy was a total failure.' How far do you agree with this statement?

What factors interact to win general elections for political parties?

The 1945 General Election

The Labour Party won a landslide victory in the 1945 General Election. During the Second World War, the UK had been run by a **National Government** led by Prime Minister Winston Churchill. He was a very popular figure and it was confidently expected that Churchill would lead the Conservative Party to victory in the 1945 Election.

However, the Labour Party ran a very effective election campaign. Voters were constantly reminded that the poverty, depression and unemployment of the 1930s was the fault of the Conservatives. Labour also held out the prospect of a new social order in the UK. Under Labour, the Beveridge Report recommendations would be fully implemented – free medical care, full employment, improved education and, above all, better housing.

Winston Churchill and the Conservatives ran a very negative election campaign. Churchill tried to scare voters into believing that Labour's socialist policies would be like having the 'Gestapo run the country' and that the UK could not afford to set up a welfare state.

Members of the Armed Forces wanted a better life after the end of the war. They believed that only the Labour Party would guarantee them this by putting the Beveridge Report into action.

Labour's landslide victory gave the Labour Party its first majority government in its history. The new prime minister was Clement Attlee. Attlee, unlike many other Labour MPs, came from a very middle-class background, and he had been educated at Oxford University. He became an MP in 1922 and by 1931 was the deputy leader of the Labour Party. During the Second World War, Attlee served in the National Government as deputy prime minister. This gave him the experience he needed to run the country. Attlee was a very modest man, but a very skilled politician and negotiator. He could appreciate the abilities of people like Ernest Bevin and Aneurin 'Nye' Bevan, and he allowed them to make valuable contributions to Labour's programme of social reform and social equality.

Figure 8 A Labour election poster from 1945, which appealed to many people in the UK

Activity

3 Read again the reasons for Labour's 1945 election victory. Make your own list of these reasons.

4 Which do you think was the most important reason for the election victory? Explain your answer.

5 Explain why Attlee was considered to be a good prime minister.

economic and social policies
es of ordinary people?

ment policies radically alter a country's economy?

ion

sation means that the
ment takes over and controls
ustry, transport and trade. By
nationalising industry, the Labour
government hoped that businesses
would become more efficient and
working conditions would be
improved. Money would be invested
in things like road- and house-
building and therefore jobs would be
created.

In 1945 the UK was virtually
bankrupt. The cost of fighting the
Second World War was enormous
and huge loans totalling over
£3,000 million were owed to the
USA. There were food shortages and
a lack of raw materials. War-time
rationing not only continued but was
extended to cover some goods not rationed during the
war. The period after 1945 became known as 'The
Age of **Austerity**'. The Labour government's first task
was to put right the UK's economic problems.

Industry needed to be modernised, and quickly.
Goods would need to be manufactured and exported
to make money for the UK. Soldiers returning from
the war would expect jobs. Labour's solution to these
problems would be nationalisation.

The Bank of England was taken over so that the
government could make money available to invest in
industry. If the government owned these industries
then any profits made would help pay for Labour's
welfare reforms. The money would benefit the people
of the UK, not just the private owners of businesses.

The policy of nationalisation was expensive. Large
amounts of money were needed to invest in industry.
As a result, taxes had to rise. Private owners of the
industries that were nationalised had to be
compensated for the loss of their property.

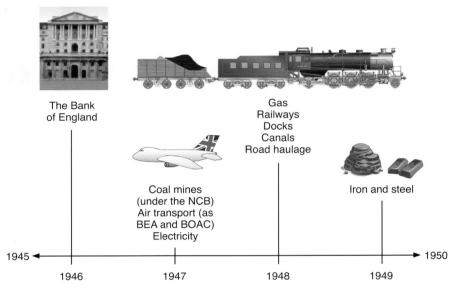

The Bank of England

Coal mines
(under the NCB)
Air transport (as
BEA and BOAC)
Electricity

Gas
Railways
Docks
Canals
Road haulage

Iron and steel

1945 ← 1946 — 1947 — 1948 — 1949 → 1950

Figure 9 Timeline of the nationalised industries

The nationalisation of the coal mines and railways
was generally welcomed because both industries
needed massive investment of the type only a
government could supply. However, many people,
including the Conservative Party, objected to the
nationalisation of road transport and the iron and
steel industries. These were seen as modern
industries that had been run very efficiently by their
private owners. The Conservative Party's attack on
nationalisation led the public to believe that the
policy was only about saving declining industries and
increasing control over people's lives.

Activity

1 Make your own list of the industries
  nationalised by the Labour government.

How can government policies radically alter people's health and opportunities?

The Labour Party elected in 1945 believed in the idea of social equality. Equality could be achieved for everybody in the UK if the nation's wealth was shared equally. Providing equality of opportunity was another of Labour's key ideals. To achieve this, better public services must be provided.

The NHS

'Disease' was one of the five 'Giants' outlined in the Beveridge Report. The new National Health Service (NHS) was to provide free medical, dental, hospital and optical care for everybody in the UK. Parliament passed the National Health Service Bill in 1946 and the NHS came into being in 1948.

The NHS would be paid for by National Insurance contributions from workers and employers and through general taxation. These contributions were crucial in supporting the welfare state. Workers in the UK were now insured against unemployment and sickness. Retirement and widows' pensions, along with maternity and death grants, were made available.

The man in charge of the NHS was Aneurin Bevan, the Minister of Health. Bevan, a coalminer from the age of thirteen, was elected MP for Ebbw Vale in 1929. He believed that health care should be free 'at the point of delivery'. This meant that nobody would have to pay to see a doctor or to receive hospital treatment. To make the NHS a success, Bevan had to ensure that doctors supported the new scheme. He did this by paying doctors a fee based on the number of patients they had. Doctors could still carry out private treatments for which they were paid directly by the patients.

The overall health of the UK's population improved dramatically. Patients who could not afford treatment before 1948 were now treated free of charge.

However, the financial burden of supporting the NHS became onerous. Charges for glasses and false teeth were introduced in 1951. The introduction of prescription charges led to the resignation of Bevan from the government.

Activity

2 Explain the arguments both *for* and *against* the policy of nationalisation.

3 Why was the NHS set up?

4 How useful are Sources A and B to a historian studying the impact of the NHS?

5 Carry out your own research into the life and work of Aneurin (Nye) Bevan. Does he deserve the title of 'The Father of the National Health Service'?

Source A

Aneurin Bevan speaking in 1948:

The rush for spectacles, as for dental treatment, has exceeded all expectations. Part of what has happened has been a natural first flush of success of the new scheme, with the feeling that everything is free now.

Source B

From *British Economic and Social History* by Philip Sauvain, a historian, published in 1987 by Nelson Thornes.

In its initial stages, the NHS was the envy of the world. The improvements in medical care were clear for all to see, most noticeably in the maternity wards, where infant deaths fell sharply. Older people benefited enormously from better-fitting teeth, the use of good quality spectacles and effective hearing aids.

How soon can society return to 'normal' after the experiences of war?

What happens to people's lives straight after the end of a war?

Between 1945 and 1951, the Labour Government did a great deal to make life better for the people of the UK. Rebuilding the UK and the creation of the Welfare State came at great cost.

Austerity

The period 1945 to 1951 became known as the 'Age of Austerity'. The government's policy was to put strict controls over industry and people. An 'export drive' was launched – shortage of goods in the shops meant that more goods could be sold abroad to earn money for the UK. The policy worked. By 1950, the UK's share of world trade in manufactured goods was 25 per cent.

However, people had to go without the things they wanted. Rationing was still in force. In 1948, rations were cut to below what they had been during the war. Bread, not rationed during the war, was rationed after it. At the same time, prices continued to rise but wages were not allowed to rise as much, so people felt worse off.

New Towns Act

The housing problem facing the government in 1954 was enormous. Few if any new houses were built during the war and the Luftwaffe had destroyed 20 per cent of existing houses.

One emergency solution had been the 'prefab'. A longer-term solution was the New Towns Act of 1946 (see page 78).

By 1950, more houses were built in the UK than any other European country, though this was still not enough, due to the 'baby boom' when the UK population began to increase after the war ended.

Source A

Mrs Ford remembers moving into Hemel Hempstead in the late 1940s. Her account was published in the book *Yesterday's Britain*, about life in the UK since 1900.

It was like a fairy tale come true. The larder was like a room to me as before I had only had one shelf. Of course, expecting the baby it was a bit hectic at first but after the baby was born we gradually got settled. To be able to put him in the garden was wonderful. The children loved it because the cows came around. They rubbed their backs up against the back door.

Activity

1 Explain why people in the UK supported the setting-up of the Welfare State.

2 Explain what is meant by the 'Age of Austerity'.

The 1951 General Election

By 1950, the UK was recovering from the effects of the Second World War. There was full employment, the Welfare State had been established and exports had increased. But there were many continuing problems. Rationing had got worse and there was a severe shortage of goods and materials. Many people felt let down by the Labour 'Homes for All' policy, which failed to meet the demand for new houses.

The UK was pressured into entering the Korean War in 1950. This, coupled with the need to rearm to face the perils of the '**Cold War**', meant a significant rise in taxation. This was resented by the wealthiest sections of society. Prices were rising due to inflation, but the government controlled wages so people felt worse off.

The nationalisation of iron and steel had not been popular. The Conservatives used this to win back public approval for their policies. Labour suffered a severe blow when the party became divided over the issue of prescription charges. Many leading members of the government resigned in protest. Despite this, Labour had transformed the UK, and many of its achievements – like the Welfare State – remain to this day.

However, in 1951 the Conservative Party under Churchill came back into power. The election success of Churchill and the Conservatives meant that the Conservative Party stayed in power until 1964.

Figure 10 Conservative Party election posters from 1951

The recovery of the economy during the 1950s and early 60s

The 1951 election success coincided with one of the greatest periods of prosperity enjoyed in the UK. The full employment created by Labour lasted until 1970. People had more money to spend. More and more goods which had once been considered luxuries, like washing machines and fridges, became cheaper and more plentiful. Cars and television sets were more easily affordable. People were encouraged to spend more by the availability of '**Hire Purchase**' and better advertising techniques, especially after ITV was created in 1955. Adverts were now beamed directly into people's homes.

The UK was fast becoming a 'consumer society'. In 1957, Prime Minister Harold Macmillan declared that 'most of our people have never had it so good'. He was right. People now saw the government's job as improving their living standards year on year. Living standards did go on rising throughout the 1950s and 60s. After the experiences of the war and the 'Age of Austerity', the people of the UK were intent on enjoying their new-found prosperity.

Activity

3 Explain why Labour lost the 1951 election.

4 What did Macmillan mean by 'our people have never had it so good'?

How can governments leave a lasting impression for future generations?

Motorways and the 'Beeching Axe'

Many families were able to buy their first car in the 1950s. One reason was the availability of cheaper family saloon cars like the Morris Minor, Ford Anglia and, after 1959, the Mini.

Increased car ownership encouraged families to travel more around the UK, which stimulated the demand for better roads.

The first stretch of motorway in the UK was the Preston By-Pass, which later became part of the M6 motorway. It was opened in 1958 and proved to be an instant success. The first motorway was the M1, begun in March 1958, and this heralded a new motoring age. Journey times were halved and manufacturers produced bigger and more powerful cars better suited to the new motorways. Motorways were fast, there was no speed limit but generally they tended to be empty. By 1974, many hundreds of kilometres of motorway had been built.

The development of private car ownership provided increased competition for the railways. Railways had been nationalised in 1948 and many millions of pounds was invested in bringing them up to date. Diesel and electric trains replaced steam locomotives, but British Railways failed to make a profit.

By 1963, the government felt that something had to be done. According to the *Sunday Times*, in the early 1960s 'British Railways are losing £300,000 a day. No doubt we ought to be disturbed by this information.'

The government was and appointed Dr Beeching as chairman of British Railways. His task was to investigate the state of the railways and make recommendations as to how they could save money. His solution became known as the 'Beeching Axe'. Losses would be cut by closing down railway lines and stations. Over 2,000 stations were closed and sold.

Many rural communities felt that they might be cut off if the railways disappeared. Many people did not own cars and relied on the railways to get about. Beeching's plans were accepted and thousands of kilometres of track were closed. This drastic remedy failed to save the railways and they continued to lose money.

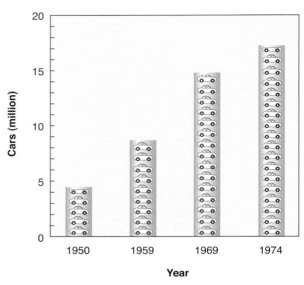

Figure 11 The number of vehicles on UK roads, 1950–74

Source A

From the Beeching Report, 1963.

Today rail and bus services serve the same purpose. Buses carry the greater part of passengers moving by public transport in rural areas. Both forms of transport are fighting a losing battle against private transport.

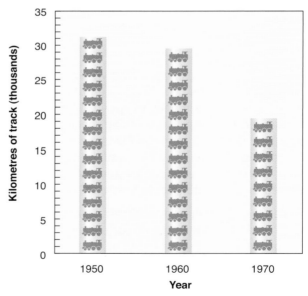

Figure 12 Distance of railway track in the UK 1950–70

Comprehensive education for all

In 1964 a Labour Government was returned to power in the UK. Doubts had been expressed about the education system since the passing of the 1944 Education Act. The main cause of concern was the Eleven Plus examination. Those who passed the Eleven Plus, about one-fifth of pupils, went to a Grammar school. Those who failed mostly went to Secondary Moderns. Many people did not like this system of education. They felt that it favoured middle-class pupils over bright working-class pupils. This left many children feeling failures at age eleven.

By the end of the 1950s, opinion in the UK was starting to shift towards the idea of one type of school for all pupils regardless of ability – the Comprehensive school. Comprehensive schools were not new. The first, Kidbrook, in Blackheath, London, opened in 1954.

The Labour government under Prime Minister Harold Wilson issued Directive 10/65. Education authorities were 'requested' to submit plans for the comprehensive reorganisation of their secondary schools. Government money for new school buildings was only given to LEAs on condition that they 'went comprehensive'.

By 1974, over 60 per cent of secondary pupils were educated in Comprehensive schools. Many of the Grammar schools and the Eleven Plus examination had gone from most parts of the UK.

The Profumo scandal

In 1963, one of the most shocking political scandals made headlines around the world. The scandal would lead to the resignation of the Prime Minister Harold Macmillan, and possibly helped the Labour Party into power in 1964.

The Secretary of State for War, John Profumo, began an affair with Christine Keeler, a prostitute. One of her other clients was a Russian military attaché and spy, Yevgeny Ivanov. It was feared that Keeler was passing on secrets about the UK's nuclear weapons from Profumo to the Russians. The Profumo affair caused great national interest and dominated the media for weeks.

What the Profumo affair clearly demonstrated was that the media, with publications like *Private Eye* and television programmes like *That Was The Week That Was*, was prepared to make fun of the government and ministers.

The lasting impression left by the Profumo scandal for future generations was that not all politicians behave in ways that are considered to be appropriate.

Activity

1 Explain why car ownership became so popular in the UK in the 1950s.

2 **a** Describe the 'Beeching Axe'.

   b Explain why it was thought to be necessary.

   c Describe its effects on different groups of people.

3 Why were Comprehensive schools introduced?

Examiner's Tips

Section A of the examination is compulsory and you need to answer all the questions.

- 2 mark questions normally ask you to look at a Source and comment on it.
- Look for the command word in all the questions: describe, explain, compare (why do Sources X and Y give different views) and make sure that you do what it tells you.
- 6 and 8 mark questions (normally Question 1f and Questions 2d and 3d) ask you to make judgments. Always remember to express your opinions. Use the pointers in the brackets to make sure that you have covered everything that you need to consider.

In Section B of the examination, you are given the option of answering either Question 2 or 3. To help you decide which question to do:

- Read both questions carefully and tick the parts that you can answer easily.
- Choose the question where you have ticked the most parts.
- Choose the question you have most interest in as this will mean you will have more to write.

The examination questions are not designed to make your life a misery. They are designed to help you show what you know and understand. Examiners want you to do your best and achieve a good grade in the examination. To be able to do this you must play your part by following some very simple advice:

- You must make sure that you have revised thoroughly for the examination.
- You must read the questions carefully.
- Where there is a choice of questions in Section B don't just answer the first question you come to, but read each question carefully and then decide which one you would enjoy answering the most.
- Make the most of the sources on the examination paper. They are there to help you.
- If there are 2 marks for a source-based question, you need to talk about about the source and use your own knowledge to make 2 points.
- Describe questions require you to give some information. There are 4 marks for this type of question so you don't have to write a lot.

- Explain questions ask you for reasons why something happened. There are 6 marks for this type of question so 3 reasons with some explanation will be enough to get you 6 marks. You can give more reasons if you want to.
- Deciding if a source is useful is easy but you must discuss the source which is in front of you on the examination paper, not sources in general. A source is useful because of what it shows or tells you about a topic. But remember, sources do have limitations. One source cannot tell you everything you need to know about that topic.
- 8 mark questions will ask you to make a judgement, to decide whether you agree with a statement or not. To achieve high marks in this question you must be prepared to discuss both sides of the argument e.g. evacuation for some children was a marvellous experience, but for others it was not so good. Give examples of both types of experiences and then decide if you agree with the statement or not.
- Don't use bullet points in your answers.
- Remember the examination is about using what you know to the best effect. Practise doing as many past examination questions as you can. You will soon get the hang of it.

Exam practice

This question is about the way in which a range of factors can interact to impact on people's lives.

1. What do Sources A and B (on page 81) tell you about the NHS? [2]
2. Look at Figure 9 (on page 80). Describe the process of nationalisation. [4]
3. Explain why the UK economy recovered during the 1950s and early 1960s. [6]
4. 'The Labour Party won the General Election in 1945 because of the leadership of Attlee.' To what extent do you agree with this statement? [8]
   (In your answer you should consider: the importance of Attlee as Labour party leader; reasons for Labour's success; and whether or not you agree with this view.)

How did changes in society affect the lifestyles of certain groups?

How radically did the nature and quality of life for women change?

Changes in the home

After the war, women were encouraged to return to their roles as housewives and mothers. The view that 'a woman's place was in the home' was still commonly held, although this view of women was beginning to change.

The introduction of modern household appliances in the 1950s radically altered housework. The widespread introduction and affordability of fridges, washing machines, freezers, electric cookers and new materials like **Formica** and plastic tiles meant housework could be done more quickly and easily. Convenience foods like breakfast cereals and tinned and frozen food, and washing-up liquid, helped ease the burden of housework.

Sainsbury opened his first supermarket in 1954, allowing women to do all of the weekly shopping in one go rather than having to shop every day. The idea of the 'supermarket' where all goods could be obtained in one shop soon caught on.

Social and cultural changes

The 1950s and 60s saw great social and cultural changes. **Contraception** probably brought about the greatest change. Women could now choose when and how many children to have. The 'Pill' brought about a sexual revolution. The 1967 Family Planning Act made contraception freely and widely available and by 1970 over one million women were using the 'Pill'. Women could now spend a few years having a family and return to or start work in the search for a higher standard of living.

Women who went out to work and looked after a family became more socially accepted, but women's magazines and the media still tended to see women as wives and mothers. Magazines like *Woman's Own* and *Woman's Realm* encouraged women to stay at home and cook, clean, sew and knit and have lots of babies. The 'Oxo' advert of the 1950s, starring Katy as the perfect housewife pleasing her man, emphasised this role. *I Love Lucy*, a television show about a housewife, was one of the most popular shows of the 1950s and 60s.

The end of clothes rationing in 1948 greatly affected women's fashion, thanks largely to younger women. Denim jeans and a sweater, soon replaced by a T-shirt, became very popular. Hemlines started to rise. Many magazines of the 1950s and 60s included sewing patterns which allowed women to make these clothes at home. New man-made fibres like nylon made stockings cheaper. The introduction of the mini-skirt, some only 30 centimetres long, in the 1960s encouraged the wearing of tights.

Activity

1 Describe the changes that took place in the home for some women.

2 What impact did the Pill have on women's lives?

3 Describe some of the social and cultural changes on women's lives in the 1950s and 60s.

Women's Lib

By 1961 there were more married women with a job than unmarried women. The government agreed equal pay for women teachers and civil servants. Novels by Iris Murdoch and film stars like Grace Kelly playing important strong roles helped change society's views about women.

The educational reforms of the 1940s and 60s meant more women were staying on in school to gain qualifications and enter higher education. The Open University allowed married women to stay at home and look after their families but study for a degree at the same time. By the mid-1970s, women had more job opportunities than ever before.

It took the Equal Pay Act of 1970 and the Sex Discrimination Act of 1975 to ensure that women were able to take their proper place in society. Despite these acts, women were still paid less than men, and posts could still be advertised by gender. This partly explains the rise of the '**Women's Lib**' movement. Women occasionally 'burned their bras' as bras were seen as a symbol of repression. Many protests were held and in 1968 the female workers at Ford, Dagenham went on strike, demanding equal pay to their male colleagues. Germaine Greer's famous book *The Female Eunuch* summed up the feminist movement.

What did all of these changes mean for the lives of women? The 1969 Divorce Reform Act allowed women to bring to an end an unhappy **marriage**. The 'Women's Lib' movement had helped to change attitudes to women and legislation made **discrimination** against women in the workplace illegal. However, many women often found that having a career brought less rather than more freedom. Often men still expected their wives to cook, clean and bring up the children, as well as work full time.

Figure 13 Women's Lib movement in Trafalgar Square

Was childhood different in the 1950s and 60s?

In the 1950s and 60s most children played outdoors and everyone seemed to know everyone else. Games were mostly played in the streets – ball games, hopscotch, bike rides, skipping, conkers, marbles, hide and seek, leapfrog, British Bulldog, tag and many others. Many games involved the chanting of rhymes like 'What's the time, Mr Wolf?'. Groups would play football, rounders and cricket with jumpers and coats used as goals, bases and wickets. Go-carts were made out of old prams and raced to destruction. These games helped to keep children fit and healthy.

Many children joined organisations like the Girl Guides and the Scouts. More than three million children were members by the 1960s. Scouts meetings, singing songs, camping and 'Bob-a-Job' week were eagerly anticipated.

The 1950s and 60s saw the introduction of many new toys. Frisbees, Hula-hoops and Space Hoppers arrived. Toys tended to be either for boys or girls. Barbie Doll was launched in 1959 and became an instant bestseller. Meccano sets and Dinky toys were very popular with boys. Mr Potato Head became an international success and was one of the first unisex toys.

Playing in parks was very popular, with queues of children waiting for their turn on slides, swings, see-saws and climbing frames. Saturday mornings provided an opportunity to visit the 'pictures'. The Lone Ranger, Davy Crockett, Zorro and Flash Gordon were idolised by millions of children as good always triumphed over evil. Smith's Crisps and Lucky Bags washed down with Vimto and Tizer were consumed in large quantities.

Hobbies like train-spotting and stamp-collecting flourished. Board games like Snakes and Ladders, Ludo and Chess remained popular.

Life for children was different compared to today. There was respect for people in authority, like the police and teachers. Discipline could be strict and enforced by large doses of **corporal punishment** at home and in schools. Nevertheless, there was something very comforting about growing up at a time when life for most children was full of games, carefree and fun.

Activity

1 Why did some women feel it was necessary to join the 'Women's Liberation Movement'?

2 Research children's toys from the 1950s and 60s. How different are they from children's toys today?

How does the development of popular entertainment contribute to society?

How did people's leisure time change in the 1950s and 60s?

Radio

During the Second World War, radio became a very important part of people's lives. Nearly every UK home had one. Programmes were a mix of entertainment, news and information. *Housewives' Choice*; *Music While You Work* and *Mrs Dale's Diary*, one of the first 'soaps', were aimed at female audiences. *Listen With Mother* and *Children's Hour*, with quizzes, serials and competitions, attracted younger audiences. Family programmes such as *Twenty Questions* and *Have a Go* were broadcast after 7p.m. Some comedy programmes were treated with suspicion. Attempts were made to ban the *Goon Show*, but by the late 1950s *Hancock's Half Hour* and *Take It From Here* attracted audiences in the millions.

Sports Report dominated Saturday afternoons, but the most popular programme was *Two-Way Family Favourites*, a record request programme which kept families in touch with relatives serving in the Armed Forces abroad.

Television

Television became popular in the 1950s, thanks largely to the coronation of Queen Elizabeth II in 1953. Manufacturers soon realised that television, 'the little box in the corner', was here to stay. By the end of the 1950s, the television set was the 'must-have' item of household equipment.

Figure 14 A family watching television in the 1950s

At first, television sets were small (9 inch or 23 centimetre screens), expensive and reception was poor. Many complaints were received about pictures being 'snowy'. There was very little daytime television, programmes finished at 11p.m, and the 'Interlude' between 6p.m. and 7p.m, when no programmes were broadcast, was designed to encourage young children to go to bed.

Only one television channel – the BBC – existed until 1955, when ITV or Commercial television was launched. BBC2 appeared in 1964 and colour programmes were first broadcast in 1967. The first television satellite, 'Telestar', was launched in 1962, and by 1969 people could watch the first moon landing on their television screens.

By 1966, over sixteen million television licences had been issued and 85 per cent of homes in the UK had television sets. These sets were still expensive, costing six times the average weekly wage of £12. Sets were usually bought on hire purchase or rented.

Programmes became more interesting and were designed to appeal to all tastes and ages. The first television 'soap' was *The Grove Family*, and this was soon followed by ITV's *Emergency – Ward 10*. *Dixon of Dock Green* was the forerunner of today's police dramas. Children's programmes proved to be very popular with all ages – *Watch with Mother*, *Andy Pandy*, *Bill and Ben the Flowerpot Men* and *Rag, Tag and Bobtail* each broadcast on a different day. *Crackerjack* and *Blue Peter* also appeared in the 1950s.

The biggest shows on ITV were *Sunday Night at the London Palladium* and game shows like *Double Your Money* and *Take Your Pick*. Many cooking, DIY and panel shows appeared for the first time.

Sports programmes appeared such as *Grandstand* and ITV's *World of Sport*.

The first *Doctor Who* episode was transmitted in the 1960s, as was *Coronation Street*, but perhaps the biggest break-through in broadcasting came with programmes specifically aimed at the new teenage audiences. *Juke Box Jury* was soon followed on the BBC with *Top of the Pops*. Many parents, however, would be shocked by pop music shows such as the *Six-Five Special* and *Ready Steady Go!*.

Source A

From the interview of a woman born in 1955 and interviewed in 2003.

I think TV must have been the biggest change in the lives of children this century. Before TV children spent so much more of their lives out playing and exploring, especially in the summer. But TV changed our lives – it gave us entertainment at the flick of a switch. I also think we discovered less for ourselves than our parents did.

Activity

1 Describe the growth of television in the 1950s and 60s.

2 Explain why there was an increasing variety of television programmes in the 1950s and 60s.

3 Watch some of the programmes mentioned in the text. Do you think television has changed since the 1960s?

Internet Research Activity

www.youtube.com

You can watch some TV shows from the 1950s and 60s using the search facility.

Films

The cinema was very popular in the 1950s, and films made in Hollywood dominated cinema screens. Film stars such as Marilyn Monroe, John Wayne and Lassie became household names. Cinema audiences numbered in the millions, and the Saturday **matinees** were very popular with children, who were allowed to go to the cinema with their 'mates', rather than under parental supervision.

By the beginning of the 1960s, the popularity of the cinema had declined. Ticket prices increased due to government taxation, and cinemas became scruffy because there was little money to repair or refurbish them.

The main reason for the decline was the increasing popularity of television. Many cinemas were forced to close and the buildings were knocked down. Some were converted to other uses, such as shops, night clubs or bingo halls. Even 'blockbuster' films such as the new James Bond films, and appearances by 'pop groups' such as The Rolling Stones, could not keep audiences up to their 1950s levels.

Year	Number of Cinemas	Weekly audiences
1951	4,600	24 million
1960	3,000	11 million
1966	1,800	6 million
1969	1,500	5 million

Figure 15 Cinema attendance 1951–69

Magazines

There were a large number of magazines and other publications in the 1950s and 60s. Women were catered for by magazines such as *Woman* and *Woman's Own*. These contained articles about being a good housewife and mother, knitting, a letters page and stories about romantic daydreams and escape from the reality of the kitchen sink.

Children's comics continued to flourish in the 1950s, with *The Beano*, *Eagle* and *Girl* proving to be very popular. Characters such as Denis the Menace, Dan Dare, Roy of the Rovers and the Silent Three of St. Kit's enthralled readers with their adventures. The success of these publications convinced many millions of children that reading was a pleasure.

Source A

A man from Somerset remembers his experiences of the cinema in the 1950s. He was interviewed in 2008 for a BBC documentary.

My dad worked on a Saturday, so he would ask me all about the matinee. I think he knew more about Tom Mix and Flash Gordon than any of my mates. I don't think there was ever a hero to match Flash Gordon.

Activity

1 Explain why the cinema was so popular in the 1950s and why fewer people went to the cinema in the 1960s.

Internet Research Activity

- www.ipcmedia.com/about/companyhistory
- www.sixtiesbritain.co.uk/lifestyle/2010/09/02/

Find out more about *Woman's Own* and read an issue of *Woman's Weekly* from 1960.

Youth clubs and coffee bars

The idea of being a 'teenager' was reinforced by the youth clubs and coffee bars of the 1950s and 60s. Most of the youth clubs at that time were organised and run by schools and churches. The idea was to sit around talking, drinking tea, coffee or lemonade, desperately trying not to appear self-conscious. Schools at this time were largely single sex and the youth club was one of the few places to meet girls or boys of your own age. The highlight was the youth-club dance. A record player and sometimes a local teenage group, desperately trying to imitate the pop songs of the day, provided the music. Activities such as table tennis and quizzes were organised under the watchful eye of the local vicar and other responsible adults, with everything coming to an end at 9.30p.m.

The coffee bars which sprang up in the 1950s and 60s were different altogether. Teenagers made these places their own, where they could dress in the latest fashion, talk, listen to the latest music and drink frothy coffee made in the Italian espresso machines. Coffee bars were very important in promoting the music of the day. They had juke boxes, and live acts sometimes played there. Musical styles such as jazz, skiffle and rock and roll were heard first by teenagers in coffee bars. The first public appearances by Cliff Richard and the Beatles were made in coffee bars. One of the most famous was the 2i's coffee bar in Soho, which is regarded as the birth place of popular music.

Sport

Sport in the UK enjoyed a revival after the Second World War. Football retained its popularity and by 1950 over 41 million people attended matches in the UK. The most successful team of this period was Tottenham Hotspur, the first team to win the league and cup double in the twentieth century. Manchester United became the first English team to win the European Cup in 1968, although the Scottish side Celtic had achieved the same feat in 1967. The greatest achievement of all came in 1966 when England beat West Germany 4–2 at Wembley to win the World Cup.

The Olympic Games were held in London in 1948, a games dominated by American athletes. English cricket suffered at the hands of the mighty Australian teams of the 1940s and 50s, and things did not get any better when the all-conquering West Indian sides arrived in the 1960s. Attendances were at record highs, and other great spectator sports like speedway, boxing, greyhound racing and horse racing enjoyed vast crowds. Henry Cooper challenged Cassius Clay for the world heavyweight boxing title in 1966.

Wimbledon had clung on to the idea of amateur unpaid competitors but this changed in 1968 when professional players competed for the first time. A UK success was enjoyed in 1969 when Ann Haydon-Jones beat the American Billie Jean King to win the ladies' crown.

Great sporting icons like Gary Sobers, George Best, Rod Laver and Henry Cooper inspired millions of young people to take up sport.

Activity

2 How did magazines, youth clubs and coffee bars help develop youth culture?

3 How did British sport develop after the Second World War?

How did changing musical styles reflect changes in society?

Most people in the 1950s turned on the radio to listen to music. Record players were common in most homes and during the 1950s sales of records increased dramatically. Young people bought singles, or listened to their favourite music in coffee bars on juke boxes. For many young people, music in the 1950s and 60s would be the greatest influence in their lives.

After the Second World War, music was dominated by artists such as Bing Crosby, Frank Sinatra and 'Big Band' music popularised by Glenn Miller during the war. In the 1950s, dance halls run by Mecca and Locarno featured bands and dance music, popular with adults.

By the mid-1950s, a new sound had arrived in the UK from America – **rock 'n' roll** – spearheaded by Bill Haley and Elvis Presley. This was music for the young. Many people predicted that rock 'n' roll was a passing phase, but by 1960 there were thousands of rock 'n' roll groups across the UK. Skiffle, another form of music popular with the young, originated in the UK. Inspired by Lonnie Donegan, this was a simpler form of music using wash boards and tea chests as musical instruments.

Elvis Presley became hugely popular after 1955, with records such as 'Heartbreak Hotel' and 'Hound Dog'. He was to be a major influence on the UK music scene. Presley's appeal to young people and his antics on stage grew when the young realised that adults did not like him or his music.

One group above all others dominated the pop scene in the 1960s. The Beatles arrived in 1962 and for the next seven years enjoyed unparalleled success in the UK and America. The Beatles influenced hundreds of other groups, including the Rolling Stones, The Who, The Searchers and The Hollies. A new term was coined – **Merseybeat**. The Beatles were awarded MBEs by the Queen for their services to pop music.

Whilst rock 'n' roll and pop music dominated the charts, other musical tastes also flourished. Soul and Motown, originating in the USA, became very popular in the UK. Artists such as Sam Cooke, the Supremes and the Four Tops travelled across the UK giving sell-out concerts. Protest songs by artists like Bob Dylan were increasingly influential at a time of political and social unrest. Flower Power took hold in many American cities and influenced young people in the UK. What shocked older people was the use of drugs by groups like the Rolling Stones, and the new sexual freedom of Flower Power. Music became a way in which young people expressed their views on a series of social and political issues and alienated them from their parents.

Source A

Captain David Evans explaining to a journalist why he returned his OBE in protest at the honour awarded to the Beatles in 1965.

At one time I was proud of my OBE but not any more. I believe that the time has come for a strong protest against these pop groups and I hope that by returning my OBE I can make someone take notice.

Source B

Lyrics from 'My Generation' by The Who.

People try to put us down
Just because we get around
Things they do look awful cold
Hope I die before I get old
Talking 'bout my generation

Activity

1 Explain how pop music influenced young people in the 1950s and 60s.

2 Read the lyrics of the song 'My Generation' by The Who. Explain how older people might react to this song.

How do political, social and moral factors influence changes in society?

How did society react to growing affluence and more liberal attitudes?

By 1960, the UK was described as an '**affluent**' society. Many more consumer goods were bought, especially by the young. In 1964, teenagers spent £1.5 billion on goods manufactured specifically for them – records, magazines, drinks, posters, make-up, clothes, etc. They had their own fashions, dances and pop music. A '**generation gap**' appeared between the young and adults. Young people imitated their pop star idols by wearing the same style of clothes – leather jackets, parkas, flowered shirts and mini-skirts. The Beatles influenced 'mop top' long hair for boys, whilst 'beehives' and page-boy cuts were all the rage for girls.

Not everyone behaved and acted in the same way, but the media soon coined the phrase 'Permissive Society' to describe the lifestyles and culture of young people – sex, drugs and rock 'n' roll. 'If you can remember the 60s you weren't there' was a famous saying. It was a time of freedom, social unrest, innocence lost, scandal and war.

The 1960s saw a relaxation in attitudes to sexual behaviour. **Abortion** and homosexuality were legalised and sex before marriage and taking drugs were tolerated, whereas previously they had been condemned as immoral and anti-social. The mini-skirt was seen as the symbol of this new sexual liberation. Films like *Saturday Night and Sunday Morning*, books like *Lady Chatterley's Lover* (which was written in 1928 but banned until 1960), and *Oz* magazine (an underground subversive magazine for young people) heralded changes in attitudes.

People had much greater personal wealth and could afford to buy things they wanted rather than needed. Full employment for most of the 1960s contributed to this growing affluence.

Some young people rejected the values of older people and some became **hippies**. Hippies spoke about free love, wanted to create a peaceful world and turned to drugs and alcohol. Drugs were illegal but became easier to buy. Hippies were mostly young white teenagers who rebelled against middle-class values, opposed the Vietnam War, promoted free sex and attended music festivals like Woodstock. They used cannabis and LSD or Acid, a **hallucinogenic** drug. They tended to live and travel together, were unmarried and adopted Scott Mackenzie's 'San Francisco' as their anthem.

Two other youth cultures achieved fame in the 1960s – Mods and Rockers. The media enjoyed highlighting their gang fights, fashion, transport, drug-taking and nudity at pop festivals. Rockers liked early rock music, wore black jeans and leather jackets, used grease on their hair and rode 'ton-up' motorbikes like Triumph Bonnevilles and BSA Gold Stars. Mods became part of the 1960s fashion revolution, wearing designer suits and Parkas and rode scooters, usually Lambrettas covered with mirrors and mascots. The two groups did not get on but rarely met, except at Bank Holiday weekends along the south coast of England. There were violent clashes reported in newspapers with headlines like: 'Day of Terror by Scooter Groups'; 'Youngsters Beat Up Town – 97 Leather Jackets arrested'; 'Wild Ones Invade Seaside Towns – 97 arrests'.

What influence did political events have on the nature and quality of people's lives?

Campaign for Nuclear Disarmament (CND)

The 1960s and 70s were two decades of protest in the UK. The era of the Cold War and the testing and manufacture of nuclear weapons seemed to make the world a dangerous place to live.

In 1949 the USA exploded its first nuclear bomb. The USSR (Russia) followed in 1955. The CND (Campaign for Nuclear Disarmament) was formed in 1957. Its aim was to stop the testing, manufacture and spread of nuclear weapons. It hoped to persuade the UK government to get rid of its nuclear weapons completely. The CND was one of the first peace movements in the UK.

In 1958, the CND organised the first protest march from London to Aldermaston, where most of the UK's atomic research took place. By 1962 almost 150,000 people were taking part in this march.

The CND's logo became very famous and was often worn on a badge by teenagers and young people to show their support. Its slogan, taken up by many teenagers and youth groups, was 'Ban the Bomb'.

The organisers of the CND developed a mass movement of demonstrations, but were opposed to unlawful violent protests. The end of the **Cuban Missile Crisis** in 1962 and the signing of the Nuclear Test Ban Treaty diminished support for the CND. Youth groups turned their attention to other protests, especially against the war in Vietnam, and so lost interest in the CND.

CND flags, showing their logo, at a protest march

Civil unrest in Northern Ireland

There had always been friction between the UK and Ireland, which led in 1948 to the recognition of Eire or the Irish Free State as a separate country independent of the UK. The six provinces of Ulster remained part of the UK as Northern Ireland.

Many Catholics living in Ulster wanted a reunited Ireland and they were suffering discrimination in terms of jobs, housing, voting and other **civil rights**. They wanted all anti-Catholic measures to be abolished and in 1968 the first Civil Rights march took place. Tension between Protestants and Catholics remained high. In August 1969 the 'Battle of the Bogside' occurred. The RUC (police) were overwhelmed and UK soldiers were sent to Northern Ireland in an attempt to restore order. Internment was introduced in 1971, which allowed suspected troublemakers and members of the IRA to be imprisoned without trial. Protests and violence against Internment followed.

On 30 January 1972, a march was organised in Derry to protest against Internment, under which Catholics were suffering more than Protestants. Soldiers put up barricades to prevent the protesters reaching the city centre. In the confusion that followed, paratroopers opened fire on the crowds, killing fourteen civilians and injuring thirteen others. This event became known as 'Bloody Sunday'.

During the 1970s, the IRA would extend its bombing campaign to the UK mainland. The violence would last for many years.

Figure 16 A photograph taken in 1972 showing one of the victims of 'Bloody Sunday'.

Activity

1 Research the history of the CND. Why do you think its campaign for nuclear disarmament was a failure?

2 Research the events of 'Bloody Sunday'. Explain why you think it was considered to be a 'turning point' in the history of the 'Troubles'.

Examiner's Tips

Sample question

This question is about making judgements and appears as Question 1f and Questions 2d and 3d.

1 'The most important development in the 1950s and 1960s was the growth of the 'Permissive Society'. How far do you agree with this statement?
- Write about the growth of the Permissive Society.
- Consider other developments in the 1950s and 1960s.
- Say whether you agree with this statement. [8]

What the examiner has to say!

1 ● It is important to follow the scaffold under the statement. This will show you how to set out your answer.
- Give some examples of the growth of the permissive society. Say what the permissive society came to be – more sexual freedom, drugs, changing attitudes and youth culture. Remember this section is worth 3 marks so you do not have to give too much information. Do not give a list; rather, explain the permissive society with one or two examples.
- Consider other developments – this can be anything from your own knowledge about developments during the 1950s and 60s. Again, this is worth 3 marks so two examples with an explanation is enough.
- Do you agree with the statement? It is important that you do decide. You may well agree but you must say why you agree. You may disagree because you think other developments were more important. This is worth 2 marks.
- The key to achieving full marks is to come to a conclusion about what was the *most important*.

Sample question

This section provides help on how to answer question 1e, which deals with historical interpretation, by analysing two sources.

2 Why do Sources A and B give different views (interpretations) about Mods and Rockers? [6]

The media made it sound much worse than it was. There wasn't as much fighting as what has been made out. The press hyped it up. There were only isolated incidents and no riots. The odd deckchair went flying through the air but there weren't any weapons. We certainly didn't go chasing after old people, even us rockers. If we saw an old lady having trouble crossing the road we would help her.

Source A This source is taken from an interview with Phil Bradley, who took part in many Rocker visits to the seaside in the 1960s. He became a Rocker at fourteen. The interview took place in 2008.

Mods and Rockers jailed after seaside riots.

Scores of youths have been given prison sentences following Bank Holiday violence between Mods and Rockers along the south coast of England. Two youths were taken to hospital with knife wounds and 51 youths were arrested for violent conduct. More than 1000 teenagers were involved, throwing deckchairs around, making bonfires and swearing at each other and passersby. Elderly residents in Margate were terrified and the police had stones thrown at them.

Source B This source is taken from the BBC news for 18 May 1964

What the examiner has to say!

2 In your answer you should refer both to the content of the sources and the authorship.

- You must read both sources carefully to see if they agree or disagree.
- Look at the content of both sources and check with your own knowledge.
- Look at who wrote the sources, when they were written and why they were written.
- Were the authors there at the time; are they writing at the time of the events or later?
- Think about why the sources were written.
- To achieve maximum marks, you need to produce a balanced answer with support from both sources and your own knowledge, together with a careful consideration of the authors.

Exam practice

This question is about how social change can affect the nature and quality of human life.

1 Study Figure 13 (on page 88). Why did some women join the 'Women's Liberation Movement'? [2]

2 Describe the variety of television programmes available in the 1950s and 60s. [4]

3 Explain how leisure activities changed society during the 1960s. [6]

4 'Young people were affected more by developments in the 1950s and 1960s than any other group.' To what extent do you agree with this statement? [8]

(In your answer you should consider: the social and cultural changes happening at the time; fashion, music, film, television, leisure activities, youth clubs and coffee bars; and whether or not you agree with this view.)

The United States of America is a country of contrasts – rich and poor, young and old, natives and immigrants. As the traditional American motto puts it – *E Pluribus Unum*, meaning 'out of many, one' or in other words 'one country made from many people'.

In the twentieth century, the USA has been the richest economy in the world. Most Americans aspired to 'a car in every garage, a chicken in every pot', as President Herbert Hoover put it in 1929. The USA considers itself to be a 'Land of Opportunity'. But not every American has been able to make the most of the opportunities.

Why do countries quarrel?

How can ideological differences between countries cause mistrust and suspicion?

One of the main reasons for the distrust that grew between the USA and the USSR at the end of the Second World War was their different **ideologies**, or ways of looking at the world.

The features of Communism and Capitalism

The USSR believed in **Communism** – complete equality and no private ownership. Everything, including land, buildings, shops and factories, was to be State controlled. The State provided free education and healthcare in return. The USSR was a state with only one political party (a dictatorship), and a ruthless secret police locked away millions of opponents of the government in labour camps. The USSR was worried that the USA wanted to destroy the Communist state and turn their country back to how it had been in the past – a very poor population exploited by a few rich people.

The USA was and still is a democracy where everyone can vote to choose their government. Citizens also get a number of freedoms, including free speech, freedom from arrest without charge, freedom to own property and to buy services like education and healthcare. **Capitalism** is the freedom to create private wealth and to make a personal profit. The USA was worried that the spread of Communism would limit their ability to expand American business and make more money.

Figure 1 Propaganda poster used by the USSR to show how they would defeat the evils of US Capitalism

During the Second World War the USSR and the USA fought on the same side. They had been able to work together because they faced a common enemy – Nazi Germany. As the war came to an end their suspicions about each other began to dictate how they behaved towards one another. This was the beginning of the **Cold War**. The expression Cold War refers to the hostile way that the USA and the USSR behaved towards each other between 1945 and 1990. It is only a 'cold' war because it did not actually involve any direct fighting between these two countries. Instead they built up connections and alliances with other countries to protect themselves, as well as building large numbers of weapons.

How can factors interact to cause bad relations to develop?

Why did bad relations in Europe after the Second World War lead to the Cold War?

During the Second World War, the USA worked with the USSR providing vital supplies to the USSR. As the war came to an end, the USSR forced Communist governments on the countries it liberated from the Nazis to protect the USSR from any more attacks from western Europe.

The Americans wanted to stop Communism spreading any further. This policy was called **containment**; in other words, trying to keep Communism inside the countries where it was already the main ideology. As Communism continued to threaten to spread to other countries, Truman, the president of the USA at the time, made a famous speech in 1947, the **Truman Doctrine**, in which he said that America would come to the aid of any country that was threatened by Communism. The Americans believed that if they allowed Communism to take over a country it would then spread quickly to other countries. This was known as the **Domino Theory**.

In 1948, believing that Communism only spread to poor countries, the American government gave lots of money, called **Marshall Aid**, to the countries of western Europe to help them rebuild after the damage of the Second World War. It was hoped that this money would help to keep these countries loyal to America and the idea of Capitalism.

The border between Communist eastern Europe and Capitalist western Europe was called the **Iron Curtain**. Germany and its capital Berlin were also divided between America and her allies (West Germany and West Berlin) and the Soviets (East Germany and East Berlin). When American money was given to West Germany and Berlin, the Communists were afraid that it would disturb their control over their parts of Germany so they closed off West Berlin from western Europe in 1948. This was known as the **Berlin Blockade** (see Figure 2). The West Berliners did not give in and they were helped by regular airlifts of essential supplies from West Germany. After eighteen months, the Soviets had to back down and access to West Berlin was re-opened. To stop people escaping, or defecting to western Europe, the Russians eventually had the **Berlin Wall** built in 1961.

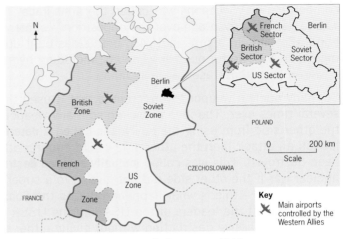

Figure 2 The Berlin Blockade in Germany, 1948

Activity

1 Describe the differences between Communism and Capitalism.

2 Explain how the USA became more involved in the affairs of Europe after 1945.

3 How useful is Figure 3 to a historian studying the division of Europe after 1945?

Figure 3 President Kennedy visiting the Berlin Wall in 1963

The end result of these conflicts and tensions was the creation of **NATO (North Atlantic Treaty Organisation)** in 1949. This was an alliance of the Capitalist countries in the West who promised to help defend each other. Not surprisingly the USSR was very angry at this new development and formed an alliance of Communist countries in 1955, called the **Warsaw Pact**. Now, instead of individual countries being hostile towards each other, large groups of countries were involved.

What were the Arms Race and the Space Race?

After the use of two atomic bombs in the war against Japan, the Soviets were scared by the Americans' superior weapons so they developed their own. This competition over weapons was called the **Arms Race**. The aim of this competition was to gain an advantage over the opposition – **strategic superiority**. From a handful of atomic bombs in 1945, both sides built up enormous arsenals of increasingly powerful nuclear weapons, including hydrogen bombs fifty times more powerful than those used against Japan.

So many nuclear weapons were created that if used they could destroy the planet several times over. The idea of having so many weapons was that it would prevent the other side from using theirs. This is called a **deterrent**. Should either side launch an attack then the other side would counter-attack until everything had been destroyed. This was called **mutually assured destruction (MAD)**. Threatening a nuclear war if the other side did not give in to a superpower's demands is called '**brinkmanship**' – this is what happened during the **Cuban Missile Crisis** (see pages 103–105), but the leaders of the USA and the USSR had realised that such a war could bring massive destruction without giving either side an advantage.

There was another competition between the USA and the USSR – over who would control space beyond the earth's atmosphere. This competition is usually referred to as the **Space Race**. It began in 1957 when the USSR launched the first satellite into orbit, called Sputnik. The USSR had another first – Yuri Gagarin became the first man in orbit in 1961. Control of space was important as it would allow countries to keep weapons directly over their enemies, as well as allowing them to spy on what was going on. Success in the Space Race was seen to prove technological superiority between the superpowers. It was also important for national pride. The Russians continued to stay ahead of the Americans until Neil Armstrong became the first man on the Moon in 1969.

The Space Race is a good example of how both sides in the Cold War used **propaganda** to persuade people around the world of the superiority of their ideology. There was a wide range of propaganda techniques employed, including annual parades through Moscow to demonstrate Soviet military superiority; chess competitions between grand masters representing both sides; and even American radio stations broadcasting jazz and rock 'n' roll music to the countries of eastern Europe.

Activity

1 Describe the Arms Race.

2 Explain why the USA and the USSR built so many nuclear weapons.

3 Explain why there was a Space Race between the USA and the USSR.

Examiner's Tips

When answering 'explain why' questions:

- you must give more than one reason in answer to the question to get beyond the lowest marks

- you need to explain in detail, with examples, exactly how the reasons you are giving explain the issue in the question

- you should EITHER try to give an indication of the relative importance of the different reasons you are giving OR find links between the reasons you are giving, to achieve the highest marks.

How are the lives of ordinary people affected by global events?

How do countries become involved in **flashpoints**?

What caused the Cuban Missile Crisis?

In the autumn of 1962, the Russians and Americans found themselves on the brink of nuclear war in the Cuban Missile Crisis.

Cuba is an island very near to the coast of the USA and was a holiday destination for many rich Americans. Until 1959 it had been run by General Batista, a cruel dictator with close connections to the USA. He was removed from power in a Communist revolution led by Fidel Castro. Castro's aim was to redistribute the wealth of the rich businessmen and plantation owners to help improve the lives of the poor in Cuba. This led him to become friendly with the USSR.

As part of their policy of containment, the Americans cut off all trade with Cuba, and Castro was forced to make an agreement with the USSR to sell them sugar, which was Cuba's main export. The Americans also helped people who had run away from the Communists on Cuba. The result was a failed attempt to invade Cuba at the **Bay of Pigs** in 1961. Whilst the American government had openly encouraged the Cuban exiles to take back their country, they stopped short of the direct military support, using the Navy and Air Force, that could have helped the invasion to succeed. President Kennedy was criticised for not acting decisively enough in support of the invasion. The leader of the USSR thought that this showed that Kennedy was too young and unsure of himself and would be easy to manipulate.

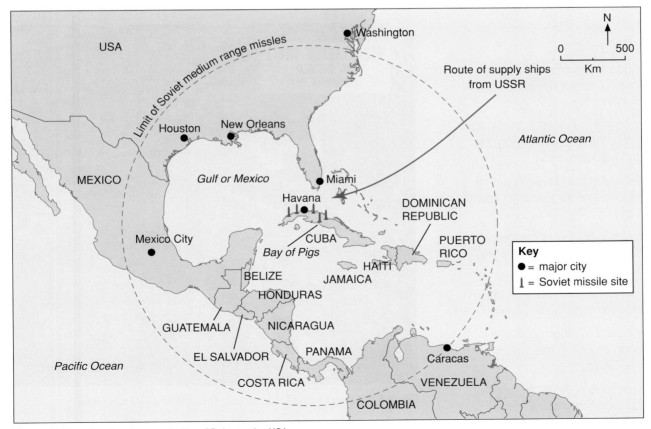

Figure 4 Map showing the proximity of Cuba to the USA

What were the main events of the Cuban Missile Crisis?

Fidel Castro asked the Russians for help to defend Cuba. Khrushchev, the Russian leader, saw this as the ideal opportunity to get his own nuclear missile bases near to the USA. As part of NATO the USA had already ensured that there were nuclear missiles pointed at the USSR from the UK, Italy and Turkey. An American U2 spy plane photographed launch sites for these missiles in October 1962. A naval plane photographed missile parts on the deck of Soviet ships heading for Cuba. President Kennedy locked himself away with his closest advisers to decide what to do. The military tried to pressure Kennedy into an all-out attack on Cuba but he resisted; he thought this would lead the Soviets to attack Berlin and would lead to a large-scale nuclear war. He preferred a more peaceful solution.

On 22 October 1962 Kennedy made a televised address to the world explaining that he intended to 'quarantine' Cuba. This involved placing the ships of the US Navy around Cuba to prevent Russian supply ships getting through. This was a **Naval Blockade**. The American Army was put on full alert and began to move to staging points in Florida and Georgia in preparation for an invasion of Cuba. Kennedy made it clear that any refusal to remove the missiles or challenge his naval blockade would be considered to be an act of war.

Kennedy wrote to Khrushchev to tell him that America would not allow these missiles to be stationed on Cuba. Khrushchev allowed the ships carrying the missiles to continue. He believed that Kennedy would back down. Khrushchev wrote two letters to Kennedy – one threatening war if the Americans did not remove their missiles from Turkey, one offering peaceful withdrawal. Kennedy accepted the terms of the more peaceful letter. Russian ships carrying the nuclear missiles passed very close to the American ships, eventually turning back to Russia. By 29 October 1962 the crisis was over. Soviet missiles were withdrawn from Cuba, the USA withdrew its missiles from Turkey. Both sides had pulled back from a conflict that could easily have ended in nuclear war.

Activity

1 Describe the problems facing ordinary Cubans before Castro's revolution.

2 How useful is Figure 4 (see page 103) to a historian studying the Cuban Missile Crisis?

3 Explain why the government of Cuba became increasingly friendly with the USSR.

4 Describe how the US government reacted to the discovery of the missile sites on Cuba.

5 Explain the role of US President Kennedy in the Cuban Missile Crisis.

6 How useful is Figure 5 to a historian studying the Cuban Missile Crisis?

7 How serious a threat to world peace was the Cuban Missile Crisis? Explain your answer.

Figure 5 CIA photo of the Cuban missile site taken by a U2 spy plane

How do ordinary people get caught up in flashpoints?

Cuba is only 90 kilometres from the coast of Florida. The Cuban Missile Crisis seemed much more threatening to the average American, not only because it could easily have ended in a devastating nuclear war, but also because it was physically so much nearer to the USA.

Newspapers, radio and television all kept Americans fully informed about the latest developments in the crisis. Radio stations also broadcast advice to Americans on how to make or where to buy nuclear fall-out shelters. Many shops had their shelves emptied of tinned food and water containers as people tried to stock up in case war did break out.

President Kennedy used television and radio to explain to Americans what was happening in Cuba and what his response was going to be. Many Americans were reassured that their president was taking such a firm stand against Communist aggression.

Results/consequences of the Cuban Missile Crisis

The Cuban Missile Crisis turned out to be an important turning point in relations between the two sides in the Cold War. It showed how brinkmanship could easily result in a nuclear war that neither side could win. To improve communications between the leaders of the USSR and the USA, a special telephone connection, known as the '**Hot Line**', was installed, providing instant communication between the White House in the USA and the Kremlin in the USSR. In 1963 the **Partial Test Ban Treaty**, ending the testing of nuclear weapons above ground, became the first of a number of international agreements to reduce the number of nuclear weapons in the world and bring the Arms Race under control.

'I call upon Chairman Khrushchev to halt and eliminate this clandestine, reckless and provocative threat to world peace and to stable relations between our two nations. I call upon him further to abandon this course of world domination, and to join in an historic effort to end the perilous arms race and to transform the history of man.'

Figure 6 President Kennedy speaking on television, 22 October 1962

Activity

8 Explain the role of the American media in the Cuban Missile Crisis.

9 Describe the consequences of the Cuban Missile Crisis for ordinary people.

10 How useful is Figure 6 to a historian studying the impact of the Cuban Missile Crisis on the American people?

How can attitudes in society affect the conduct of conflict?

Why do countries become involved in conflicts?

Why did the USA become involved in Vietnam?

During the Second World War, the CIA trained a secret Vietnamese army called the **Viet Minh** to fight against Japanese occupation. Once the war was over, the Viet Minh expected Vietnam to become independent. The Americans did not want this because the Viet Minh were Communists. They put the French back in control. The Viet Minh then attacked the French and defeated them at **Dien Bien Phu** in 1954. The Americans arranged for Vietnam to be divided in half at the peace conference in Geneva. The Geneva **Accords** stated that the Communists would control the North and the pro-America Ngo Dinh Diem would rule the South.

The Communists of North Vietnam, led by Ho Chi Minh, planned to reunite both halves of Vietnam into one single Communist country. Their supporters began to make secret attacks on South Vietnam as soon as the country was divided in 1954. They had lots of support in the South because the rich Catholic government officials of Diem and their friends exploited the poor Buddhist peasants.

America was worried that if Vietnam became fully Communist, Communism would spread right through South East Asia following the Domino Theory. China had already become Communist in 1949, then North Vietnam in 1954. The US government was worried it would continue to spread through South East Asia – to Laos, Cambodia, Thailand, etc. American support for the government of South Vietnam followed the Truman Doctrine, which meant that they would give military support to the South Vietnamese government to contain the spread of Communism. The Americans first sent money then, from 1961, thousands of US military advisors to train the army of South Vietnam to

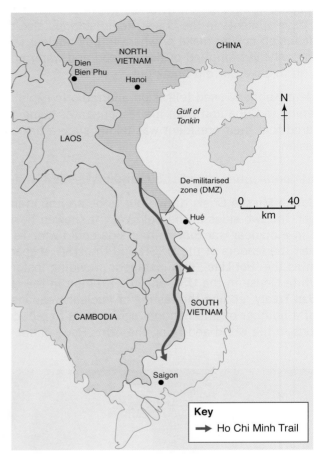

Figure 7 Map showing the Cold War division of Vietnam

fight the Communists. In 1964, American ships were attacked off the coast of Vietnam in the **Gulf of Tonkin**. President Johnson sent hundreds of thousands of American soldiers to help keep the Communists, who the Americans called the **Viet Cong**, out of the South.

Activity

1 Describe the division of Vietnam in 1954.

2 Explain why the USA became involved in the conflict in Vietnam.

3 How useful is Figure 7 to a historian studying the problems that led to the Vietnam War?

How was the Vietnam War fought?

The war was fought in two very different ways. The Americans used their wealth and technological superiority to try and defeat the Viet Cong. The Viet Cong used the covert tactics of **guerrilla warfare** to convince the Americans that they could not win.

The Viet Cong	The American response
The Viet Cong wore black pyjamas when attacking at night but hid amongst the peasants wearing normal clothes during the day. They laid booby traps and hid in the jungle and let the Americans injure themselves while trying to find them. A complex series of tunnels had been dug to allow the guerrillas to escape from American foot patrols and hide during air raids. They were kept supplied with basic weapons from North Vietnam along the **Ho Chi Minh Trail**, a pathway of villages throughout the jungle who were secret supporters of the Viet Cong. They also became very skilful at stealing or reusing discarded American weapons. The peak of the Viet Cong campaign came during the **Tet Offensive** in 1968, which convinced many Americans that the war could not now be won.	The American response to the Viet Cong's guerrilla tactics was to use technology. Fleets of American bombers were sent to attack targets in North Vietnam and on the Ho Chi Minh trail in **Operation Rolling Thunder** from 1965, dropping more bombs than during the whole of the Second World War. **Napalm**, a burning jelly, was dropped to clear out hostile areas of jungle and **Agent Orange**, a chemical weapon, was sprayed onto trees to strip them of their leaves so that Viet Cong movements could be observed from the air. Much of this was far less effective than the Americans intended. Simple air raid shelters protected many from bombing, indiscriminate use of napalm killed many innocent civilians and chemical weapons poisoned many and led to birth defects in Vietnamese children.

The relationship between Americans and the Vietnamese people was complicated. Many Americans were convinced that they were fighting the war in Vietnam to help the Vietnamese people, not just in fighting off a Communist dictatorship, but by bringing them medicine, modern technology and education as well. Most Americans did not bother to learn the Vietnamese language and never showed any appreciation for their culture. They failed to understand that most people did not support the Viet Cong because they were Communists, but because they hated the government of South Vietnam.

The Viet Cong often used women and children to lure American soldiers into dangerous situations, and as the war dragged on the Americans trusted the Vietnamese people less and less. The fact that it was impossible to tell friendly and hostile Vietnamese people apart from each other made this worse. Sometimes American frustration would boil over and civilians would suffer. The Americans never won the 'hearts and minds' of the Vietnamese people, and eventually realised that they could never win the war.

Activity

4   Explain how the Viet Cong fought the Vietnam War.

5   Describe the tactics used by the USA in the Vietnam War.

6   How important were the guerrilla tactics of the Viet Cong in winning the Vietnam War?

How can a range of factors interact to affect government policy?

The role of the media and public opinion on the Vietnam War

The media played a vital role in the outcome of the Vietnam War. It was the first conflict to be televised, and as the war progressed through the 1960s more and more American households had uncensored footage of the conflict broadcast into their homes. People were horrified by the destruction to Vietnamese property and the suffering of the people, especially the women and children, whilst the USA seemed to be making little progress against the Viet Cong. It was newspaper and magazine journalists who broke the stories of American atrocities against the Vietnamese people, most notoriously the massacre of women and children in the village of **My Lai** in 1968.

Peace protests against the war became increasingly common, especially amongst young people. Young men who refused to go and fight when they were ordered to were known as '**Draft Dodgers**'. President Johnson was increasingly associated with this misguided war – 'Hey! Hey! LBJ! How many kids did you kill today?' was just one of many chants that rang out from crowds of protesters. His '**Great Society**' programme for improving the lives of the poorest people in America was sidelined and underfunded as resources were directed towards the war effort.

The cost of the war and its impact on domestic policies

President Johnson resigned in 1968 because of the war, and his successor President Nixon withdrew the Americans from Vietnam as soon as he could, following on from his election promise to bring '**Peace with Honour**' to the conflict in South East Asia. Nixon followed a policy of '**Vietnamization**' – making the soldiers of South Vietnam fight instead of Americans. He also increased American 'carpet bombing' of civilian targets in the North and in the neighbouring countries of Cambodia and Laos to force the Viet Cong into a ceasefire.

The official peace saw the Americans withdraw from Vietnam and the North Vietnamese promise to leave the South alone. The Americans left but the Viet Cong broke their part of the agreement. South Vietnam was overrun by the Communists in 1975.

Activity

1 Explain why the USA withdrew from the Vietnam War.

2 Was the portrayal of the war in the media the most important reason for the USA's withdrawal from Vietnam?

3 How useful is Figure 8 to a historian studying why the USA withdrew from Vietnam?

Figure 8 Young students protesting against the Vietnam War

Examiner's Tips

To help with your preparation for the exam, make sure you know:

- the differences between Communism and Capitalism – and in particular why the USA was so determined to stop the spread of Communism
- the different ways in which the USA and the USSR tried to convince the world that their ideology was the best – the Berlin Airlift, the Berlin Wall, the Arms Race, the Space Race, propaganda, etc.
- the causes, events and consequences of the Cuban Missile Crisis
- the causes of the Vietnam War, the different ways it was fought by the USA and the Viet Cong, and the reasons why the USA withdrew from the war.

A very common mistake is that candidates get very confused between the Cuban Missile Crisis and the Vietnam War. Candidates can also be very one sided when thinking about the Cold War – it is vital that they remember that there were *two* sides in each conflict.

Sample question

'The Vietnam War was the most serious crisis for the USA during the Cold War'.
Consider the arguments for and against this statement:

- Consider the importance of the Vietnam War for the USA.
- Explain other problems the USA faced around the world during the Cold War.
- Decide how far you agree with the statement. [8]

What the examiner has to say!

- You need to explain why the Vietnam War was important for the USA.
- You need to identify and explain at least one other crisis that the USA faced in this period of time (eg. Berlin, Cuba, arms race, etc.).
- A top-level answer will explain why Vietnam was important for the USA, and why other crises were also important to the USA, finishing with a clear judgement explaining which was the most important crisis and why it was the most important.

Exam practice

1 Give two differences between Communism and Capitalism. [2]
2 Describe the arms race between the USA and USSR after 1945. [4]
3 How useful is Figure 4 (on page 103) to a historian studying the Cuban Missile Crisis? [4]
4 Explain why there was a crisis over Cuba in 1962. [6]
5 Explain how the Cuban Missile Crisis affected ordinary people in the USA in 1962. [6]
6 'The cost of the war was the main reason that the USA withdrew its troops from Vietnam.' To what extent do you agree with this statement?
   Give arguments for and against this statement by:
   - *explaining why the Vietnam war was so costly for the USA*
   - *considering any other reasons why the USA withdrew from Vietnam.*

   Conclude by saying how far you agree with the statement. [8]

Why is there a need for racial equality?

How do society's attitudes and values affect people's lives?

Black people in the USA were descended from African men and women who had been captured and brought to work in America as slaves on large plantations in the Southern States. In 1861 President Lincoln had granted all slaves their freedom. This resulted in the American Civil War in which the Southern States fought against the rest of the USA to keep their slaves.

Jim Crow Laws

After racist white people lost the war in **the South** they decided to live completely separate lives from black people as far as possible. This was called **segregation**. In the 1890s, southern states had passed the **Jim Crow Laws** which said that black people were to be treated 'separate but equal'. This kept black people away from white people in schools, on public transport, in restaurants and in public toilets. The presidents of America were always reluctant to deal with the poor treatment of black people. Even the highest court in America, the **Supreme Court**, which was supposed to prosecute people for breaking the **Constitution**, would not deal with this problem. Why? Because presidents and senators and judges all relied on the votes of the southern Americans who were causing these problems in the first place.

Segregation

Segregation took many forms. It did not just mean keeping black and white people apart in public. Black people were not as well educated as white people because schools for black children were usually over-crowded and under-funded. It was often difficult for black people to find decent places to live because many landlords and estate agents would only deal with white people. Many employers would only employ black people as a last resort and might only pay them half of what they would pay a white person to do the same job, and black people would be the first to lose their jobs if businesses started to struggle. This even extended to voting. Even though the US Constitution gives the right to all of its adult citizens to vote,

Figure 9 Segregated public washrooms and water fountains in the Deep South

by 1960 only 20 per cent of black people were registered to vote. The white people who controlled voter registration introduced written tests to make sure that poorly educated black people would not be able to vote.

The Klan

White Americans, particularly in the south, had a very particular view of what the ideal American should be: **White Anglo-Saxon Protestants** (or **WASPs**). One organisation, known as the **Ku Klux Klan (KKK)** took these ideas to the extreme. They dressed in white cloaks and hats to conceal their identities. They frightened black people by placing large burning wooden crosses outside their houses. Sometimes they would even take black people and **lynch** them. The Klan were rarely prosecuted for their crimes because many of their members were local policemen, lawyers and judges.

Activity

1 Describe the ways in which black people in America were discriminated against.

2 Explain why black people in America were discriminated against.

3 Explain how the Second World War started to change attitudes towards black people in the USA.

4 How useful is Figure 9 to a historian studying segregation in the Southern States of the USA.

Progress by 1950

Some progress had been made towards ending segregation during the Second World War. As well as the founding of a new **civil rights** organisation called **CORE (Congress of Racial Equality)**, which had worked to improve working conditions for black people during the war, President Truman had passed a law in 1948 which officially ended segregation within the US Army. The Second World War had a considerable impact on Americans' attitudes towards black people, who were now more widely respected for their bravery in battle and their hard work on the Home Front.

How can people campaign against inequality and injustice?

Education

By 1954, twenty states in America had segregated schools keeping black and white children apart. They were supposed to be 'separate but equal' according to the segregation laws but schools for black children were never as good as those for the white children. One organisation, the **National Association for the Advancement of Colored People (NAACP)**, challenged the laws in the courts when a black girl called Linda Brown was told she was not allowed to go to her nearest school, which was an all-white school. They managed to persuade the highest court in America, the Supreme Court, to rule in their favour, declaring separate schools unconstitutional and unequal.

By the end of 1956 there were still six states in the south of America that had not allowed a single black child to attend an all-white school. This situation in the south was finally challenged in 1957. The Governor of the state of Arkansas tried to use the local army, the National Guard, to stop nine black children, including a fifteen-year-old girl called Elizabeth Eckford, attending Little Rock School (see Figure 10 on page 112). The law said the children were allowed to attend.

The Governor of Arkansas lost that battle and withdrew the National Guard, leaving the black children at the mercy of an angry mob of white parents who did not want these black children in their schools. In the end, President Eisenhower, who was forced to support the laws made by the Supreme Court, had to send in 1,000 paratroopers with fixed bayonets to protect these children as they went to school. Again, many people from outside the South were horrified that such anger and hatred existed against black people.

Figure 10 Elizabeth Eckford being harassed by the white mob on her way into Little Rock High School, 1957

Public transport

Segregation on public transport was another humiliation that black people had to suffer regularly. The front seats of all buses were reserved for white people only and black people could only sit in the middle of a bus if no white people wanted to sit there.

In December 1955, in a town called Montgomery, in the state of Alabama, Rosa Parks, a black woman, refused to get up to stand at the back of the bus so a white man could sit in her seat. She was arrested, thrown in prison and fined $10. Her friends were so angry that they organised a protest where no black people would ride on the buses until segregation was ended. This became known as the **Montgomery Bus Boycott**. The slogan of the Montgomery Bus Boycott was 'People don't ride the bus today. Don't ride it for freedom'.

The bus companies were hit very hard as 75 per cent of their passengers were black people. Supporters of the bus companies used all kinds of intimidation to try and get black people back on the buses, but without any success. After nearly a year, short of money and under orders from the Supreme Court, the bus companies gave in and segregation on the buses was ended. After this first success, the campaign moved all around America.

People who used the buses to help end segregation became known as '**Freedom Riders**'. The Freedom Riders were activists who rode interstate buses into the southern states to test out the ruling that had outlawed racial segregation. They faced a lot of violence from white people, even the police, who wanted to keep segregation going.

The first Civil Rights Act 1957

In 1957 President Eisenhower passed a Civil Rights Act to encourage more black people to be able to vote. Because of opposition in the Senate, and a number of last-minute changes, it was not very effective because it was difficult to enforce. However, it did pave the way for future laws which would end segregation and discrimination in housing and improve black people's voting rights.

Activity

1 Describe the main events of the campaign to desegregate education.

2 Describe the main events of the campaign to desegregate public transport.

3 How useful is Figure 10 to a historian studying events at Little Rock High School?

4 Explain why education and public transportation were desegregated.

How can protest movements affect attitudes in society?

How important are leaders in protest movements?

Martin Luther King

One of the key figures in the campaign for civil rights was Martin Luther King. King's experiences earlier in his life formed the basis for his determination to end segregation in the USA. At school his best friend was white, but his friend's parents disapproved of their friendship. At college King heard about the work of Mahatma Ghandi, who had helped break unfair laws in British India whilst always being peaceful and polite. This type of protest is known as '**passive disobedience**'.

After college he became preacher at a church in Alabama and was one of the black ministers who organised the Montgomery Bus Boycott in 1955. He began to receive threatening telephone calls and his house was mysteriously firebombed. King moved to Atlanta and began the first '**sit in**'. He was arrested three times in 1960 and 1961 for taking part and organising these **non-violent protests**.

In 1963 Martin Luther King organised a massive protest march in Birmingham, Alabama. The police met this non-violent protest with vicious attacks on the protesters. In August, Martin Luther King led the **march on Washington** for 'jobs and freedom'. One quarter of a million people turned up to hear his famous 'I have a dream …' speech at the Lincoln Memorial (see Figure 11 on page 114). In 1964, the work of Martin Luther King gained international recognition when he was awarded the **Nobel Prize for Peace** (see Source A). He gave the $54,000 prize money to civil rights organisations.

King was arrested in the town of Selma in 1965 after he led a march to demand that black people should be allowed to vote. The police viciously attacked protesters. Sixty people were seriously injured and the public were so horrified that the **1965 Voting Rights Act** was soon passed. In 1967, during the Vietnam War, King said that no one should be sent off to fight for freedom in other countries until everyone in America was free. As with his work over civil rights, all he wanted was peace.

In 1968 Martin Luther King went to Memphis to organise a march in support of the local dustmen who were being treated unfairly by their new mayor. He made another one of his famous speeches about how black people would soon reach their 'promised land'. He was shot dead on 4 April by James Earl Ray as he stood on his motel balcony.

Martin Luther King's protests and speeches turned public support around the world in favour of granting equal civil rights to black people. President Johnson attended his **funeral**, and his family received over 150,000 messages of condolence from around the world.

King proved to be an important figure in the civil rights movement. He was energetic and enthusiastic and was able to inspire those who worked with him. His impassioned speeches won him many supporters.

Source A

From the Nobel Peace Prize citation for Martin Luther King, 1964.

He is the first person in the Western world to have shown us that a struggle can be waged without violence. He makes the message of brotherly love a reality in the course of this struggle, and he has brought this message to all nations and races. He has never abandoned his faith in the struggle he is waging, he has been imprisoned on many occasions, his family has been threatened, but he has never faltered.

Examiner's Tips

Question – how important was Martin Luther King in the success of the Civil Rights Movement? *Consider* the qualities that make someone a good leader, e.g. influential ideas, setting a good example; powerful public speaker, *but* don't forget there are other explanations for success, e.g. media coverage, actions of politicians, economic pressure, etc.

'I have a dream that one day this nation will rise up and live out the true meaning of its creed: We hold these truths to be self-evident, that all men are created equal … I have a dream that my four little children will one day live in a nation where they will not be judged by the color of their skin but by the content of their character.'

Figure 11 Martin Luther King giving his famous 'I have a dream …' speech in Washington, 1963

Activity

1 Describe Martin Luther King's 'dream' (see Figure 11) in your own words.

2 Explain why the ideas of Martin Luther King appealed to many white people.

3 Explain why Martin Luther King was an important leader of the Civil Rights Movement.

4 How useful are Source A (on page 113) and Figure 11 to a historian studying the importance of Martin Luther King in the struggle for civil rights?

How can protest movements affect government policy and attitudes?

What the Civil Rights Movement needed was a new president and a new set of circumstances to change the segregation laws. This new president was John F. Kennedy. Kennedy was committed to doing everything he could to help the Civil Rights Movement. He sent troops to enable the black student James Meredith to attend university in Mississippi in 1962. He sent out 500 US Marshals to protect the Freedom Riders. And in 1963 he closed the last of the segregated schools in Alabama, ordering the local governor and police chief to end their campaign of violence against the civil rights protesters. He also ordered that they release Martin Luther King from prison.

In August 1963 Martin Luther King led his March on Washington, whilst this bill was still being discussed. Kennedy had to ask him to call it off so that **Congress** could not use it as an excuse to vote against the bill. Martin Luther King refused. He said that if he called the march off it might lead to violence.

Opposition to Kennedy's civil rights bill caused many of his other important laws, on the space programme and foreign aid, to be held up. Congress was finally forced to pass the bill as a mark of respect after Kennedy's **assassination** in November 1963. His successor, Lyndon B. Johnson, was a southern Democrat. He had always opposed civil rights for black people. He had voted against an anti-**lynching** bill in 1937. However, once he had become president, Johnson helped to push through Kennedy's civil rights bill and oversaw many bills being passed, including the 1965 Voting Rights Act.

CIVIL RIGHTS LAWS	
1964	CIVIL RIGHTS ACT outlawed racial discrimination in jobs, restaurants, hotels and amusement arcades; made sure all schools were equally funded; an Equal Employment Opportunity Commission was set up to investigate complaints.
1965	VOTING RIGHTS ACT stopped racial discrimination over voting.
1967	SUPREME COURT RULING said state law is not allowed to prevent inter-racial marriages.
1968	CIVIL RIGHTS ACT made discrimination in housing illegal.

Many things have changed for black Americans since these acts were passed, culminating in the election of America's first black president in 2008. Although civil rights improved for many black people in theory, some problems still remain:
- many poor black people still live in poor-quality urban ghettoes (in 1999, 55 per cent of black people lived in run-down urban areas)
- black Americans are much more likely to be unemployed than whites (in 1999, 9 per cent of black people were unemployed, compared to just 4 per cent of white people)
- on average black people still earn much less than white people (in 2008, black Americans earned an average $10,000 less than the national average wage)
- black people are still the victims of racially motivated violence (e.g. the beating of Rodney King by police officers in California in 1991)
- there is still a much higher proportion of black people in prison and on 'death row' in America compared to white people (black people make up 12 per cent of the US population but 35 per cent of criminals in 2010).

Activity

5 Explain why American presidents passed civil rights laws in the 1960s.

6 How effective were the civil rights laws passed in the 1960s?

How do the attitudes of some groups influence the nature of their protest?

Why are some protest groups more radical than others?

New laws did not change people's opinions over night. Many white people still feared and hated black people. The Ku Klux Klan still operated. Many black people thought that the new laws had not gone far enough. These included Malcolm X and Stokeley Carmichael. Malcolm X was the most famous member of a group, the Nation of Islam, whose supporters called for separatism, a total separation of blacks and whites, or a separate black state. Members of the Nation of Islam believed that the solution was a separate nation for blacks to develop themselves apart from what they considered to be a white nation destined for destruction.

Many members of the mainstream civil rights groups did not like the Nation of Islam and felt that they had a 'hate-white doctrine' which was as dangerous as any white racist group.

Case Study

Malcolm X

Malcolm Little's father had been murdered by the Klan. His mother became so ill her children had to be taken away from her. After growing up in foster homes and reform schools, Malcolm ended up in prison for burglary where he joined an organisation called the **Nation of Islam**. They wanted black people to live apart from white people completely. He had changed his surname to 'X' saying that he would not recognise the slave name his family had been given by the white men.

By the early 1960s, the Nation of Islam had become well known and Malcolm was their most prominent spokesperson. The media portrayed Malcolm X as a 'dangerous black racist' because he had said that, if necessary, black people were to use violence to protect themselves and their interests. In 1963, however, the Black Muslims silenced Malcolm for his remark that the assassination of United States President John F. Kennedy was like 'the chickens coming home to roost'. In the following year, Malcolm broke with the Nation of Islam and formed a new black nationalist group, the **Organization of Afro-American Unity (OAAU)**.

In 1964 Malcolm made a hajj (pilgrimage) to the Islamic holy city of Mecca, Saudi Arabia. Based on this trip, and other travels to Africa and Europe, he renounced his previous teaching that all whites are evil, and adopted the Arabic name El-Hadj Malik El-Shabazz. On 21 February 1965, while addressing an OAAU rally in New York City, Malcolm was assassinated. Some believe he was killed by rivals within the Nation of Islam movement, but some extremists believe that his murder was the result of a conspiracy between the New York City Police and the FBI who were worried about the political threat that he posed.

'We don't go for segregation. We go for separation. Separation is when you have your own. You control your own economy; you control your own politics; you control your own society.'

Figure 12 Malcolm X describing how black people should be totally separated from white people in the speech 'We go for separation' at Michigan State University, 23 January 1963

Case Study

Stokely Carmichael

Stokely Carmichael had been influenced by Malcolm X. He had been a member of the **Student Non-Violent Co-Ordinating Committee** which organised sit-ins. After Malcolm X, Carmichael took over the idea that black people needed to live separate from but equal lives to white people, and be proud of their differences and their heritage. He called this '**Black Power**'. He toured America giving speeches to raise support amongst black people for his ideas.

Carmichael had many important supporters. The boxer Mohammed Ali refused to go and fight in Vietnam and was stripped of his Olympic gold medal and sent to prison. And at the 1968 Olympics in Mexico, two black American athletes, Tommy Smith and John Carlos, made a Black Power salute during the American national anthem as they were awarded their medals. It was shown to a worldwide television audience of hundreds of millions of people. Black Power ideas are still very influential in many parts of the USA today.

> 'We have got to get us some Black Power. We don't control anything but what white people say we can control. We have to be able to smash any political machine in the country that's oppressing us and bring it to its knees … We have to organize ourselves to speak for each other. That's Black Power. We have to move to control the economics and politics of our community.'

Figure 13 Extract of Stokely Carmichael's speech on 'Black Power', 1966

Activity

1 Explain the part played by Malcolm X in the movement for civil rights for black people in America.

2 Explain why some black leaders did not agree with the aims and methods of the civil rights campaign.

3 How useful is Malcolm X's speech (see Figure 12) to a historian studying the campaign for civil rights in 1960s USA?

4 Describe the aims of the Black Power movement.

5 How useful is Stokely Carmichael's speech (see Figure 13) to an historian studying the Black Power movement?

6 'The Black Power movement made the biggest contribution to the civil rights campaign.' How far do you agree with this statement?

Do radical protest groups influence the attitudes, values and beliefs of society?

Race riots

Throughout the 1960s, there were outbreaks of violence from black communities in the USA because of their frustration that not enough was being done quickly enough to help them. In 1964, there were race riots in Harlem and in areas of other northern cities. In 1965, 33 people were killed in the **Watts riots** in Los Angeles. Many black people refused to fight in the Vietnam War. Stokely Carmichael argued that it was pointless for black men to fight for the freedom of Vietnamese people when they did not have freedom at home. In 1967 there were further riots in Newark, Detroit and other cities, where 83 people were shot dead. This peaked in 1968 when there was a strike by black people in Memphis, Tennessee to campaign for equal pay. The police savagely attacked the protesters and a Black Power group attacked the local police station. Martin Luther King was assassinated while trying to organise peaceful marches through Memphis. The riots across America that followed the news of his death saw 30 people killed and thousands more injured. Many of these riots were spontaneous acts of desperate and angry black people, rather than organised by radical groups.

The Black Panthers

The most notorious black organisation was the **Black Panther Party** which was founded in 1966, with its membership reaching a peak in 1968. Its aim was to organise groups of black men to defend black communities against violence from white people, especially the police. To advertise their support, members would dress completely in black, almost like a military uniform, and patrol in black neighbourhoods. The group came to be less about violence and more about how to improve conditions for black people.

The White Backlash

Some white people continued to maintain some form of segregation after civil rights laws were passed. This is called the '**White Backlash**'. Politicians tried to use 'redlining' to ensure that white communities got more funding and better facilities than those dominated by black people. White people organised protests against 'busing' – the use of transportation to move black students into schools previously exclusively for white children. George Wallace was elected as Governor of Alabama in 1963, with the promise that his policies would be dominated by 'Segregation now, segregation tomorrow, segregation forever!'. He even stood as a candidate for president in 1968.

Activity

1 Describe how some black people responded to discrimination with violence.

2 Explain the reaction of the white population in the Deep South to the campaign for civil rights.

3 'Rioting and violence made it more difficult to persuade white people to support civil rights.' Do you agree with this statement? Explain your answer.

Examiner's Tips

To help with your preparation for the exam, make sure you know:

- the problems black people faced before civil rights
- the non-violent Civil Rights Movement
- the more aggressive Black Power Movement
- the reasons why white people, and the US government, supported civil rights
- the reasons why many white people continued to oppose civil rights for black people.

A very common mistake is that candidates focus just on the non-violent Civil Rights Movement and forget that there were several movements involved in the civil rights struggle, including the Nation of Islam and supporters of Black Power.

Sample question

Why do Sources A and B give different views of the value of the work of Martin Luther King?
(In your answer you should consider the authorship and content of the sources.) [6]

> 'Martin preached about black people being equal to white people. He knew it would be hard but he wanted no violence. We went on marches, listened to his speeches, sat down on the roads and in restaurants. We wanted the same rights. It was because of him that we got our rights.'
>
> [A civil rights activist, speaking to a journalist in 1968, just after Martin Luther King was assassinated]

Source A

> 'Martin Luther King was seen as being too moderate and his non-violent approach was regarded by many people as weak and ineffective. Blacks were becoming increasingly frustrated by King's approach and many felt that violence was the only way to achieve civil rights. The decision to grant civil rights to blacks owed very little to King.'
>
> [Neil de Marco, a historian writing in school history textbook *The USA: a divided nation* (Longman, 1992)]

Source B

What the examiner has to say!

- You must identify what the differences are between the two authors of the sources – who they are, when they are writing, why they are writing, what evidence they will have used, etc. – BECAUSE this will give you the reasons why these views are different.
- You must identify the differences between what the two views actually say (in this case, one author thinks that civil rights was the result of non-violent protest, while the other thinks it was more to do with violence).
- A top-level answer will accurately describe the differences between what the two authors have said and then explain those differences using the information about the authors (e.g. one author was writing at the time of a lot of anger towards non-violent protest as King had just been killed, but the other author has the benefit of hindsight and is less affected personally by events).

Exam practice

1. Give two examples of the ways in which people protested against racial inequality. [2]
2. Describe the ways in which black people were segregated in the USA. [4]
3. How useful is Figure 10 (on page 112) to a historian studying the struggle for civil rights for black people in the USA? [4]
4. Explain why the Montgomery Bus Boycott was important to the struggle for black people's civil rights in the USA. [6]
5. Explain how the Civil Rights Act of 1964 improved the lives of black Americans. [6]
6. 'The methods used by the Black Power movement were the most important reason for black people gaining their civil rights in the USA.' To what extent do you agree with this statement?
   Give arguments for and against this statement by:
   - *describing the methods used by the Black Power movement*
   - *considering other methods used to achieve civil rights for black people.*

   Conclude by saying how far you agree with the statement. [8]

How do political and economic conditions help to bring about increased prosperity?

How do favourable economic conditions give opportunities for human societies?

Mainland America was not invaded or bombed in the Second World War, and had made a lot of money selling weapons to her allies. By the end of the war America was richer than it had ever been. Having such a lot of money to spend on luxuries is known as **affluence**. As prices fell after the war, wages rose. By 1960 the consumer had 40 per cent more to spend than they had a decade earlier.

There was a post-war 'baby boom' which increased the population by 40 million people. It happened because the new affluence of America meant that people could afford to have more children. The population of America grew from 151 million in 1950 to 179 million in 1960. This meant an even greater economic boom as it meant there was more demand for industrial goods.

Consumerism is the idea that buying goods makes people happy and keeps the economy strong. After 1945, Americans were only saving 5 per cent of the money they earned. People were encouraged to spend. Shopping became a leisure activity. As people became more affluent they moved out to new homes in planned communities in the suburbs, at the edge of towns and cities. By 1960 a quarter of all Americans lived in suburbia. Between 1945 and 1960 the number of private cars increased from 25 to 62 million. America produced more than half of the world's oil and steel, so cars were cheap and becoming cheaper all the time. Goods that had once been thought to be too luxurious – washing machines, televisions, refrigerators – came to be seen as everyday necessities. By 1960, 90 per cent of homes in America had a television set. Advertising appeared everywhere, encouraging people to spend more and more money. Attitudes to spending changed. Rather than spending what they had on essentials, people were encouraged to borrow. Hire purchase increased by 800 per cent between 1945 and 1957.

How can government policies help to improve standards of living?

In 1959, 22 per cent of the population lived below the '**poverty line**', so could not afford to feed and clothe themselves or their families. They included the black and immigrant communities who were given badly paid jobs; farm workers from the south and east who had fewer job opportunities; and the old and sick who had expensive medical bills to take care of.

Americans had no unemployment, sickness or old-age benefits paid by the government because richer Americans did not want to pay higher taxes and many did not want to see the government giving charity to the poor.

In the early 1960s, *The Other America* by Michael Harrington was published. He showed that a large number of people in America continued to live in poverty even though the country was becoming richer all of the time. He claimed that between 40 and 50 million Americans were poor because of lack of education and medical care, poor housing, old age and alcohol.

Both Kennedy and Johnson implemented policies to help improve standards of living.

Kennedy's 'New Frontier'

Kennedy told Americans he would:
- provide money to educate the poor
- pass laws to grant equal civil rights to black people
- improve government care for the sick and the elderly.

Kennedy failed to achieve this because:
- crises in Berlin and Cuba distracted him
- many Democratic Southern senators supported segregation
- he was assassinated in 1963.

Johnson's 'Great Society'

After Johnson won the 1964 presidential election, he passed:
- the Economic Opportunity Act to provide training to disadvantaged youths aged 16 to 21, to help poor students go to college and to recruit volunteers to teach in slum areas
- Medicare and Medicaid to provide medical insurance for the over 65s and hospital care for the poor
- the Development Act to provide money to replace city slums with new homes
- Civil Rights laws to end racial discrimination.

By the end of the 1960s the number of Americans living below the poverty line had been halved. But there was a lot of opposition to the 'Great Society' plan. Some schemes were badly planned and in some areas government funds were used to protest against the government's own policies in Vietnam. The cost of the war in Vietnam also prevented Johnson from completing his plan to end poverty.

Activity

1 Explain why there was a growth of the consumer society in America after 1945.

2 What was Johnson's 'Great Society'?

3 Explain why it was considered necessary in the 1960s to bring in a policy such as the 'Great Society'.

How do developments in popular culture contribute to changes in society?

How did entertainment and leisure develop after 1945?

Young people in the 1950s had a lot more money to spend on themselves than any other young people before them. Companies even designed special products for them such as designer clothes and teenage magazines. More and more young people could afford to buy radios and record players to follow new trends in fashion and music.

Popular music

In the early 1950s there was a revolution in popular music. Big bands and crooners like Frank Sinatra became known as 'Mom and Dad' music.

Young people instead turned to music of black people, experimenting with drums and the twelve bar blues. Out of these experiments came a new and exciting form of music called 'Rock 'n' Roll'. The first records of this kind to be produced for a mass audience came from people like Bill Haley, who with his group the Comets had a number of hit records including 'Rock Around the Clock'. In 1956, Elvis

Figure 14 Bob Dylan performing

Come mothers and fathers throughout the land
And don't criticize what you can't understand
Your sons and your daughters are beyond your command
Your old road is rapidly agin'.
Please get out of the new one if you can't lend your hand
For the times they are a-changin'

A verse from 'The Times They Are a-Changin' by Bob Dylan, 1964

Presley entered the pop music scene. His music was a mixture of country and western and rhythm and blues. He was very successful with teenagers but their parents and teachers did not like him. They criticised his long sideburns, his sneering expression and the sexual way he performed.

In the 1960s American music was invigorated by the arrival of '**Beatle Mania**', a hysterical reaction to the music of the Beatles from Britain. Many American bands tried to imitate the style and sound of the Beatles and other British bands who followed them.

The Monkees were created for American TV to be the American equivalent of the Beatles. A revived interest in folk music also saw the rise of musicians like Bob Dylan who sang inspirational songs about important issues like the struggle for civil rights or the war in Vietnam. As the 1960s progressed the hippy movement also had its own music, including bands like the Grateful Dead.

Cinema and television

Cinema struggled to hold on to the massive audiences it had gained during the Second World War. The old Hollywood '**star system**' where film studios could hold actors to long contracts and block-book studios for their films was brought to an end by a Supreme Court ruling which allowed actors and small-scale film-makers more freedom. There was also the rising threat to cinema audiences from television, which brought a wide range of entertainment right into people's homes. Comedies like 'The Honeymooners' and 'I Love Lucy', serial dramas – also known as soap operas – like 'Peyton Place', entertainment programmes like 'The Ed Sullivan Show', even national network news shows anchored by star reporters like Walter Cronkite, were broadcast to more and more homes by new local and national television networks.

In response to other changes in America, cinema began to change. **Technological innovations** such as full-colour films, stereo sound, widescreen images and even 3D glasses were introduced to increase audiences.

The opening of **drive-in movie cinemas** provided cheap films on a large scale in the 1950s and 60s. Because of the freedom and privacy they offered, drive-in movie cinemas became very popular with young people.

While adults continued to enjoy musicals like 'Singing in the Rain', or romantic comedies starring Rock Hudson and Doris Day, with their clean-cut and sensible characters, young people preferred Marlon Brando in 'The Wild One' and James Dean in 'Rebel Without A Cause'. These were films where young people turned against the sensible world of their parents. The 1960s saw more films that reflected changing youth culture, such as 'Easy Rider', a film about two young drug dealers and their journey across America, and 'Woodstock', the film about the free music festival that took place over four days in 1969.

Activity

1 What changes occurred in American popular culture after 1945?

2 What does Figure 14 (page 121) tell us about the changing relationship between children and their parents in the 1960s?

3 How useful is Figure 15 to a historian studying changes to US popular culture in the 1950s?

Figure 15 Poster for the film 'Rebel Without a Cause'

How can different social groups react to developments in popular culture?

Young and old

Many did not understand changing attitudes amongst young people in the 1950s and 60s. Some people said that Rock 'n' Roll music encouraged teenage crime. As time passed, rebellious teenagers joined new groups with new ideas.

Many of these angry young people were middle-class white college students. They were disgusted by the struggle for Civil Rights and the war in Vietnam. They dropped out of college and did not aim to get well-paid jobs. They did not trust politicians. This set of radical ideas is often referred to as the **counter-culture**. Some were involved in open demonstrations against the war, such as the one at Kent State University in Ohio in 1970 that ended with four students shot dead by the National Guard.

Adults in the 1950s and 60s were confused. They had grown up being told to respect their parents and each other. The '**Generation Gap**' that had opened up between adults and young people made it difficult for older people to understand. It is important to remember that not all young people rebelled. Many continued to follow the values that were important to their parents.

> **Beatniks (1950s)**
> - Young people who rejected the conservative values of their parents.
> - Inspired by authors like Jack Kerouac and his novel *On The Road*.
> - Summed up by the phrase 'Live fast, die young, and have a good-looking corpse'.

> **Hippies (1960s)**
> - Young people who turned completely against the affluent lifestyle and politics of their parents.
> - Inspired by thinkers like Timothy Leary.
> - Took drugs and engaged in more open sexual behaviour.
> - Summed up by the phrase 'Turn on, tune in, drop out'.

Activity

4 Describe how young people's attitudes changed in the 1950s and 60s.

5 Why did some Americans dislike the changes in popular culture?

Women

The lives of women were greatly changed during this period of American history as well. The Second World War had introduced many women to work and wages for the first time in their lives. These jobs were usually in traditionally male areas, but despite their wartime experiences many women preferred to return to life in the home once the war was over.

Women were supposed to stay at home, but the needs of consumerism meant that they were expected to go out and earn some wages too. Whilst men were expected to buy cars, women were supposed to want fitted kitchens and cooking devices. Although more women than ever were going out to work in the 1950s, almost all were in low-pay 'women's occupations', such as office and shop work.

By the 1960s these views were beginning to change. A new kind of feminism was inspired by the ideas and tactics of the Civil Rights Movement. Women had been theoretically granted equal rights to men under the 1963 Equal Pay Act and 1964 **Civil Rights Act**. Many employers in particular were slow to acknowledge this. Women needed to take further action to ensure they were given equal rights to men.

The women's movement was launched in 1963 by *The Feminine Mystique*, a book by Betty Freidan. She wrote that women were not happy being the housewives that society told them they should be. She explained that families were equal partnerships between men and women. She encouraged women to develop themselves through education and work outside the home. The book became a bestseller.

By the mid-1960s the phrase '**Women's Liberation**' came into use. In 1966, the **National Organization for Women (NOW)** was set up. Feminists used petitions, strikes and legal action to push employers to increase wages and open top-level jobs to women. One widely publicised protest took place at the annual beauty contest, the Miss America Pageant in 1968.

Figure 16 Feminist protesters outside the 1968 Miss America Pageant

The idea that sexual discrimination was wrong was becoming more widespread. In 1972 the Supreme Court ruled that any discrimination against women in employment, education or any other aspect of life was illegal.

Religious groups

Many religious groups reacted angrily to what they saw as the open sexuality and blasphemy of the counter-culture and Women's Liberation. Many saw religion as a way to stop the spread of Communism, and church attendance increased from 50 per cent of adults in 1940 to 65 per cent of adults in 1960. Many believed 'the family that prays together, stays together'. Evangelist preachers like Billy Graham started using radio and television to spread their message and became an important influence in American life.

Activity

1 Explain why the role of women in the USA changed after 1945.

How important are political events in influencing people and society?

How can iconic political events affect the attitudes and values of society?

The assassination of President Kennedy

President John F. Kennedy is one of America's best-remembered presidents, and yet during the 1,000 or so days he was president he actually managed to achieve very little in America itself. His main focus was on tackling the Cold War with the USSR – the Berlin Wall, Cuba, the Space and Arms Races. Kennedy was deeply concerned by the problems of poverty in America and by the lack of civil rights for black people. He was assassinated before he could pass any laws to deal with these problems, although these problems were eventually dealt with as a mark of respect to his memory.

President Kennedy was shot and killed in Dealey Plaza, Dallas while on a tour of the city on 22 November 1963. There was a lot of confusion about what happened at the time, even though the 'Zapruder film', taken by a by-stander, very clearly documents the moment of Kennedy's death. Many of the eye-witnesses to the event subsequently died under strange circumstances, including Lee Harvey Oswald, the man believed to have shot Kennedy, who was himself killed by local Mafia thug Jack Ruby before he could be interviewed by police. All records and evidence from the assassination, including the autopsy report, were sealed for 75 years under a secrecy act, so it is very difficult to know what happened.

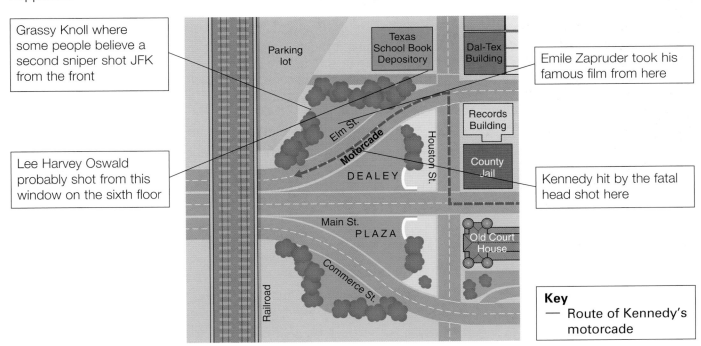

Grassy Knoll where some people believe a second sniper shot JFK from the front

Emile Zapruder took his famous film from here

Lee Harvey Oswald probably shot from this window on the sixth floor

Kennedy hit by the fatal head shot here

Parking lot

Texas School Book Depository

Dal-Tex Building

Records Building

County Jail

Elm St.

Motorcade

Houston St.

DEALEY

Main St.

PLAZA

Old Court House

Commerce St.

Railroad

Key
— Route of Kennedy's motorcade

Figure 17 Diagram of the Dealey plaza scene showing the positions of the motorcade during the shooting and the potential location of shooters

Different explanations for the Kennedy assassination

The '**Lone Gunman Theory**' says that Kennedy was shot dead by a single assassin, Lee Harvey Oswald, who was firing from the sixth floor of the Dallas School Book Depository. A rifle found at the scene was identical to one that Oswald had recently bought by mail order. Oswald was on record as opposing Kennedy's policies on Cuba and he had been dishonourably discharged from the US Army, which would give him a motive. This theory was supported by the Warren Commission Report, the official government investigation which was published in 1964.

Because of difficulties with the evidence, many people have come to believe in **conspiracy theories** which suggest that someone tried to cover up the real reasons for Kennedy's assassination. They have tried to show that Oswald could not have killed Kennedy from his position (as Kennedy's car was a long way off and moving downhill and away) and have suggested that he was killed by snipers who shot Kennedy from behind the hill by the railway yard (known as the 'grassy knoll'). There have been a number of further court cases and commissions set up to re-examine the evidence. The lack of hard evidence to prove these theories wrong has meant that more and more people have come to believe that they are true. No one can prove these theories right or wrong until the evidence is finally released in the 2030s.

Impact of the assassination

Public reaction to the assassination was immediate. It is estimated that 54 per cent of Americans stopped what they were doing when they heard the news. Schools closed. People cried openly in the streets. Many consider it to be one of the great shared experiences of Americans, as memorable and important as hearing of the Japanese attack on Pearl Harbour in 1941, or of the 9/11 attacks in 2001.

The political impact of the assassination was far reaching. Lyndon Johnson became President and pushed through civil rights laws and measures to reduce poverty, using the death of Kennedy as a way of persuading Southern opponents to give their support in honour of his memory. It also led to Johnson's more aggressive policy against the Communists in Vietnam and an escalation in American involvement. He believed that you needed to take a stand before it spread quickly into America.

As a young President, Kennedy had been an inspiration to many young people who now became more interested and involved in politics, particularly through protest movements. This would ultimately lead to the US voting age being reduced to 18 in 1972.

Activity

1 Describe the Lone Gunman theory of the Kennedy assassination.

2 How useful is Figure 17 (on page 125) to a historian studying the Kennedy assassination?

3 Explain why it is difficult to find out the truth about the Kennedy assassination.

How can political scandal affect the attitudes and values of society?

The Watergate Scandal

Richard Nixon, representing the **Republican Party**, became US president in 1968. For four years he ran America and made himself very popular. He was the president who spoke to the first US astronauts on the moon, he was the first president to visit Communist China, he brought US troops home from Vietnam and he made an agreement with the USSR to limit nuclear weapons.

The **Democratic Party** were using offices in the Watergate complex in Washington to run their election campaign. On 17 June 1972, five burglars were caught inside these offices with the equipment needed to plant listening devices. All of them worked for the Republican Committee for the Re-election of the President (known as CREEP).

The Democrats accused the Republicans of 'a blatant act of political espionage', but Nixon and his staff denied all involvement in the break-in. Democrat politicians always called Nixon 'Tricky Dicky' because of the way he always avoided answering their questions.

Nixon was still popular. In 1972 he won by a landslide, the largest vote any Republican president had had in American history. There is no evidence to suggest that Nixon knew about the break-in before it happened. The crime that he committed was that he tried to cover it up afterwards so that no one could blame him for it. Nixon used his presidential powers to help the cover-up, blocking police, Justice Department and Congressional investigations.

The investigation

The media slowly began to uncover the truth. Woodward and Bernstein from *The Washington Post* received a lot of information about Watergate from a secret contact they called '**Deep Throat**'.

After the burglars had been sent to prison, a special **Senate Watergate Committee** was set up. During the trial of the burglars, one of them had said that important men in the White House had been involved and that he had been offered a lot of money to say nothing about it.

The Senate committee investigation was televised and everyone was shocked when one witness, John Dean, turned on Nixon and accused him of obstructing justice. Nixon had to go on television to deny this. He said that no one would try to hide anything: 'There can be no whitewash at the White House'.

In the summer of 1973 it was revealed that President Nixon kept tapes of all the private conversations he had in the Oval Office of the White House. These tapes would prove that Nixon was lying about the cover-up in just the same way as a smoking gun would give away a killer, and became known as **smoking gun tapes**.

Nixon tried to resist having to hand these tapes over. In the end, public demands for his **impeachment** (removal from office) were growing. Investigators were angered when they found that eighteen minutes of conversation about Watergate had been erased. People were upset by the way he acted more like a gangster than a politician. He seemed to think that the law did not apply to him. Nixon faced the possibility of going to prison.

Figure 18 Nixon is greeted by movie star John Wayne during 1972 election campaign

Resignation

On 8 August 1974 Nixon became the only American President to resign from office. The reason he gave was that he could not run America and fight to save his reputation both at the same time. He was replaced by Gerald Ford.

The effect of the **Watergate Scandal** was that people did not trust their presidents as much as they had done previously. As the new president, Gerald Ford, said at the time 'our long national nightmare is over. Our Constitution works. Our great Republic is a government of laws and not of men'.

After Watergate was over, the US Congress passed new laws to limit the power of the president. Jimmy Carter was elected as president in 1976 because he was a local politician who had nothing to do with corrupt Washington. He promised the American people 'I will never lie to you'. Opinion polls showed that only 14 per cent of Americans trusted the US government in 1974. It had been 57 per cent in 1958.

Activity

1 Describe the political event known as the Watergate Scandal.

2 Explain the role of President Nixon and his advisers in the Watergate cover-up.

3 What effect did Watergate have on America?

Examiner's Tips

In preparation for the exam, make sure you know:

- consumerism made many Americans more wealthy, but many Americans were too poor to benefit from this new affluence
- Presidents Kennedy and Johnson made a number of attempts to improve the lives of deprived Americans
- there were many changes in popular culture in the 1950s and 60s but many young people and most older people did not support or follow some of the more extreme changes

- the lives of many, but not all, women changed in this period of time.

A very common mistake is that candidates are too vague when answering questions on this topic, for example making statements like 'young people listened to Rock 'N' Roll' without giving a specific example. Many candidates also write as if everyone followed every change – not all young people in the 1960s were hippies.

Sample question

How useful is Source A as evidence to a historian studying the growth of the 'affluent society' in the USA in the 1950s? [4]

	\multicolumn{4}{c	}{Families owning (%)}
	Cars	Televisions	Refrigerators	Washing machines
1948	54.0	2.9	76.6	67.4
1949	56.0	10.1	79.2	68.4
1950	60.0	26.4	86.4	71.9
1951	65.0	38.5	86.7	73.5
1952	65.0	50.2	89.2	76.2
1953	65.0	63.5	90.4	78.5
1954	70.0	74.1	92.5	81.3
1955	71.0	76.1	94.1	84.1
1956	73.0	81.0	96.0	86.8

Source A

What the examiner has to say!

- You need to identify what this source does tell us about what the historian is studying (in this case the growth of the 'affluent society').
- You need to identify what important elements of the topic the historian is studying are not covered by the source (in this case, for example, it does not tell the historian why this is happening or who is able to afford these products).
- A top-level answer will show the ways in which the source is both useful in some ways, and yet limited in others, for the historian.

Exam practice

1. Describe the living standards of some Americans in the 1950s. [2]
2. Describe the development of cinema in the USA after 1945. [4]
3. How useful is Figure 16 (on page 124) to a historian studying the women's rights movement? [4]
4. Explain why the government introduced such policies as the 'New Frontier' and the 'Great Society'. [6]
5. Explain why many American women supported the Women's Liberation movement in the 1960s. [6]
6. 'The most important event in the USA after 1945 was the assassination of President John F. Kennedy.'
   To what extent do you agree with this statement?
   Give arguments for and against this statement by:
   - *explaining the importance of the assassination of President Kennedy*
   - *considering other important events or development which took place after 1945.*

   Conclude by saying how far you agree with this statement. [8]

What are the main beliefs and teachings that underpin Christian attitudes?

Being a Christian is not just a case of reading the **Bible** or going to church; it is following a set of beliefs and values that have a real impact on the way that people live their lives.

Jesus' life and teachings are at the very heart of Christianity. We find out about Jesus in the New Testament of the Bible; the story of the birth of Jesus can be found in two of the **Gospels**: Matthew (1:18–25, 2:1–12) and Luke (1:26–38, 2:1–20).

During his time on earth Jesus did many amazing things; Christians believe that he even worked **miracles**. This is further evidence to them that Jesus was the son of God. There are over 30 miracles in the New Testament – find out what happens in Luke 5:18–19. One of the most famous miracles is the Feeding of the 5,000 (Mark 6:30–44). Many Christians think that the point of this miracle is that if everyone shares what they have, even if it is very little, then everyone will be alright.

What beliefs underpin the Christian religion?

Holy week

The events of the last week of Jesus' life (Holy Week) were amongst the first things to have been written down. Each of the Gospels tells of Jesus' suffering in the hours before he died. Figure 2 is an overview of the week; you can read the full account in Luke 19:28–23:38.

Figure 1 Jesus walks on water

Activity

1 Read both accounts of the birth of Jesus in the Gospels. Make a note of the differences. You should think about each of the unusual occurrences: the angels visiting Mary and Joseph; the three kings (Magi); the angel visiting the shepherds and their claims proving to be true; the warning of the Magi in a dream. What significance does each have?

2 What do you think Gospel accounts of the birth of Jesus are trying to tell us? Christians believe that these events are important not only because some of them probably saved the young Jesus' life, but they are also signs that Jesus truly was the Son of God.

3 Find two Biblical accounts of Jesus performing miracles. Make a note of what happens. What do you think Jesus is trying to teach through these miracles?

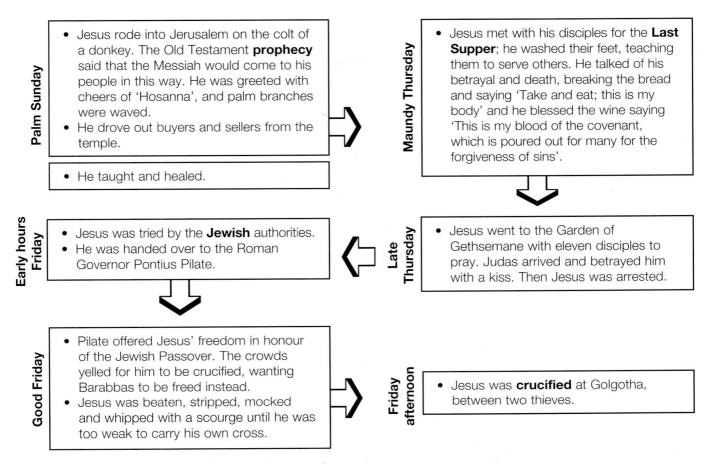

Palm Sunday
- Jesus rode into Jerusalem on the colt of a donkey. The Old Testament **prophecy** said that the Messiah would come to his people in this way. He was greeted with cheers of 'Hosanna', and palm branches were waved.
- He drove out buyers and sellers from the temple.

- He taught and healed.

Maundy Thursday
- Jesus met with his disciples for the **Last Supper**; he washed their feet, teaching them to serve others. He talked of his betrayal and death, breaking the bread and saying 'Take and eat; this is my body' and he blessed the wine saying 'This is my blood of the covenant, which is poured out for many for the forgiveness of sins'.

Early hours Friday
- Jesus was tried by the **Jewish** authorities.
- He was handed over to the Roman Governor Pontius Pilate.

Late Thursday
- Jesus went to the Garden of Gethsemane with eleven disciples to pray. Judas arrived and betrayed him with a kiss. Then Jesus was arrested.

Good Friday
- Pilate offered Jesus' freedom in honour of the Jewish Passover. The crowds yelled for him to be crucified, wanting Barabbas to be freed instead.
- Jesus was beaten, stripped, mocked and whipped with a scourge until he was too weak to carry his own cross.

Friday afternoon
- Jesus was **crucified** at Golgotha, between two thieves.

Figure 2 An overview of the last week of Jesus' life (Holy Week)

Beliefs about life after death

What happens when we die?

Christian beliefs

- If God judges that a person has had a good life, they will go to heaven.
- There are different opinions about what heaven is like and who will be there.

- Purgatory is for souls who have sins to be dealt with, but they may still proceed to heaven.
- Catholic Christians believe that this is like a waiting room for souls.

- If God judges that a person has led a bad life then they will go to hell.
- Different opinions exist about whether it is a place, or a state of not being with God.

God judges — Heaven — Purgatory — Hell

Figure 3 Christian beliefs about life after death

The Trinity

Christians believe in one God. God the Father, God the Son and God the Holy Spirit make up God. This is the Trinity.

God the Father created everything. He is all-powerful, all knowing and all-loving.

God the Son, Jesus, came to earth in human form and sacrificed his life so that Christians could get to heaven.

The Holy Spirit is all around, to guide and give strength to Christians.

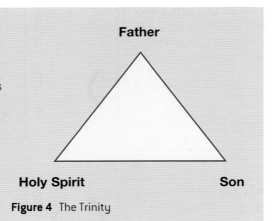

Figure 4 The Trinity

Why are holy books important to a religion?

The Bible

The Bible is very important to Christians; it tells them about God and about how they should live their lives. It is a great source of comfort to believers, and it is an important part of Christian **worship**.

As you have already learned, the way a Christian behaves during their life affects what happens to them in the afterlife. The Bible tells them how they *should* act; if they follow the teachings, then they are promised that they will gain eternal life in heaven.

The role of parables

Jesus taught in many ways. Sometimes he spoke directly, sometimes he used **parables** or miracles, and he taught by example through the way that he lived his life.

Parables are stories with a meaning about how Christians should behave. Jesus used them because they made his teachings easier to understand, especially as many of the people he taught were not well educated, and they found it difficult to understand teachings about the Kingdom of God.

Throughout the Bible, Christians are told that they should 'love their neighbour'; this teaching is given eight times, and is the most repeated command in the Bible. When asked 'who is my neighbour?' Jesus replied with the Parable of the Good Samaritan.

The main points of the Parable of the Good Samaritan are that it was a Jewish man who had been attacked, and a Jewish priest and a Jewish Levite did nothing to help. A **Samaritan**, who was a sworn enemy of the Jewish race, did stop, and he went out of his way to help the injured man.

This parable makes it easy to see the answer to the question 'who is my neighbour?'. Your neighbour is anyone who needs help, regardless of where in the world they are from, or which religion they follow. In order to 'love your neighbour' you need to go out of your way to help people who need your help.

Activity

1 Find out what Christians believe about God. Copy Figure 4 and explain it using your findings.

2 Imagine you have gone on a school trip to a remote location. The car carrying the food supplies has broken down and will not be there until the morning. What do you do? Discuss. Could the teaching of the miracle in Mark 6:30 be of any use?

3 Why do you think Jesus used parables to deliver some of his teachings?

4 Read the Parable of the Good Samaritan (Luke 10:27). Make a story board to show the key events.

The Sermon on the Mount

At the Sermon on the Mount Jesus gave his teachings to the crowd. He told them how to live their life so that they could go to heaven. His ideas challenged many beliefs of the time.

Beatitudes

At the Sermon on the Mount, Jesus delivered his teachings directly to the crowds. Firstly, Jesus gave the **Beatitudes**, or 'blessings'. He offered blessings to those who society often forgets, like the poor and the meek. This gave hope to those who were struggling in life that they would get to heaven in the end. It made the point that being rich or successful in life had nothing to do with your chances of going to heaven.

Antithesis

Jesus then delivered the **Antithesis**, where he talked about the teachings of the Old Testament. He took specific teachings and added to them, completing them. For example, he took the Old Testament teaching 'An eye for an eye, a tooth for a tooth', which was designed to limit revenge, and said instead you should 'turn the other cheek' (Matt 5:38–39), therefore taking no revenge at all. The teaching 'Do not commit adultery' was also added to: '... everyone who looks at a woman lustfully has already committed adultery with her in his heart' (Matt 5:28).

These teachings offer clear guidance on how to live a good life; following them would surely be a good thing. They are not easy to follow, though; many feel that they are not relevant in the modern world. Can you think of examples of modern day Christians who have lived up to these teachings?

Figure 5 John Terry was relieved of the captaincy of the England football team in 2010, following revelations about his adultery with a fellow player/friend's ex-girlfriend

Activity

5 Find out which groups received blessings in Matt 5:3–10. Which groups in society today would find comfort in the Beatitudes?

6 Look up the following references to find other key Antithesis teachings: Matt 5:31–32, 5:38–39, 6:9–15. Find some newspaper headlines that discuss people breaking Jesus' teachings.

7 What modern examples of Jesus' teachings being ignored or broken can you think of? Think about current news stories, or things that you have watched on TV, and examples from your own life.

8 Look at Figure 5. What does it tell us about adultery in the modern world? What would you expect a Christian to think about this? Why?

9 Make two columns, headed 'relevant' and 'outdated'. Place the teachings that you have studied into the columns. Discuss the reasons for your choices with the class.

What are the main features of Christian worship?

Why is worship important?

Prayer

When you think of a Christian at prayer, you may imagine this: a person with their hands together and eyes closed, perhaps kneeling at a pew in a church or at their bed side at night. You may think of someone holding a set of **Rosary beads**, a **prayer book** or the Bible. You may imagine someone standing with their arms outstretched, looking to the sky. These are all typical of Christian prayer.

There are different approaches to prayer and different reasons for it, but there is a common belief among Christians that they pray to a God who hears and who loves them. Prayer is one of the ways in which Christians express their beliefs.

Some pray simply to show their love to God – this is called worship. It is an important part of Christian life. Others pray because they want advice on how they should live their life, hoping that God will guide them in making the right choices. Some are keen to thank God for all the good things that he has provided, others want to own up to things that they have done wrong and ask for God's forgiveness.

Some Christians prefer to pray in a church, whilst others prefer to pray alone at home or in another place. When Christians come together to worship God it generally takes one of two forms: **sacramental** or **charismatic**. You will find out more about these ideas and think about the different reasons for choosing different types of prayer on pages 138–139.

Figure 6 Examples of charismatic worship

Words from the Lord's Prayer:
Give us this day our daily bread,
and forgive us our trespasses,
as we forgive those who trespass against us.
And lead us not into temptation,
but deliver us from evil.

Eucharist

The word 'Eucharist' comes from a Greek word meaning 'Thanksgiving'; it may also be called Communion or Mass. The Eucharist is the church service that remembers the events of the Last Supper, when Jesus breaks the bread, saying 'Take, eat, this is my body', and blesses the wine, saying 'Take, drink, this is my blood'. Jesus instructed his disciples to 'do this in remembrance of me'.

The **minister** blesses the bread and wine, and members of the congregation come to the front of the church to receive a sip of wine and a small piece of bread or wafer. You should look up the order of service and make a note of what happens and what is said.

This is a hugely important church service reminding Christians of the ultimate sacrifice that Jesus made for them. It is a symbol of God's promise of eternal life to the faithful. It brings Christians closer to God and helps them to understand their faith. For many Christians it reminds them of what it means to be a Christian, challenging them to live a good life.

Figure 7 Taking Communion

Activity

1   Discuss the importance of the Eucharist for Christians, and make notes.

2   Discuss the following statements with a partner:

'The Eucharist is essential to being a Christian; it is one of the last things that Jesus asked of his followers.'

'There are more important things than taking the Eucharist, like working to relieve poverty, and living out Jesus' teachings.'

Why are festivals important to people?

Festivals are important to Christians as they help Christians *remember* and *celebrate* events in the religion, and they reinforce Christian teachings. It is a time when believers can come *together* to worship and express their faith.

Easter

Easter remembers the death and resurrection of Jesus; it is the most important event in the Christian calendar. The time of preparation (Lent) lasts for about six weeks, and for Christians this should be a time of prayer and reflection. Some will **fast** and many will give up something that they enjoy.

During Holy Week, Christians often attend special services. During each service there is a distinct remembrance of key events in the last week of Jesus' life. Look back at page 131 for more details.

> **A Christian Easter**
> - Palm Sunday: Palm crosses are given out in churches.
> - Maundy Thursday: Priests wash the feet of worshippers.
> - Good Friday: Christians often meditate on Jesus' last words: 'Father forgive them, for they do not know what they are doing' (Luke 23:34). In some places there is a procession or even a re-enactment of the crucifixion.

Easter Sunday is a time of celebration for Christians: Jesus came back, and because of this Christians believe that they too can have eternal life. Churches are decorated in white and gold, with flowers and banners.

> **A social affair**
>
> Easter is also a time of chocolate eggs and Easter bunnies. It is a time when shops can make a lot of money, and people feel pressured to buy Easter goodies because that it what is expected. Easter is also a time off school and work as Good Friday and Easter Monday are both Bank Holidays; many families see this as an ideal opportunity to spend time with family or friends, or to go on holiday. Many Christians enjoy church services and exchange chocolate eggs, spend time with family and enjoy the break.

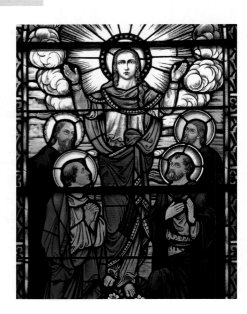

Figure 8 Images of Easter – Easter eggs or death and resurrection?

Christmas

Christmas is the most widely celebrated of all religious festivals; it celebrates the birth of Jesus, God's greatest gift to Christians.

Because of its wide appeal, Christmas is also the most **commercialised** of all festivals. Shop floors are crammed with gifts and all the trappings and trimmings months before **Advent** even begins, making it clear how people are expected to prepare for Christmas in the modern world. Many families feel pressure to find money for expensive gifts at this time of year.

Advent is when Christians prepare to celebrate the birth of Jesus, and look forward to the time when Jesus will come again. Churches will have an Advent Crown – an evergreen wreath with four candles around the edge and one in the centre, which are lit as Christmas draws closer. There are carol services, nativities and Christingle for children. Often the most well attended service of the season is Midnight Mass on Christmas Eve, where candles are lit to symbolise the coming of Jesus, and worshippers make the sign of peace. This is a very joyous occasion.

At church services on Christmas Day, the final candle on the Advent crown is lit. The minister bids the congregation to go and do good like Jesus did. For some Christians this may mean volunteering some of their time on Christmas Day to help the needy. Many Christians leave this service determined to live out their Christian beliefs. Some Christians think you must go to church on Christmas day and keep it as a sacred day; others spend the day with family, exchanging gifts and sharing a meal.

Activity

1 Why is Easter important to Christians?

2 Draw a flow chart of the events of Holy week and Easter.

3 Research church services during Advent. Compare these to other Christmas traditions that you know of.

4 Make a list of ten things that you look forward to at Christmas in order of their importance to you. How does your list compare to an ideal Christian Christmas?

5 Think of the advertisements that you see in the run up to Christmas: expensive gifts, decorations, clothes, food and drink, charity appeals. What does this tell us about attitudes to Christmas in the modern world?

Figure 9 A Christian Christmas, or a commercialised Christmas?

How do Christians express their beliefs?

How can Christianity influence people's lifestyles and identities?

Following Christian teachings means adopting a certain lifestyle, which gives people a sense of identity. How closely individual Christians follow the teachings in their daily lives differs, which means that there are different ways of living a Christian life.

There are two guiding principles in the Bible that all Christians try to follow: 'Love God' and 'Love your neighbour'. The Bible made it clear that giving and helping others are essential to getting into heaven (see also pages 133 and 150–152).

'It is easier for a camel to go through the eye of a needle than it is for a rich man to enter the Kingdom of God.' (Matt 19:24)

A camel cannot pass through the eye of a needle. Even if you imagine that the eye of the needle is some type of 'kissing gate' in the wall of the city as some people do, it is still impossible! The teaching is that a rich man cannot get into heaven.

It is not wealth in itself that is a bad thing – it can be used for great good – but in the Bible it says that it is the *love* of money that causes a problem. There is no value in storing up wealth on earth (see page 146 for further discussion).

To follow a Christian lifestyle means attending church or praying **privately**, celebrating religious festivals, following key religious teachings. They should also give time and resources to help others and they should not store up riches.

How are Christian beliefs expressed in contemporary society?

Today only about 10 per cent of the adult population of the UK attend church regularly, but when asked 72 per cent of the UK population claimed to be Christian in the 2001 census. Many people who consider themselves to be Christians do not worship in a church; maybe they do not practise their faith at all, or maybe they choose to pray in private.

Worship

Those who choose **public worship** do not all do the same things:

Sacramental worship is very traditional. It follows a set pattern and varies little from week to week. The minister leads the service, and the congregation respond at set intervals. It involves traditional prayers, Bible readings and singing hymns. Sacraments are highly important to many Christians. Many enjoy this type of worship; it makes them feel close to God and it is a comfort to them that it is unchanging.

Charismatic worship is often lively, and it may involve singing, dancing, clapping and the raising of hands, and people speaking out when they feel like it. It is a very free form of worship that varies from week to week. Many Christians enjoy this type of worship; they feel close to God and they hope that through it they will receive the gifts of the Holy Spirit.

There are different attitudes to worship: some believe that you *must* worship publicly in a church, while others prefer to worship in private.

Take part in church services

Speak to the minister

Meet other Christians

More powerful communal prayer

Christian teachings provide a moral code. They show people how they should act. Christianity offers answers to deep and meaningful questions, and the promise of eternal life with God. As fewer people attend church and religion plays a less important role in the lives of many, do you think they are missing out?

We live in an increasingly **secular** society, where many people do not hold religious beliefs. Some worry that this has a negative impact on the moral and spiritual health of society.

Activity

1 Arrange the following words into two columns, headed 'Charismatic' and 'Sacramental':

hymns	dancing	clapping	kneeling
Eucharist	arms outstretched		
Lord's Prayer	speaking in tongues		
set pattern	free	lively	

Which would you prefer? Why?

2 Use Figure 10 and your own knowledge to explain why Christians have different attitudes towards church attendance.

3 Do you think that you need to have religious beliefs in order to live a good moral life? Give reasons for your answer. Why might someone disagree with you?

Enjoy a private relationship with God

God hears prayers anywhere

Worship through good deeds

Can't get to church because of work, family or health issues

Figure 10 Public and private worship

Examiner's Tips

To help with your preparation for the exam, make sure you know that:

- The Bible is important to Christians; it teaches them about God, the life of Jesus and it tells them how they should live their lives. If they follow the teachings, they are promised that they will be rewarded with eternal life in heaven.
- Worship is an important part of a Christian life. Christians pray in different ways and for different reasons. They all believe that they pray to a God that listens and cares about them.
- Religious festivals are celebrated in religious and non-religious ways in the modern world; some believe that they are losing their religious significance, others believe that they still have a very important religious role.
- A Christian lifestyle involves worship, observing religious festivals and following the teachings from the Bible and the church.
- Christians should try to follow a Christian lifestyle, but this can be difficult in the modern world. Fewer people go to church than used to and patterns of worship are changing. Some worry that this will have a negative impact on the moral and spiritual health of society.

A common mistake is that candidates do not give enough information when they are describing Christian teachings, e.g. making statements like 'Christians should not be rich', without stating a specific teaching such as 'It is easier for a camel to pass through the eye of a needle than for a rich man to enter the kingdom of heaven'. You should go on to explain what the teaching means for Christians. Many candidates do not explain the impact that teachings have on the lives of different people.

Sample question

'Festivals like Christmas and Easter have little religious importance in the modern world.' How far do you agree with this statement? [8]

What the examiner has to say!

- You need to look carefully at what the statement is saying. Always do this when attempting this type of question.
- You may wish to plan your answer, to make sure you are giving a *balanced* discussion.
- What reasons are there for agreeing with this statement? What evidence is there that festivals have no religious importance in the modern world?
- What reasons are there for disagreeing? What evidence is there that festivals do have religious importance in the modern world?
- You need to weigh up the arguments and evidence that you have given and make a decision – how far do you agree with the statement? Why?

Exam practice

1. Explain why Holy Week is important to Christians. [4]
2. What does Figure 3 (on page 131) tell us about Christian beliefs about life after death? [4]
3. Describe the Parable of the Good Samaritan. [4]
4. Explain the meaning of the Parable of the Good Samaritan. [4]
5. Describe Christian prayer. [4]
6. Explain why prayer is important to Christians. [4]
7. Use Figure 7 (on page 135) and your own knowledge to describe what happens at a Eucharist service. [6]
8. 'To be a good Christian, you must take part in the Eucharist service regularly.' To what extent do you agree with this statement? [8]
9. Use Figures 8 and 9 (on pages 136 and 137) and your own knowledge to describe the pressures faced by families at Christmas and Easter. [6]
10. Explain why Easter is important to Christians. [4]
11. 'Festivals like Easter and Christmas have lost their religious meaning in the modern world.' How far do you agree with the statement? [8]
12. Describe Christian teachings about helping others. [4]
13. Explain the impact that Christian beliefs have on lifestyles. [4]

How do Christian churches interact with the local community?

How can the Christian Church interact with the community?

Church leaders claim that the church has a vital role to play in any community. The church is certainly important to many Christians; it is where they go to worship God, meet up with others to celebrate important events in their lives and celebrate religious festivals. There are prayer meetings and classes for adults, and 'young church' and Bible classes for children. We know that many people are not practising Christians; what does the church do to interact with these members of the community?

Churches often run activities for children and young people, like Brownies, Guides, Scouts and Boys Brigade. There are support groups for adults; for example, Bury and Bolton **Methodist** Church runs a support group for people suffering from ME/EFS, and 'Babyloss' is a Catholic support group for people who have suffered a miscarriage. Many churches get involved in youth work and helping people to overcome their problems, which may range from drugs to bereavement.

The church building is often in use, for various activities that appeal to different people in the community. There are often baby and toddler groups, which provide a service and bring people together in the local community who otherwise may not meet. Church halls are often used for jumble sales and fundraising events, appealing to people of all ages. There are sometimes coffee mornings and bingo for senior citizens.

How can the local minister impact on the attitudes and values of the local community?

Ministers have certain religious duties. They must prepare and lead church services, including the Eucharist. They prepare people for and lead wedding ceremonies and **baptisms**. They conduct the funeral service, and offer support to the dying and bereaved. In their religious role, ministers mainly support Christians, but many people who do not have strong religious beliefs still like to get married in a church, or may find the minister supportive when they have lost someone close to them.

Ministers also have a **pastoral** role in the community. They should offer support to anyone in the community who has been affected by tragedy, or who is ill or alone or suffering in any way.

Some ministers act as chaplains to the armed forces, hospitals, prisons or in education. Think about their role in these situations; why do you think they are important?

Although far fewer people in the UK attend church regularly than they did fifty years ago, it remains for many a focal point in their community. The impact that the local minister has on community life and on the views of the people in the community will depend on how many people they come into contact with. In some communities this is clearly more than in others, which means that the role of the church and the minister may vary from being an integral part of the life of the community to having little or no input into community life.

Figure 11 Busy life of a minister by pupil Tony Canon (year 7)

Activity

1 Make a list of all the different things that can happen in a church. Divide them up into those that are religious and those that are not. For each one, think about which members of the community will be there.

2 Investigate church support for different members of the community. Draw up a table.

3 With a partner, discuss each of the following statements. What do they tell us about different attitudes to the church?

'I am a Christian, I pray regularly, and I live according to Christian teachings, but I don't go to church.'

'I am not a Christian, and I do not go to church services, but I go to the church regularly to meet up with my friends at a coffee morning.'

'I am not a Christian, I never go to church; it has no impact on my life.'

'I go to church regularly, I got married in the local church, and have had my children baptised there – it is a special place for me.'

How does Christianity impact on the day-to-day lives of individuals and families?

How does the Church celebrate events in people's lives?

A **rite of passage** is the ritual or ceremony that marks a time when a person reaches a new and significant change in their life. The Christian Church celebrates four rites of passage: birth, coming of age, marriage and death.

Baptism

The baptism service welcomes people into the church and into the Christian faith; the font is often near the entrance to the church to illustrate this. Most Christians practise infant baptism, but some prefer to leave it until a person is old enough to know and understand what they are doing: 'believer's baptism'.

During an infant baptism service, the parents and godparents make promises on behalf of the child, and promise that they will bring them up in the Christian faith, with the teachings of Jesus. The minister baptises the child at the font, marking the sign of the cross onto their forehead with water and saying 'I baptise you in the name of the Father, and of the Son, and of the Holy Spirit'. The water is a symbol of spiritual cleanliness, as during the baptism service it is believed that a person is cleansed of all sin so that they can start a new life with God. A candle is lit, to mark the child moving from darkness into the 'light' of Jesus' teachings.

The water symbolises spiritual cleansing. Through baptism a person is brought from darkness into light.

A baptism service welcomes the child or adult into the Christian faith.

Figure 12 Infant and adult baptism

Confirmation

'Coming of age' means the time at which a person is old enough to take on the duties of their faith. For Christians this is the **confirmation** ceremony, where a person confirms that the promises that were made on their behalf at their baptism hold true for them now that they are old enough to understand their meaning. This is important as it is at this point that Christians take on the responsibilities of their faith more seriously.

This is an important ceremony, conducted by the Bishop rather than the local minister. During the service, the Bishop 'lays on hands' and says prayers asking for the Holy Spirit to guide and help the person to keep their promises.

Marriage

The wedding ceremony marks a couple starting their life together. The ceremony comprises the following key parts (other things may also happen):
- The minister states Christian beliefs about marriage.
- Declarations: the couple make promises that they will love, comfort, honour and respect one another.
- Vows: 'To have and to hold from this day forward, for better for worse, for richer for poorer, in sickness and in health, till death us do part.'
- Exchange of rings.
- **Proclamation**.
- Prayers and readings.
- Signing the register.

Weddings are also important because a couple want God to bless them, to join them and to help them to stay together through the challenges of life.

Funeral

A funeral marks the close of a person's life on earth. It is a time for family and friends to grieve, to give thanks for the life of the deceased, and to pass them over to God's keeping. Readings like 'Blessed are those who mourn, for they will be comforted'; Psalm 23 'The Lord is my Shepherd'; and prayers all offer comfort to mourners, and hope of resurrection.

> 'We therefore commit his/her body to the ground; earth to earth, ashes to ashes, dust to dust, in the sure and certain hope of the resurrection to eternal life.'

The funeral service is a great comfort to Christians, as it is not only a time for them to say goodbye to a loved one, but to entrust them to God. This service offers hope of resurrection, which is really important to Christians.

Activity

1. If you were going to celebrate an important event in your life, who would you want to be there? List them in order of importance. For each one, think about why you would want them to be there. Do you think a Christian would add God to their list?

2. Look up Psalm 23. Why do you think this is often read or sung during a funeral service?

What are Christian attitudes, values and beliefs about family life in the modern world?

Marriage

In the Bible it says that people are expected to marry (see Mark 10:6–9). Marriage is seen as the *ideal* situation for sexual relationships, and for family life. All churches encourage marriage, although many accept that couples choose to live together without being married, or '**cohabit**'.

The Church of England hopes that this is a 'step along the way to the fuller commitment of marriage'. The Roman Catholic Church, however, does not accept cohabiting couples, seeing sex outside of marriage as a grave sin. They do not accept that it helps to prepare a couple for marriage; it should be all or nothing.

Figure 13 A church wedding

Divorce

Jesus gives two teachings on **divorce**:
- in one, he allows divorce on the grounds of 'marital unfaithfulness' (adultery) only (see Matt 19:3–9)
- in the other, he says that couples should not divorce at all (see Mark 10:1–12).

Many churches do allow divorce and remarriage because they realise that humans can make mistakes and they should not be forced to suffer for their lifetime in an unhappy marriage.

The Roman Catholic Church does not allow divorce because they do not believe that humans have the power to dissolve something that was made by God. They do, in some circumstances, grant an annulment, which means that the marriage was never real.

Family

Family is important to Christians. It is the place where many of our beliefs and values are formed. The following references look at Christian attitudes to family life: Exodus 20:14, Ephesians 6:3, 6:4, Proverbs 23:22–24, Exodus 20:12.

The Bible teaches that it is the responsibility of children to care for their parents when they are old. Christians are told that they should not try to escape this burden (Mark 7:10–13). Some Christians follow this teaching and invite their parents to live with them and be cared for by them in their old age; many, however, do not.

The church supports family life: they welcome babies through the baptism service, and young people through confirmation; people marry there; and often say goodbye to their dead. There are many family services to attend, and Sunday School. The church offers moral support through difficult times, and useful advice through marriage guidance.

Should the church support all families in the modern world? Think about the following:

> The Bible suggests that a family consists of two married parents and their children, living in a loving environment following Christian teachings; ideally, this should last for life.

Many families in the UK today do not follow this pattern: there are many unmarried parents; many divorced parents who have remarried, creating '**reconstructed families**'; many single-parent families; and a growing number of same-sex couples with children.

All of these family situations are against the teachings of the Roman Catholic Church.

The Church of England accepts divorce and remarriage, as do many free churches. The Church of England accepts gay couples and has plans to allow gay marriages in church.

Figure 14 Different family types

Activity

1 Find out the conditions for annulment.

2 In the UK today more than one in every three marriages ends in divorce. How many reasons can you think of for a couple wanting to get divorced? Do you think marriage should be for life?

3 Copy out and complete the table with your own thoughts:

Marriage for me …	Cohabitation for me …
I believe it is wrong to have sex without being married.	I do not attend church often, so I wouldn't get married in church anyway, and I can't see the point in marriage.
I want God to bless me and my partner at the beginning of our life together.	I am fully committed to my partner, we have a loving relationship, we don't need a piece of paper to prove it.

4 Who do you think is responsible for caring for the elderly? What reasons might someone have for not taking care of their parents? Do all elderly parents want to be cared for by their children?

How does poverty impact spiritually and morally on Christians today?

What are Christian attitudes, values and beliefs about poverty?

Absolute poverty is a state of poverty where the base needs of human beings are not met. People do not have access to food, water, shelter or medicines. This results in millions dying of malnutrition or diseases that could be avoided. Many people living in the countries of sub-Saharan Africa live in absolute poverty.

Relative poverty is different. It means that people may be poor compared to other people around them. This may mean that they cannot have or do the same things as other people or have the same chances. This is the type of poverty we see in the UK and other countries in Europe.

For hundreds of years before the twentieth century, absolute poverty was a fact of life in the UK. The poor were treated badly; they were not important and there were very harsh laws about vagrancy. Poverty was accepted because poor people were not seen as important to society and because most people believed that it was their own fault. Paupers were sent to the workhouse. The church did offer some support, but mainly to the old or disabled; the able-bodied poor were left to fend for themselves. Towards the end of the nineteenth century people started to realise that poverty was not entirely a person's fault, and the chances of their being able to escape poverty without help were very small. In 1906, poor children were granted a 'free school meal', and in 1945 'child benefit' was introduced.

Jesus was poor; he lived a poor person's life with few possessions. He taught that people should not seek money in life but instead seek God and care for the poor. You have already looked at some key Bible teachings relating to this: 'Blessed are the poor', 'love your neighbour', 'the eye of a needle' and 'the feeding of the 5,000', but there are many more. In fact, there are more teachings in the Bible about the poor than just about anything else! Look up Luke 16:19–31, 21:1–4 and Matt 25:31–46.

Christians believe that the world and all in it belong to God, and they are supposed to care for God's creation – this includes other people. Everyone is of equal worth to God.

The average annual expenditure of an American is $16,500, in Japan it is $19,700, in Somalia it is just $17. Bill Gates has a fortune amounting to around $30 billion; some countries barely have this much! These are just a few examples to show us that wealth is not shared out fairly; this goes against key Christian values like love, justice and equality. Think back to the feeding of the 5,000; if everyone shared what they had, everyone would have enough.

Activity

1 Make a list of things that you use every day that you couldn't do without. From this list, how many things do you think someone living in absolute poverty would have?

2 Do you think the accumulation of these things has been important to life in the UK?

Christians believe that wealth should be used to do good: 'Command them to do good, to be rich in good deeds, and to be generous and willing to share.' (1Timothy 6:18).

Sir John Templeton, who died in July 2008 aged 95, was a very successful Christian. He boasted one of the longest and most successful records on Wall Street, making a huge amount of money. He donated lots to education, and set up the Templeton prize worth nearly £300,000 for progress in religion. He saw this as God's plan for him.

How can Christians respond to the problems of poverty?

Christian churches and individual Christians often respond by fundraising or giving up time to work for charity organisations, as well as praying for the poor. There are famous Christian charities such as Christian Aid, CAFOD and the Salvation Army.

These organisations offer practical help and moral support to people in need in the UK and in the poorest countries of the world, regardless of faith or background. They try to educate people who are not poor about the needs of poor people around the world, raising awareness and encouraging people to help.

These organisations also provide emergency aid to save lives in the immediate aftermath of a disaster, and they try to help people to rebuild their lives, teaching them skills and providing equipment so that people can help themselves to gain a better standard of living.

Christian Aid runs community groups for children and adults offering moral support to help communities work together to overcome their problems and their differences. They work with women and girls in Afghanistan who have been denied an education by the Taliban and with children in the Sudan where fewer three in every 50 children finish primary school.

'FAITH BY ITSELF, IF IT IS NOT ACCOMPANIED BY ACTION, IS DEAD'
James 2:17

Martha Talavera plants trees and collects-up rubbish – improving the environment her family and community depend on for coffee farming in Nicaragua. Christian Aid faithfully supports people such as Martha to work towards a better life. www.christianaid.org.uk

Figure 15 Christian Aid poster: one Christian response to poverty

Internet Research Activity

CAFOD:

www.cafod.org.uk

Christian Aid:

www.christianaid.org.uk

The Salvation Army:

www1.salvationarmy.org.uk

Find out more about the work of some Christian charities.

Examiner's Tips

Christian charities offer practical help, moral support and education – you should be able to discuss all of these in the exam.

Case Study

Mother Teresa

Figure 16 Mother Teresa working in Calcutta

Born Agnes Bojaxhiu, in Macedonia in 1910, she died in the headquarters of the Missionaries of Charity in Calcutta in 1997. Agnes came from a religious family and felt the call to work for God at the young age of 14. Later known as Mother Teresa, she was an inspirational woman who gave tirelessly of her time and dedicated her effort and love to helping the poor, the sick and the dying. In her lifetime she was often spoken of as a saint. She administered treatment to lepers who were cast out by the rest society, and she welcomed people suffering all manner of illness.

Not everyone was supportive of her; she faced opposition to her work and questioning of her motives, especially in the beginning. She had some very strong views on issues like abortion, which some people found offensive.

Timeline:

- **1928** Went to Ireland to join the Sisters of our Lady of Loreto in Ireland, where she was given the name Teresa.

- **1929** Sent to India, where she became a teacher in the convent school in Calcutta.

- **1937** Made her final profession as a nun, and has been known as Mother ever since.

- **1948** The Catholic Church granted permission for her to leave the convent to go and help the poor. She went to live in the slums. She managed to persuade the local authorities to give her a building; this became 'Nirmal Hirday' – 'Place of the Immaculate Heart'. This was somewhere people could go to die with dignity; here she comforted people of all faiths in their last hours.

- **1950** Founded the religious order 'Missionaries of Charity'. This provides hospitals, schools and orphanages, and shelters for lepers and the dying. There is a food distribution programme, a children's home and a 'Town of Peace' for rehabilitating lepers. There are now 50 branches in India and 30 in other countries.

- **1979** Awarded the Nobel Peace Prize for 'Work undertaken in the struggle to overcome poverty and distress, which also constitute a threat to the peace'.

Activity

1 Discuss with a partner: Which Christian teachings are being followed by charities like Christian Aid, and people like Mother Teresa?

2 Look up Christian Aid or CAFOD on the internet and find out what they do.

3 Discuss the following statement: 'Christians must share what they have.'

Examiner's Tips

To help with your preparation for the exam, make sure you know:

- what the minister does in the local community and how the church building is used. In some areas the church is a focal point for the whole community; in other areas it has less of an impact.
- there are important ceremonies to mark the key changes that a person goes through in their life: baptism, confirmation, marriage and funeral. The significance that these have on people's lives varies.
- that family life is important. The Bible teaches about marriage, divorce and family life and churches provide teachings as well. There are many different beliefs about what constitutes a family and there are different attitudes to family life in the modern world.
- there are more Bible teachings about helping others than anything else; Christians should help people who live in poverty. There are major Christian organisations like Christian Aid, and individual Christians also help in their own ways.

It may be helpful when revising to look for Bible references on the internet to support your learning on Christian teachings.

Sample question

Describe a Christian wedding ceremony.   [4]

What the examiner has to say!

A common mistake is that candidates make generalised statements assuming that all Christians act in the same way, e.g. 'Christians should not get divorced'. It is important to explain that some Christians believe this, while others do not, and you need to explain why this is. For example, some Christians will not accept divorce because of teachings from the Bible and the Roman Catholic Church (you could include a quote: 'Therefore what God has joined together, let not man separate.' Mark 10:9); other Christians believe that divorce is acceptable because the Bible teaches about being compassionate and the Church of England accepts divorce.

- You need to *describe what happens* at a Christian wedding; you do not have to explain why things happen.
- This is a straightforward question; be accurate and give as much detail as you can. Describe the location and what different people do and say. Put events in the correct order.
- A top-level answer will use correct terminology throughout.

Exam Practice

1   Describe the role of the church in the local community.   [4]

2   Use Figure 11 (on page 141) and your own knowledge to describe the role of the minister.   [6]

3   Use Figure 12 (on page 142) and your own knowledge to describe a baptism service.   [6]

4   Explain why the funeral service is important to Christians.   [4]

5   Use Figure 14 (on page 145) and your own knowledge to describe different family types.   [6]

6   Describe Christian teachings about care for the elderly.   [4]

7   'The church should support all families.' To what extent do you agree with this statement?   [8]

8   Describe Christian teachings about poverty.   [4]

9   Explain Christian attitudes to wealth.   [4]

10 Use Figure 15 (on page 147) and your own knowledge to describe Christian responses to poverty.   [6]

11 'There should be no such thing as a rich Christian.' To what extent do you agree with this statement?   [8]

12 Describe the work of Christian Aid or CAFOD.   [4]

13 Explain why charity is important to Christians.   [4]

What are the Christian approaches to the issue of racism in Britain today?

What do Christians believe about racism?

An overriding principle for Christians is that God created the world and he created human beings in his own image. Christians believe that God loved the world and people so much that he sent his only son to die for them.

Despite years of campaigns and legislation, racism remains a problem in the modern world. **Racism** goes directly against the Gospel teachings. Christianity developed into what it is today simply because it accepted people of all races.

Racism is making a judgement that one race of people is superior or inferior to others. People who make such judgements *often* do so because they are prejudiced. **Prejudice** means making a judgement about something or someone without knowing enough about it or them to support the judgement. If people act upon their prejudices and treat people unfairly, it is **discrimination**. Racism is one form of discrimination; can you think of any others?

For Christians there should only be one race – the human race. They believe that all people were created in the image of God, they are all loved by God, and humans have a duty to care for God's creation.

> 'From one man he made every nation of men' Acts 17:26

Jesus did not treat people differently because of their race or religious beliefs. He healed a Centurion's servant and a Samaritan woman; and of course he used a Samaritan as the hero in the famous parable. Jesus died to save all people, everywhere in the world, and his death breaks down the barriers between nations:

> 'There is neither Jew nor Greek, slave nor free, male nor female, for you are all one in Christ Jesus.' Galatians 3:28

> 'Love one another as I have loved you.' John 13:34

All churches condemn racism as it goes against Christian teachings. This does not mean, however, that the church has never been involved in racial discrimination: many Christians were involved in the slave trade. Today church leaders are sorry about this; Pope John Paul II asked for forgiveness for 'past acts and omissions of the Church', which have led to the unfair treatment of some groups.

What are the Christian responses to racism today?

The church was largely responsible for the Race Relations Act in 1976, and many churches are involved in human rights and charity work around the world. The church may still be accused of institutional racism, where the structure of the church makes it difficult for some groups of people to become church leaders. The churches are aware of this and are making efforts to put an end to it.

The Race Relations Act makes it illegal to discriminate against people on grounds of race, but this does not mean that racism does not exist today. For some it can be that they cannot access good housing, education or jobs; for others it can take the form of violence, and even murder (see the Stephen Lawrence case study).

Case Study

Stephen Lawrence

Figure 17 Teenager Stephen Lawrence

Stephen Lawrence was murdered in a racially motivated attack in April 1993. The 18-year-old A level student was stabbed by a gang of white youths while he waited at a bus stop near his home in south-east London with a friend. Stephen was stabbed twice, and he later died in hospital.

A 1997 inquest ruled he had been 'unlawfully killed in a completely unprovoked racist attack by five white youths'.

The original investigation brought no charges, raising questions about the police commitment to solving the crime. The Macpherson inquiry in 1999 reported that the police force was 'institutionally racist' and made 70 recommendations for improvement. This has worsened poor relations between the police and ethnic minority groups. Senior officers are now trying to rectify this.

This case has been high profile, and has raised important questions for the criminal justice system.

Eighteen years after the death of Stephen Lawrence it has been announced that two men will finally stand trial for his murder. His parents have never given up the fight for justice; they are relieved by this news but realise that there is a long way to go.

One of the recommendations of the inquiry report was to improve the way that the police relate to the community. The church has had a role in this, working with the police to improve the service they offer the community. The church also works with the community, encouraging people to come forward and report racially motivated crimes.

'Love your neighbour'

'Love your enemies'

'You are all one in Christ Jesus'

James 2:4 describes those who discriminate as: 'Judges with evil thoughts'

Figure 18 Bible teachings

'Heaven above is softer blue,
Earth around is sweeter green;
Something lives in ev'ry hue
Christless eyes have never seen;
Birds with gladder songs o'erflow,
Flow'rs with deeper beauties shine,
Since I know, as now I know,
I am his and he is mine.'

Figure 19 An old Christian hymn

Case Study

Martin Luther King

Figure 20 Martin Luther King engaged in peaceful protest

Martin Luther King was born in Atlanta, Georgia in 1929, the son of a Christian minister. He was taught at home and at church that God created all people equally, in his image, and he loves them dearly; yet when he went outside he saw black people being treated badly.

Martin Luther King followed Christian teachings in his mission. He believed that it was unacceptable to treat God's people unfairly, and it was his Christian duty to make a stand. He refused to use violence despite the violence that he met, following the Christian teaching 'turn the other cheek'. Peaceful methods such as sit-ins, freedom rides and marches were used to get the point across.

King campaigned tirelessly despite threats to his life. He took strength from his Christian faith. He stressed the need to 'love your enemies and pray for those who persecute you' (Matthew 5:44).

Activity

1 There are different reasons for prejudice. Discuss the following reasons that might cause someone to be prejudiced and put them in order according to how likely they are to make someone prejudiced: ignorance, fear, upbringing, following friends, unemployment, jealousy.

Most likely ————————————————➤ Least likely

2 Look at Figures 18 and 19 on page 151. What do the Bible teachings and hymn tell us about racism?

3 Discuss with a partner the problems caused by racism in the UK today. Do you think the situation has improved?

4 What could Christians do today to address racism in society, and institutional racism in the church?

5 Find out about another Christian response to racism.

What are the individual and communal implications of exploitation?

What are Christian attitudes concerning exploitation?

Exploitation means to use someone or something for personal gain. It includes the overuse of the world's resources, the devastating damage being done to the environment, the poor treatment of animals and denial of human rights.

The planet simply cannot cope with the levels of exploitation of its resources we are currently experiencing, the rainforests will be gone in forty years if the current rate of destruction is not stopped. This creates issues for all people; global warming and overuse of resources affect everyone. What will be left for future generations? For Christians this is not just the destruction of something functional – it is the destruction of God's beautiful creation.

Christians believe that God created the world carefully, bit by bit over six days, and each part of it was 'good'. Mankind was created last, and given dominion over all the creatures of the world. Some have used this teaching to justify exploitation of the planet, but most believe that they were given a duty to look after creation on behalf of God. This is called **stewardship**.

'The earth is the Lord's, and everything in it.' (Psalm 24:1)

Many Christians celebrate the environment by holding harvest festivals.

Christians are given guidance in the Bible on how they should treat the land, the things that grow from it and animals. They are told to rest the land, not to cut down trees, and to rest animals and treat them well.

In the UK most chickens are reared on battery farms. Chickens are kept in appalling conditions, in wire cages, with no room to flap their wings, unable to perch and with their beaks trimmed. They are given an artificial sunrise and sunset, and fed nutrients so that they produce an average of 338 eggs per year, twice as many as an average hen. They are then slaughtered for pet food or pies.

Figure 21 Battery farming

What can Christians do to help fight exploitation today?

Christians should try to use the planet sensibly, through sustainable development and sustainable use of resources. This can involve finding alternative resources, using existing ones more efficiently, and sustainable resource management (including recycling and limiting carbon emissions).

Internet Research Activity

www.christian-ecology.org.uk

Find out more about Christian Ecology Link.

Christians may choose to buy Fair Trade goods, which are sustainable because farmers gain enough money to keep growing things. The retail price is higher; despite this, more people are choosing to buy them. Estimated retail sales have risen from £16.7 million in 1998 to £799 million in 2009.

The whaling industry has had a devastating effect on the world's whale population. The blue whales of the Antarctic are now fewer than 1 per cent of their original number. The West Pacific grey whale is close to extinction. Greenpeace are actively working to bring an end to the whaling industry.

There are Christian charities and organisations which focus on conservation, investigation of sustainable resources, saving specific animals or habitats, poverty relief, etc. They all tackle aspects of exploitation.

Case Study

World Vision

World Vision is a Christian humanitarian organisation that works to transform the lives of the world's poorest children in almost 100 countries. It serves thousands of communities regardless of religion, race, ethnicity or gender. World Vision wants to help create change that lasts, demonstrating God's unconditional love for all people in everything it does.

Many thousands of children are exploited daily through mental or emotional abuse, physical violence, human trafficking, recruitment as child soldiers and much more. Every year 1.2 million children are trafficked for use in child labour or for sexual exploitation, while across the world 300,000 children serve as child soldiers.

Motivated by its faith in Jesus Christ, World Vision works to tackle these issues as well as the root causes of exploitation such as poverty and lack of education. As part of its work, World Vision campaigns to influence the way that societies and nations think to ensure that the world's most vulnerable children can always be heard.

Figure 22 A photo taken by a child in Pakistan of two girls walking to school. World Vision's work in Pakistan highlights the importance of education – which provides children with life opportunities to escape cycles of poverty and exploitation.

Activity

1 Make a list of the ways in which human activity could be described as 'exploiting' the planet, animals or people. What do you think a Christian would say about them?

2 Research whaling or battery farming; in what ways do they go against Christian teachings? You should consider the following in your answer: 'God created the world for himself; he filled it with life, including human life, and said that it was all good. Humans lived in harmony with animals in the Garden of Eden. God is not indifferent to creation; wronging the planet wrongs God.'

3 Find out more about World Vision, or another Christian charity working to eradicate exploitation. Make a note of what they do. Which Christian teachings and values are they following?

How can the Christian faith be reconciled with advancing technology?

What are Christian attitudes towards contraception and abortion?

Contraception is something that prevents a pregnancy (pill, condoms, IUDs, etc.). The Bible has little to say about contraception; Christians look to the teachings of the church. The Church of England accepts contraception within a marriage because it is responsible family planning: all children, after all, should be wanted. They do not accept contraception if it is used to promote promiscuity.

The Roman Catholic Church does not accept artificial contraception, as they believe that every sexual act should be open to the possibility of pregnancy. They do allow the rhythm method, which means avoiding having sex when the woman is most fertile. Many Catholics choose to ignore church teachings in this area of their life.

The use of condoms is encouraged in the modern world as they protect from STIs. Condoms can stop the spread of HIV, which could save many lives. Some would say that Christian teachings are out of date as they do not account for STIs.

In the UK there have been high levels of teenage pregnancy, which has led to government campaigns for safe sex.

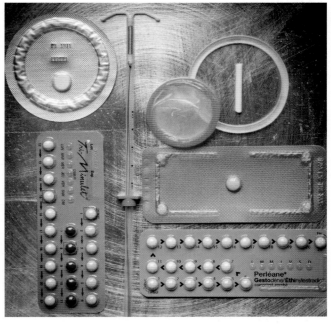

Figure 23 Artificial contraception

Abortion is the deliberate ending of a pregnancy. In the UK, abortion is legal provided that two doctors agree that one of the following conditions apply:

There is risk:
- to the mental or physical health of the mother
- to other siblings
- of severe disability
- to the mother's life.

For the first two conditions, the time limit is 24 weeks; there is no upper limit for the third and fourth conditions. In the UK in 2008, 195,296 abortions were carried out, 90 per cent of which took place under 13 weeks, and 38 per cent of which were 'medical' abortions. Some believe that the legal guidelines effectively offer abortion on demand in the UK. The Pro-life Alliance takes this view (Figure 24) and wants to change the law. In 2008, MPs voted to keep the 24-week time limit when given a choice of reducing it.

Liz Davies of Marie Stopes International described the two-doctor rule in the UK as 'archaic': 'Contrary to popular belief, we do not currently have abortion on request in Great Britain, unlike most other European countries, and reform is long overdue.'

When does human life begin? What quality of life will a child expect if they are born with severe disabilities or into dangerous situations? Is the life of the foetus as important as the life of the mother? Does UK law mean that we have abortion on demand? There are no clear answers, but responses to these questions will affect views on abortion.

Christians believe that life is God-given, and is precious. They are told 'you shall not kill', and given numerous teachings on the importance of human life. There are passages in the Bible – including Psalm 139:13, Jeremiah 1:5 and Luke 1:9–44 – which suggest that God knows and loves people before they are born.

The Roman Catholic Church teaches that abortion is always totally wrong because they believe that life starts at conception, and that God has a plan for every life – it is in God's hands whether or not the pregnancy is successful. They say that at conception there is not just a potential human life, but a human life with potential. You should find out about 'dual effect'.

> 'I declare that direct abortion ... always constitutes a grave sin.' Pope John Paul II, 1995

The Bible teaches Christians that they should love one another, and show compassion to others. The Church of England, Methodists and the Quakers oppose abortion, but recognise that there are times when it is the most loving course of action, in cases such as rape or risk to the life of the mother.

Activity

1 Why do you think the Roman Catholic Church is upset about government campaigns for safe sex?

2 Make a list of reasons why someone might want to have an abortion, and a list of reasons why people should not have an abortion. Do you think that the UK law on abortion is fair?

3 Look up the development of a foetus. At what point do you think life begins? Give reasons for your answer.

4 Discuss the following points with a partner: What is 'abortion on demand'? Do we have abortion on demand in the UK? Do you think it is too easy to get an abortion, or do you think it should be made easier? Why might a Christian oppose abortion? Why do you think there are different views on abortion within Christianity?

Make a note of your responses.

'With abortion provided on demand in the UK, and the annual figures escalating, we should surely be seeking better ways to reduce this tragic loss of life and providing better solutions in crisis pregnancy situations.'

Figure 24 Julia Millington of the Pro-life Alliance

What are Christian attitudes to modern medical advances?

Christians believe in the **sanctity of life:** the preservation of life is important to all Christians.

In medieval times there was tension between the church and folk medicine, as there was a belief that God gave illnesses and God would take them away if and when he chose. In the Bible, however, Jesus is said to have healed or raised someone from the dead on 23 occasions. Furthermore, the Bible instructs people to look after their bodies (Proverbs 12:18), and to take medicine when they are ill (1 Timothy 5:23).

Medical advances, especially since the establishment of the NHS in 1945, have benefited many millions of people, saving lives and giving people a better quality of life, from simple things, like taking antibiotics, to advanced surgery. In recent years advances in science and technology mean that increasingly complex operations can be performed, and this has led to some interesting questions for Christians.

Organ transplants

Organ transplants involve taking the healthy organs from a 'donor' and putting them into another person, in the hope that it will save their life. Nowadays transplants are commonplace, and if properly matched have a high success rate. There is nothing in the Bible that says that people should not donate organs, indeed Jesus gave up his body for the good of others.

Some Christians though have had worries that this 'mutilation' of the body goes against Bible teachings; others have concerns that they need their body to remain whole so that it can be resurrected.

In 1997 the Church of England declared that organ donation was a Christian duty: body parts should not be mistaken for the person; donating them is the most loving thing to do. The Roman Catholic Church also supports organ donation but is unlikely to claim that it is a duty.

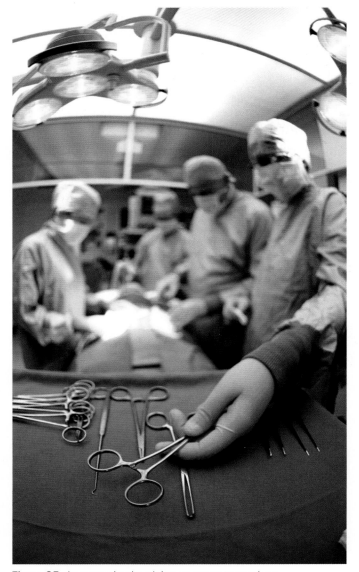

Figure 25 An operation involving an organ transplant

Activity

5 There are some interesting moral issues connected with transplants. Discuss the following with a partner:

In 1968 the Harvard Committee suggested that doctors should use 'brain death' as the way to determine death; in the 1980s there were calls for this to be updated.

- Is the thirst for donors so strong that it will change the definition of death?
- With demand being so high, who should get the organ when it becomes available?

Genetics and stem-cell technology

Genetic engineering has the potential to do great good, for instance getting rid of hereditary diseases. For Christians it begs the question of whether humans should be interfering with the design process; are they trying to play God? It offers the possibility for parents to choose the sex of a child so as to avoid passing on gender-specific illnesses. It could also offer the possibility of choosing a child's characteristics – creating designer babies.

There are warnings in the Bible about the created putting themselves above the creator. If the *reason* for genetic engineering is good, and it is aimed solely at helping people, then it does not go against Christian teachings. One of the worries is that it will go too far, like with human cloning: if humans meddle too much with God's 'natural order', then who knows what will happen?

Stem-cell technology can be used in the treatment of Alzheimer's, diabetes, cancer, strokes and paralysis. It may use adult stem cells, but embryonic ones are preferred because they can grow into any human cell. In order to get the stem cells, the **embryo** is destroyed. This creates a moral dilemma, like the issue of abortion, as to whether or not an embryo should be protected as a human life.

Activity

1 With a partner, make a list of the benefits and the potential worries concerning genetic engineering.

2 Why are embryonic stem cells favoured? Why does this create a moral dilemma? Is there an alternative?

3 What are the Christian teachings that can be applied to each of these issues? Make a table:

Issue	Teaching	Application
Transplants	'Love your neighbour'	May feel that it is the most loving thing to do
Genetic engineering		

Examiner's Tips

In preparation for the exam, make sure you know that:

- Christian teachings show racism to be wrong. God created all people in his own image. There are lots of relevant Bible teachings; you will need to know several. The church today is totally against racism, but this has not always been the case. Christians should make a stand against racism; Martin Luther King is a good example.
- Christians have a duty to care for the planet on behalf of God ('stewardship'). In the face of exploitation of the world's resources, Christians should take action on an individual level to ensure sustainable use of resources. Christians should also take action against the exploitation of people; World Vision is a good example.
- Christians believe in the sanctity of life, and there are several Bible teachings that support this. There are a range of Christian views about contraception and abortion. Christians look to the teachings of the churches. You will need to know about these.
- Modern advances in medicine can raise questions for Christians. Those advances that are clearly beneficial and definitely save lives are accepted by most Christians. Stem-cell research and genetic engineering are more complicated. You will need to know a range of views on these issues.

Sample question

Use Source A and your own knowledge to explain why there are a range of views about abortion. [6]

> 'I do not like the idea of abortion – I would definitely see it as a last resort – but if I had been raped then I would consider having an abortion. The Bible teaches about love and compassion. No one should be forced to have a baby.'
> Protestant woman

> 'The Bible teaches that life is sacred. I believe that life starts at conception; abortion is not an option for me. If I had been raped I would consider adoption.'
> Roman Catholic woman

Source A

What the examiner has to say!

- Look at what the sources tell you – they give clear reasons for their views.
- Now think about the things that the source does not tell you. What do the different churches teach about abortion? The Bible does not teach about abortion directly, but there are important teachings about the sanctity of life that you should mention.
- Use this information to *explain why* some Christians would consider abortion, while others would not.

Exam practice

1. Read the Stephen Lawrence news story. Use the article and your own knowledge to explain the problem of racism. [6]
2. Describe the work of Martin Luther King. [4]
3. Explain how non-violent methods of protest reflect Christian teachings. [4]
4. Use Figure 24 (on page 156) and your own knowledge to explain different views on abortion. [6]

Christianity What are the main beliefs and teachings that underpin Christian attitudes?

What beliefs underpin the Christian religion?

Beliefs about God

Christians believe in God. They believe that Jesus is the Son of God. These beliefs can be found in the Bible. Christians believe that there is only one God and that he created everything and that humans are created in his own image. It is also a Christian belief that God knows everything.

The Trinity

Another important belief is the Trinity. This is the idea that God is one but with three separate parts: God the Father, God the Son (Jesus) and God the Holy Spirit. God the Father is the creator, Jesus is God in human form and the Holy Spirit is God's presence on earth.

Jesus

The birth of Jesus is the time that Christians believe is the start of the religion. His birth was a miracle and Mary gave birth to him without having sexual intercourse. Jesus' birth is celebrated at Christmas. You can read the story in the Gospel of Mark in the New Testament.

Holy Week

Holy Week is the time from Palm Sunday to the arrest and resurrection of Jesus. Jesus entered Jerusalem on Palm Sunday on a donkey. He was welcomed by crowds waving palm branches. Jesus then preached and overturned the tables of people trading in the Temple. He was arrested and tried by the Sanhedrin (Jewish religious court) and the Romans. It was the Roman governor, Pontius Pilate, who sentenced him to death.

Jesus was tortured and then placed on the cross (crucifixion). After his death he was placed in a tomb but he rose again three days later. This is called the resurrection.

Life after death

Forty days later Jesus rose up to heaven. This is called the Ascension. It is the resurrection that gives Christians their belief in life after death. Jesus said he would rise from the dead and he did. Jesus performed many other miracles and this is another important belief to Christians.

Miracles

Miracles are an important part of Christian belief. Jesus performed many including curing people of blindness and leprosy. Leprosy is a very unpleasant disease that was misunderstood. People who suffered from it were kept apart from others. Jesus spent time with them and was prepared to help them, as he was with all people who were poor, sick or on the outside. The most important thing to remember about miracles is that the person who would benefit from it had to have faith in Jesus and God. By overcoming death at the resurrection Jesus shows Christians that, with faith, anything can be overcome.

Activity

1 Describe the events of Holy Week.

2 Debate: 'The Christian belief in the crucifixion of Jesus is the most important belief for Christians.'

3 'Miracles do not happen. They are just stories and they have no purpose in the world today.' To what extent do you agree with this statement?

Why is the Bible important for Christians?

Holy books are important to a religion as without them the religion would probably not exist. They provide the story of the foundation of the religion and tell followers what to believe.

The Christian holy book is called the Bible. It has two sections: the Old Testament and the New Testament.
- The Old Testament tells the story of creation, contains the Ten Commandments and many other rules and, Christians believe, predicts the coming of Jesus. It also includes poetry and stories.
- The New Testament starts with the birth of Jesus. The four Gospels of Matthew, Mark, Luke and John tell us about the life and teachings of Jesus.

The Bible provides Christians with guidance on how to live and an understanding of how their religion started. It also tells them about the creation of the universe.

Jesus only taught for the last three years of his life. He chose twelve disciples to help him in this task. He used many different methods to spread his message of eternal salvation. He taught people how to pray. A good example of this is the **Lord's Prayer**.

He suggested how they should behave and how they might get to heaven in the Sermon on the Mount. This very important speech included the **Beatitudes**, meaning 'blessed' or 'happy' (Matt 5:1–12, see also page 175), some of Jesus' most famous sayings. Another important thing to remember about the Sermon on the Mount is that it was for everyone who wanted to listen. Jesus made no difference between people wherever they came from.

In a time when most people could neither read nor write, Jesus was very good at helping them understand his message. There are many sayings of his that we still use commonly today, such as 'let he who is without sin cast the first stone' or 'do unto others as you would have them do unto you'.

He told interesting stories with a meaning, called '**parables**'. Anyone, whatever their age, could understand these simple stories. The most famous example of a parable is probably the Good Samaritan, but other examples are the Sheep and the Goats, and the Prodigal Son.

The Parable of the Good Samaritan tells the story of a Jewish man walking along a road when he suddenly gets attacked by robbers. He is beaten badly. First a priest comes by and then a Levite. Both of these men are religious Jews. They both walk past the man. A little later a Samaritan comes by. Samaritans and Jews thought of themselves as enemies. The Samaritan stopped and tended the man's wounds and took him to an inn where he asked the innkeeper to look after him. The Samaritan added that he would pay for any costs on his return journey. You can read the whole story in Luke 10:25.

Activity

1 Describe what Christians mean by the Trinity.

2 Why is the birth of Jesus important to Christians?

3 Write a modern-day version of a parable of your choice.

Examiner's Tips

Make sure that you look at the command word in the question, such as *describe* or *explain*. *Describe* questions require you to give some information. *Explain* questions ask you for reasons why something happened.

Figure 1 The Good Samaritan by Chinese Christian artist He Qi. He has done several paintings of stories from the Bible.

Islam What are the main beliefs and teachings that underpin Muslim attitudes?

What beliefs underpin the Muslim religion?

Muslims believe in **Allah**. This is the Arabic word for God. Islam is a monotheistic religion which means that Muslims believe in one God. The most important Muslim beliefs are found in the five pillars: Shahadah, Salah, Zakah, Saum and Hajj (see Figure 2).

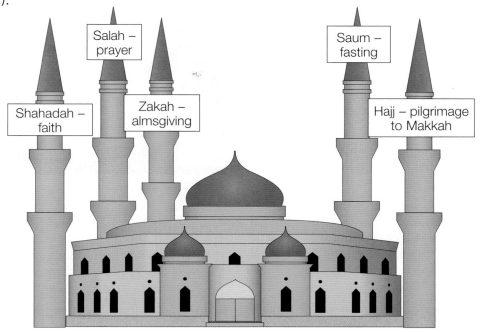

Salah – prayer

Saum – fasting

Shahadah – faith

Zakah – almsgiving

Hajj – pilgrimage to Makkah

Figure 2 The Five Pillars of Islam

The first pillar, Shahadah, is the first thing every new-born Muslim should hear. It describes the most important thing that Muslims believe:

'There is no God but Allah, and Muhammad is his messenger.'

Islam means 'submission' and this means that Muslims must give themselves up to Allah. One of the main ways of doing this is through daily prayer – salah. Muslims must pray five times a day. The actions in the prayers show that they give themselves up to Allah.

All Muslims who can afford to should give 2.5 per cent of what they earn to charity (Zakah). This shows that they are prepared to help those less fortunate than themselves.

Every year Muslims should fast (Saum) during the month of **Ramadan**. This is done in the hours of daylight. However, if a person is ill, pregnant, breast feeding or travelling they are not expected to fast.

If a Muslim can afford it they should go on a pilgrimage to **Makkah** (Hajj). Makkah is the holy city for Muslims. This is where Muhammad founded Islam. It is the city where he started receiving messages from Allah.

Muslims believe in life after death. They believe that all people will be judged on the Day of Judgement. They believe in heaven and hell. They must follow the rules laid down by Allah in the **Qur'an**, in order to get to heaven.

Muslims show their faith in Allah through worship (Shahadah and Salah). It is also important to do practical things: fasting reminds Muslims of those who cannot afford to eat and also makes them realise that Allah will always look after them; the pilgrimage to Makkah is to remind them where the religion started (only Muslims are allowed to go to Makkah); and almsgiving is a practical way of helping the poor.

Why is the Qur'an important for Muslims?

The Muslim holy book is called the Qur'an. It is written in Arabic and Muslims believe this to be a holy language. The Qur'an can only be used in worship if it is written in Arabic. Muslims believe the Arabic in the Qur'an to be special and holy. This is because they believe that Muhammad received messages from Allah in Arabic. Muhammad received these messages from Angel Jibril (Gabriel) on Mount Hira, near Makkah, to begin with. He then received more messages in Madinah when the first Muslims moved there in 622CE.

Muhammad could not read or write so he had to recite these messages to **scribes** who could then write them down. *Qur'an* is the Arabic word for 'recite'.

The Qur'an actually provides a strict set of rules to live by as well as providing guidance and advice. Many Muslims believe the Qur'an tells them all they need to know about how to live.

Muslims believe that Muhammad is the last of all the great prophets. They believe he was a normal human being asked to do a special job. At first many people did not want to believe his message. The first person who did was his wife, Khadijah. She was a rich businesswoman.

After many disagreements with the people of Makkah over his message of one God, Muhammad moved his band of followers to Madinah as the people there were more supportive. This happened in 622CE. This is known as the Hijra (migration). The people of Makkah did eventually accept Muhammad as Allah's messenger. This was important as Makkah was the most important city in the region at that time.

The Qur'an is split into 114 suras (chapters). When it is used it is placed on a stand called a kursi. Muslims must wash before touching it. It is used in the mosque by the imam who may give a reading from it at Friday prayers.

When it is not in use it is kept in a high place with nothing on top of it. It is placed in a cover to keep it clean.

Figure 3 Reading the Qur'an

Activity

1   What are Muslim beliefs in life after death. Explain, in your own words, why this is so important to Muslims.

2   Why are the five pillars so important to Muslims? Think about what each one of them stands for. After you have done this, you need to think about how they affect Muslims in their daily lives.

3   Muslims believe the Qur'an, in its original Arabic version, to be holy. Why do you think the Arabic language is so important to them?

4   Many Muslims are not Arabs. They may not understand Arabic. What difficulties might they face? How could these difficulties be resolved?

5   Muslims believe Muhammad was only human. Explain why they think his life was so important by what he did whilst he was alive.

6   Debate: 'The Qur'an should only be read in Arabic.'

Examiner's Tips

When building an argument in a debate, always think of what people who might disagree with you would say.

What are the main similarities and differences between Christian and Muslim worship?

How and where do Christians worship?

Christians worship in a church. Churches come in many shapes and sizes but most older churches are built in the shape of a cross. In this kind of church you will usually find the nave, the sanctuary, the font, the altar and pews. Most church services happen on a Sunday. This is because it is the day that Christians believe that Jesus was resurrected from the dead. The minister leads the service from the altar. He or she will bless the bread and wine and then share it amongst the congregation. It is important to remember that not all Christian services are the same.

The minister does a lot of other work too. He/she will take other services throughout the week, as well as baptisms, weddings and funerals when the need arises. He/she may also run Bible classes, along with clubs for the elderly, the young or parents, such as mother-and-toddler groups. The minister also visits schools, hospitals and individuals in their homes if they cannot make it to church.

The minister therefore has two different roles: **pastoral** and religious. His pastoral role is anything that sees him working in the wider community amongst people who may not go to church. His religious role is one that sees him carry out all the services mentioned above and more.

The church is a focal point for the community as well as a religious building. The building is used to worship God. However, the church may also have a hall attached to it where many other community activities take place that may not be religious; it may be the base for youth clubs, Cubs and Brownies or for coffee mornings for the elderly.

Figure 4 A typical parish church in the UK. Many modern churches can look very different.

How and where do Muslims worship?

Muslims worship in a mosque. The first mosque was built in Madinah by the Prophet Muhammad. This first mosque has become the model for all mosques.

Mosques come in many shapes and sizes but in many Muslim countries they are built with a dome for a roof. Therefore many in the UK have been built in this way. They also have minarets (spires) from which the **muezzin** gives the call to prayer. In a mosque you will find the minbar (pulpit), mihrab (niche that indicates the qiblah), qiblah (the direction of Makkah) and wall and wash basins for performing **wudu**. This is the washing before prayer. There are separate prayer halls for men and women. Muslims should pray five times a day but they can pray anywhere as long as they have washed and are facing Makkah. If they can, however, they should try and get to the mosque on a Friday for special communal prayers. The **imam** leads the prayers and gives a sermon from the minbar.

The imam does a lot of other work too. He rarely works full time as the imam and may be the caretaker of the mosque too, for example. He may also run special classes called madrassahs where Muslim children learn Arabic and about the Qur'an. The imam also visits schools, hospitals and individuals in their home if they cannot make it to the mosque.

It is important to remember that the imam therefore has two different roles: pastoral and religious. His pastoral role is anything that sees him working in the wider community amongst people who may not go to the mosque. His religious role is one that sees him carry out all the work mentioned above and more.

The mosque is not only a building but also provides a base for the community. It gives support and advice to people, many of whom may have just arrived in Britain. It will help them learn English and about life in Britain. The building is used to worship Allah. However, the mosque may also have a hall attached to it where many other community activities take place that may not be religious, such as youth clubs.

Figure 5 A mosque in Abu Dhabi

Activity

1 Compare and contrast a mosque and a church. What do they have in common? How are they different? Why are they both important?

2 Compare and contrast the role of a minister and an imam. Why is it that the imam often has another job?

What are the most important stages in a Christian and a Muslim life?

How are birth and coming of age marked in both religions?

The birth of a new child is important to both Christians and Muslims. When a Muslim baby is born, the baby should hear the **adhan** (call to prayer) and then have something sweet rubbed on their teeth. Usually at seven days old Muslims celebrate the aqiqah ceremony, where the baby's head is shaved and the hair weighed, with the equivalent weight being given in money to charity. A sheep is sacrificed, or, in Britain, the meat is usually ordered from a **halal** butcher. The meat is shared between family, neighbours and the poor.

Later in a boy's childhood, Muslims carry out the rite of **circumcision**. This can take place at seven days of age or any time up to puberty. In Turkey, for example, circumcision often takes place when a boy is nine or ten. It is done to remember the fact that Ibrahim followed Allah's order to circumcise himself and his son, Ishmael.

Many Christians, especially Roman Catholics, believe it is important to baptise a baby. When they are teenagers, these Christians then repeat the vows made for them by their godparents at baptism in a ceremony called confirmation.

A baptism ceremony usually takes place at the font, which is found at the front of the church. The font contains holy water, and the minister will bless the baby by pouring the holy water over his/her head or by making the sign of the cross with the water. Godparents will make promises to help bring up the child in the ways of the Church.

Figure 6 An infant baptism ceremony

Other groups of Christians, such as Baptists, believe people should make the choice of being baptised when they are old enough to decide for themselves, as Jesus himself did. This ceremony takes place in a baptismal pool where the person is fully immersed in the water by the minister as blessings are said. This is known as total immersion.

How are marriage and death marked in both religions?

Weddings

Muslims and Christians both believe marriage to be very important. Weddings are significant ceremonies and very happy occasions. However, in any religion, there are going to be very different ways of celebrating a wedding, depending on where you are from and what part of the religion you belong to. For example, a Roman Catholic wedding looks quite different from many Protestant weddings.

All religious weddings, however, represent one thing: the joining together of a couple in the eyes of God.

Activity

3 Describe circumcision.

4 Why do some Christians wait until they are older to get baptised?

Muslim weddings are often arranged, though this is not always the case in Britain today. Before any wedding, the husband must agree a mahr (dowry). This is a sum of money that the wife keeps and spends as she wishes, even after a divorce in most cases.

Some people brought up as Muslims may decide they do not want to follow traditions such as arranged marriage. This could cause tension in the family between generations. Younger people will have always different views from their parents and this may be made more difficult if they have been brought up in a non-Muslim country like Britain.

The Muslim ceremony itself is known as **nikah**. Marriage is a contract and the ceremony reflects this. Sometimes the wife does not attend but has to send witnesses. Prayers are said and passages read from the Qur'an, as well as vows being exchanged. Weddings do not have to take place in a mosque.

A large feast is usually held. Dress varies according to the country the couple come from, though many brides wear a white dress. Many couples also decorate their hands with henna.

In a Christian wedding, the couple stand at the altar and make vows to spend the rest of their lives together. This is done in front of the minister and witnesses. Rings are exchanged. It is still customary for the bride to wear white. The wedding is followed by a reception where celebrations take place.

All marriages in Britain, regardless of their religion, should also be registered at the local registry office. This makes the marriage legal in the eyes of the government.

Funerals

Funerals are important to both religions as they mark the passing of a person into the next life.

Most Christians still believe that a body should be buried as it is believed that it will be resurrected when Jesus comes again. However, cremation is becoming more common. At a Christian funeral prayers are said, hymns are sung and the person is remembered in speeches given by friends, family and the minister.

For Muslims, a funeral is a simple affair with the body buried in a simple wooden coffin facing Makkah. If at all possible the body should be buried within 24 hours of death.

Figure 7 A Muslim wedding

Activity

1 Describe a Christian wedding ceremony.

2 Describe a Muslim wedding ceremony.

3 What are the problems facing Muslim parents who may want their children to follow the traditional way of getting married in Britain today?

4 'Living together before getting married is a good thing.' To what extent do you agree with this statement?

5 Research a Muslim or Christian funeral service.

6 Debate: 'Arranged marriages are better than people choosing their own partner.' (You might like to note that in arranged marriages the couple should also give their consent.)

Examiner's Tips

Always make sure you give at least one reason for the opposing argument when you are asked 'to what extent' or 'how far do you agree'. This matters even if you do not agree with what you are writing. It shows you understand there is more than one point of view. This is a very important skill in life.

Why are celebrations important in both Christianity and Islam?

How do Christians demonstrate their attitudes, values and beliefs through their celebrations?

Figure 8 Christmas midnight mass

Christmas

Christmas is the time when Christians celebrate the birth of Jesus. It is celebrated in Britain on 25 December. Advent starts on 1 December and marks the beginning of the time when Christians start thinking about the birth of Jesus. The story of Jesus' birth can be found in the Gospels. These are the books that describe the life and teachings of Jesus in the New Testament. They are named after the people that probably wrote them: Matthew, Mark, Luke and John.

Mary, the mother of Jesus, was visited by the Angel Gabriel and was told that she would give birth to a son and she would call him Jesus. This was despite the fact she was a virgin. The father of Jesus was God. Mary and her husband, Joseph, went to Bethlehem where Jesus was born. He was visited by shepherds and three wise men who had travelled a long distance. All brought him gifts. These visitors symbolise that Jesus was born for everyone, whether they were rich or poor; foreign or native.

Today, during Advent, Christians go to church for special services. Some even go to a service known as midnight mass on the night of Christmas Eve. Presents are given and received and it is a special time to spend with family and to think about God and Jesus. Many of the decorations we have today were added much later and are not linked to the birth of Jesus.

Easter

Easter is the most important festival in the Christian calendar. Without it there is no Christianity. Jesus told his twelve disciples that he would sacrifice himself for the sins of all humans and then rise again. Believing in this means that Christians believe they get the chance of eternal life.

On Palm Sunday, Jesus rode into Jerusalem and was welcomed by the crowds, who were waving palm branches. In that week, he overturned the tables of the merchants in the Temple. Jesus had the Last Supper with his twelve disciples, where he told them he would be betrayed. Judas Iscariot was the one who would do this and he was present at the meal.

Later in the Garden of Gethsemane Jesus was arrested by the Romans, who had been led to him by Judas Iscariot. Jesus was questioned by the religious authorities as well as by the Romans under Pontius Pilate, the Roman governor of Judea. He was tortured and beaten and then sentenced to death by the Romans.

He was crucified on the cross on Good Friday and then rose from the dead on Sunday. He had been buried in a cave belonging to a rich friend.

The culture of materialism

The culture of materialism in our society – seeing Christmas trees in supermarkets in early November, decorations and presents for sale in the run-up to festivals and seemingly longer run-ups every year – puts pressure on families of all backgrounds. Advertising can make it difficult to manage the expectation of children. It is important to remember that for truly religious people these festivals are about worshipping God and spending time with family and friends.

The culture of materialism we live in is a real problem for many families. There are always new toys and gadgets to buy as technology is changing so quickly. Many parents simply cannot afford the things their children may want. The pressure this puts on families can be felt in more than one way. It may be financial. It may be emotional as parents try and reason with their children that the toys they want for Christmas are not affordable.

At Easter time the financial issues may be less of a problem. However, there is still the issue of people not understanding the origins of what they are celebrating and then going to excess. This may be through something simple like having too much chocolate at Easter! It may be more serious by drinking too much alcohol at Christmas time.

How do Muslims demonstrate their attitudes, values and beliefs through their celebrations?

Eid-ul-Fitr is a three-day holiday that comes at the end of the month of fasting, which is the Muslim month of Ramadan. Muslims fast during the hours of daylight, not eating or drinking anything. Because the Muslim calendar is a lunar calendar, Eid-ul-Fitr can fall in the height of summer during the very long days. The festival starts when the new moon is sighted. Fasting during Ramadan is one of the five pillars.

This festival is celebrated by wearing best or new clothes. Presents are exchanged. There are special ceremonies at the mosque, and some people go for a retreat in the mosque for ten days before the end of Ramadan. Houses are decorated. Muslims thank Allah for giving them the self-control to have fasted for a month. Fasting reminds Muslims that there are many people who cannot afford to eat every day.

Eid-ul-Adha remembers the time when Ibrahim was prepared to sacrifice his son Ishmael at Allah's command. In the end, Allah stopped Ibrahim from doing this and he was given a sheep to sacrifice instead. At this time, Muslims remember the sacrifices they make for Allah and their submission to him. *Islam* means 'submission' or giving in to Allah. As at most festivals, presents are given and received and special prayers and services are held at the mosque. An animal is slaughtered and shared between family, friends and the poor.

Being a minority faith in Britain sometimes makes it hard for Muslims to celebrate these festivals. They might have trouble getting time off work or school as the dates of the festivals change from year to year and usually fall during term time. It might be hard to find halal meat, or they might live a long way from the nearest mosque.

Figure 9 Eid-ul-Fitr celebrations in Trafalgar Square, London

Activity

1 Why is Christmas important? Why is Easter important? Compare and contrast the importance of Christmas and Easter. Give reasons for you answer.

2 Explain why Eid-ul-Fitr and Ramadan are not the same thing.

3 'Muslims and Christians both have the same problems when celebrating festivals these days.' To what extent do you agree with this statement? Give reasons for your answer.

4 Debate: 'A child's favourite reading at Christmas is a toy catalogue. This is a reflection of our times. We have never been more materialistic.'

Examiner's Tips

When you debate an issue, always give a reason for why you think something.

What are the implications of practising faith in modern Britain?

What are the problems facing Christians in practising their faith in today's society?

There are many issues that arise from being religious in Britain today. Some schools and work places may not allow Christian symbols to be worn, and it may be hard to get time off work if there are special ceremonies to attend. This is less likely to happen to Christians as the main religion of Britain has been Christianity for many centuries. This means that, for example, the school calendar works around the Christian faith. There are Christmas and Easter holidays.

One of the biggest problems facing many Christian denominations is declining attendance. In many areas ministers have to cover several churches as there are simply not enough people going to church. Many of the people going to church are elderly and cannot travel great distances.

Another problem is the increasing **secularisation** of society. In short, most of us are becoming less religious. There are many reasons, including that there are so many more things for us to do with our time. For example, shops did not always open on a Sunday – now they do. The church used to have much greater control over society than it does now.

What are the problems facing Muslims in practising their faith in today's society?

Muslims must pray five times a day. This doesn't mean they have to go to the mosque; they can pray anywhere as long as they have a mat and have performed wudu. They must pray in the direction of Makkah. Muslims can have problems getting time off work or school to do this. Although many employers understand the issue and provide suitable arrangements, this may not always be possible. Every Friday Muslims must try and attend the mosque for communal prayers. Here the imam gives a sermon and reads passages from the Qur'an. Again, getting time off work in a non-Muslim country like Britain can sometimes be difficult, and if you are a Muslim living a long way from a big town where there is a mosque it is even more difficult.

Islamophobia is the hatred or fear of Muslims. Some people feel this way towards Muslims for a number of reasons. They may think that Muslims are a security threat or that they do not want to adapt to life in Britain. It is a very unfortunate problem as most of the things Muslims are accused of are simply not true.

Muslims have special food laws known as halal. The most important rules are regarding meat: animals must be slaughtered in a special way and all the blood drained. Muslims are not allowed to eat any kind of pork. Obeying the rules of halal can be problematic for Muslims who do not live in a big town where there is a halal butcher.

Internet Research Activity

Visit this website

www.whychurch.org.uk/trends.php

for more on declining attendance of churches.

Activity

5 Why do you think society in Britain is becoming less religious? Give reasons for your answer.

The question of the way Muslims dress has become an issue in recent years, symbolised by the headscarf (**hijab**). It must be noted that Muslims often dress according to the country which they are originally from, as opposed to what their religion is. Many Muslims dress in a way we could typically describe as British. The headscarf can be a problem if it covers the whole face, especially in places like banks and airports where identification is important. Most Muslim women, however, wear a scarf that allows their face to be clearly seen.

Headscarves

France has a very different approach from the UK to religion in schools. The Church in France was separated from the state in 1905. Since the separation of church from state in France, no religion is meant to have a higher status than any other. This is why all religious symbols are banned in all places run by the government, including schools.

In Britain this is not the case. Usually Muslim girls, for example, can wear a headscarf as long as their face is visible. Interestingly, the headscarf is banned in government buildings in a Muslim country: Turkey.

Figure 10 A Muslim lady wearing the traditional hijab

Activity

1 Describe what happens at Friday prayers.

2 Compare and contrast the problems faced by Muslims and Christians in trying to practise their faith in Britain today.

3 Debate: 'It does not matter what you wear to school.'

How does religion impact on the day-to-day lives of individuals and families?

What are Christian attitudes, values and beliefs about marriage, divorce and family life?

Christians believe that the Bible gives them the guidance they need to live their lives. They believe it is the word of God. Amongst the most important passages in the Bible is the Ten Commandments. This is a set of simple instructions that Christians can live by and they are considered to be some of the most important for the religion. They are split into two categories: the first four commandments are religious and the following six are secular. In this way they provide rules on how to be a good religious person as well as how to be good in everyday life. This is because Christians believe that all their actions should be religious, so being a Christian has an impact on every single aspect of life.

There were not many rules that Jesus himself laid down. Much of his teaching was in the form of parables. However, he was very clear on marriage and divorce. He said 'But I tell you that anyone who divorces his wife, except for marital unfaithfulness, causes her to become an adulteress, and anyone who marries the divorced woman commits adultery.' (Matthew 5:32).

Jesus taught 2,000 years ago in what is now called Israel. Things have changed immensely. Whilst the most common family in the UK is still the nuclear family, there are now many different types of family. There has been a large rise in the number of single-parent families, which usually consist of a mother bringing up children by herself. However, there are fathers who bring up children by themselves too. One of the main reasons for this rise in single-parent families is that divorce is easier to obtain than it was in the past and partners can easily leave if they are not married. Many parents **cohabit**. This means they live an ordinary family life without ever getting married.

The changes in family life in Britain have affected our relationship with elderly relatives. In previous generations, it was the norm for elderly relatives to live with their families. This still occurs but is less common than in the past. Again, there are many reasons for this. Amongst the main reasons are that people are living longer and enjoying active retirements. Medical advances have meant that those with the means can live independent retirements. Another factor is that people often do not live near their parents. They move to another part of the country or even abroad.

Figure 11 The Ten Commandments, which appear in the Old Testament in the book of Exodus

Activity

4   How many of the Ten Commandments could you follow if you were not religious? Explain why this is the case.

5   What did Jesus teach about marriage and divorce?

6   Society has changed a lot in recent years and this has affected the way we look at family life. What different types of family life can you think of? Does it matter in what type of family a child is brought up?

What are Muslim attitudes, values and beliefs about marriage, divorce and family life?

Although it is not compulsory, many Muslim marriages are arranged by the parents. No one can be forced to marry against their will. The couple should consent to the marriage and should be given time to get to know each other. In modern Britain many Muslims choose who they marry, whilst others continue with the traditional practices of their parents' generation.

Divorce is allowed in Islam, but is discouraged.

Many of the Muslim communities that have settled in Britain since the Second World War try to maintain a way of life that is in keeping with the country from which they originate. This means attitudes vary to all issues, including family. For example, a Muslim could come from Pakistan or Turkey. These are two very different countries with different languages and cultures. Therefore some of the things we associate with being 'Muslim' may actually be Pakistani or Turkish.

Family life is just such an issue. In the main, Muslims try to live near each other, in the same town if not in the same house. This has as much to do with the fact that when the first Muslims arrived many could not speak English, so it helped to pool their efforts as a community. Whilst it is true that many people from abroad still live in the same community it is also true that many younger people are much more integrated into life in Britain.

This means that Muslims, as well as Christians, have the same issues surrounding different types of family life mentioned above, though divorce rates amongst Muslims are low and this can lead to more stability. Elderly relatives are often cared for within the family. There may be issues surrounding the rights of women in some communities but a lot of work is being done to improve this situation.

Activity

1 What are Muslim perspectives on arranged marriage?

2 Debate: 'The care of elderly relatives must be the responsibility of the extended family.'

Examiner's Tips

Always remember that there is often more than one possible correct answer to a question or an issue. Many questions that ask about people's beliefs have more than one answer – that is why there are so many different religions.

What are the religious and moral standpoints regarding inequality in society?

What are Christian attitudes, values and beliefs about poverty and inequality?

Beatitudes (Matthew 5)

Jesus taught that anyone can go to heaven and these teachings can be found in the Gospel of Matthew (Chapter 5). These are a series of blessings known as the Beatitudes. It tells us that the people who are blessed do not have to be rich or powerful but they can be peacemakers. The Beatitudes were taught at the Sermon on the Mount. It gives Christians a very good idea of how to behave to those less fortunate than them.

'... eye of a needle'

The conversation that Jesus has with a rich man in Matthew 19 is clear in that he states that: 'Truly I tell you, it is hard for someone who is rich to enter the kingdom of heaven. Again I tell you, it is easier for a camel to go through the eye of a needle than for someone who is rich to enter the kingdom of God.'

This is a very clear statement of what Jesus thought about worldly wealth. That said, Jesus also had rich friends such as Nicodemus in whose tomb he was buried after his crucifixion. What this tells us is that Jesus made it clear that becoming rich should not be an ambition in itself and that there are more important things in life than money. Remember also that Saint Paul said that the *love* of money is the root of all evil.

Jesus' disciples

Jesus chose twelve special people to be with him at all times throughout his teaching. They are known as the twelve disciples. Twelve is an important number in the Jewish religion and Jesus was Jewish. It represents the twelve tribes of Israel who are talked about in the Old Testament.

The disciples were men from many different backgrounds. Peter, regarded by Catholics as the first Bishop of Rome (Pope), was a fisherman. Matthew was a tax collector. They led very simple lives, travelling from one place to another, preaching and helping people. They worked a lot with the poor and the sick. Their behaviour has become a role model for Christians throughout history. From Mother Theresa to Martin Luther King, so many people have tried to live up to the example set by Jesus and his disciples in the fight against poverty and inequality.

Jesus also set another example in his life. He had friends from a range of backgrounds. He would help anyone. He helped a Roman centurion – the Romans were considered enemies in Judea at the time. Indeed, it was Pontius Pilate, the Roman governor, who sentenced Jesus to death.

Parables

To help reinforce his message about equality in the eyes of God, Jesus used stories called parables. It is important to remember that there were not many people who would have stood up for the rights of the poor, the sick, foreigners or even people who were considered criminals. Jesus was not liked by many people in authority as he criticised many of them for being more concerned with enriching themselves than with helping others.

Amongst the most famous examples of a parable is the Good Samaritan found in Luke, Chapter 10 (see also page 162).

This parable is told in answer to the question 'Who is my neighbour?'. The golden rule in the Jewish religion is 'love your neighbour as you love yourself'.

Internet Research Activity

www.christianaid.org.uk

www.cafod.org.uk

Find out more about these Christian charities and their work to help end poverty and inequality.

Activity

3 Make a list of the Beatitudes and explain, in your own words, what each one means and why it is important.

4 Read the parable of the Good Samaritan. Explain why many people feel it is still so relevant today.

What are Muslim attitudes, values and beliefs about poverty and inequality?

Muslims believe firmly in fighting poverty and inequality. The fasting month of Ramadan is partly about a symbolic gesture of giving up food and drink in the daytime in order to understand how lucky they are to have these things. At festivals or when a baby is born and an animal is sacrificed some of the meat is given to the poor.

The five pillars are also an important guide to attitudes, values and beliefs about poverty and inequality. The last pillar is the hajj, which is the pilgrimage to Makkah. Everyone wears the white robes called **ihram** and no leather or jewellery is worn; communal prayer and the declaration of faith are all statements that everyone is equal in the eyes of Allah. The prophet Muhammad led a very simple life, which reflected his teachings.

In **Surah** (chapter) 9 of the Qur'an it states 'take from their wealth so that you might purify and sanctify them'. **Zakah**, one of the five pillars, means 'to purify' (see below). This is represented by charity. Those who are wealthy should consider it a blessing from Allah; it is these people's duty to give some of this back to those who need it most. In a rich country like Britain, many people would be expected to give something back. It is important to remember that what passes as poverty in Britain would, in many countries, be considered as fairly well off.

The most important pillar in helping the poor and destitute is Zakah. It is the belief that all Muslims should give 2.5 per cent of their disposable income to charity. Zakah has inspired the growth of many great charities such as the Red Crescent and Islamic Relief, whose website gives many useful examples of how Muslims combat poverty and inequality.

Muslims would consider the struggle against poverty and inequality as jihad, which is a struggle to be a good Muslim and to build a good Muslim society.

Words from the Islamic Relief website: *Whoever saved a life, it would be as if he saved the life of all mankind.* Qur'an 5:32

Islamic Relief is an international aid and development charity that aims to alleviate the suffering of the world's poorest people. It is an independent Non-Governmental Organisation (NGO) founded in the UK in 1984 by Dr Hany El Banna.

Activity

1 Explain why Zakah is so important to Muslims.

2 Debate: 'All religious people should just give all of their money anyway.'

Figure 12 Islamic charities work to combat poverty and inequality and help in times of need and natural disasters. Here the Turkish Red Crescent are distributing supplies in Bagdad, Iraq

Examiner's Tips

Explaining something you have written means that you should tell the reader your thoughts in clear and simple terms.

How can religious groups develop practical responses to inequality?

What can Christians do to help fight inequality?

A simple thing that any Christian can do in order to help fight inequality is pray, which can be done either privately or communally. Jesus taught Christians how to pray, and they believe in the power of prayer. There are some important types of prayer, the most important prayer for many Christians being the Lord's Prayer, found in Matthew, Chapter six. Thanksgiving and **supplication** are also very important types of prayer, especially in the fight for equality.

Christians can also campaign for change, and this has led to the foundation of some great Christian charities such as CAFOD and Christian Aid. As well as doing practical things such as running fundraising campaigns and helping people with short, medium and long-term aid throughout the world, they also campaign for change by persuading governments and other organisations to do more to fight poverty and inequality. In Britain, another very famous example of a Christian charity is the Salvation Army, founded by William Booth in the nineteenth century. The Salvation Army also does a lot of good work in other countries.

Figure 13 CAFOD are a Catholic charity. In this photo, Moises Tipula, Vice President of a project CAFOD is supporting in Peru, high up in the Andes, is testing the water quality in his local area that has been affected by a tungsten mine. The community is also receiving legal support to take the company to court for damages to the environment, livestock and health.

Case Study

Lebanon

During the 1948 Arab–Israeli war, tens of thousands of Palestinians fled to surrounding countries – including Lebanon, where an estimated 400,000 are still living in camps.

Most people live in overcrowded, poor conditions, are unemployed, do not have proper rights and are unable to access public services. CAFOD supports local organisations that train and educate refugees so they can find work and are not reliant on aid.

Many people also come to Lebanon from other countries to get jobs as domestic workers. Most have legal work permits, but some employers abuse them physically and sexually, refuse to pay their wages and withhold their passports.

When they try to escape they are often arrested as their legal status is dependent on their being employed. CAFOD supports their local partner to provide a safe house, legal support and counselling for detained migrants.

CAFOD spent £68,000 in Lebanon in 2008/09.

www.cafod.org.uk/about-us/where-we-work/lebanon

What can Muslims do to help fight inequality?

Muslims wishing to fight inequality can do many of the same things as Christians. They can pray both individually and communally. Muslims believe they belong to the ummah, the worldwide community of Muslims, and prayer connects them to each other. This means that they do everything they can to fight inequality as they are all part of the same whole.

Muslims can campaign for change. The work to fight inequality could be considered a **jihad** as it is a struggle to improve things. They can donate money and join charities.

The organisation of much of the work against poverty and equality is very similar for Muslims and Christians. The work often starts locally and is based around the mosque or church. The minister or imam leads the effort, but it is a true community effort. The wonderful thing about this work is that it shows God's work in action. This means that many people, who may not even be very religious, get involved with these efforts.

The effectiveness of these efforts can vary but they almost certainly do some good. It is often better to give money than clothes or other heavy goods that you might think are useful. This is because the money can be spent where the problems are and it employs local people to help solve them. This has two advantages. Firstly, it means that local people get jobs. Secondly, local people know the area in which they live, which means they often know how to deal with the problems better.

There are always going to be issues when fighting inequality. Sometimes, for a number of reasons, the money may not reach the people it was intended to help. This might be for reasons of poor administration or corruption. Sometimes local issues can cause problems. This might be because of the lack of good roads or other poor transport connections. The weather or time of year may be a problem too. It is always better to try and overcome problems though and this means that people of all religions are always trying to work hard to make sure that the fight against inequality continues.

Activity

1 Why do you think religious people believe prayer helps those who are suffering? Give reasons for your answer.

2 Explain how campaigning for change could help.

3 Choose an example of a charity or an organisation you have studied and describe the work they have done to tackle inequality. How successful do you think they have been?

4 Debate: 'We should help people in Britain before we help people in other countries.'

Examiner's Tips

Where possible, use a case study to help you explain what you have learned. This means you can show the examiner or your teacher that you have looked at how a specific person or organisation has put the teachings of their religion into practice.

Case Study

Islamic Relief East Africa Crisis Appeal, 2011

The drought in the Horn of Africa is affecting over 10 million people from across Somalia, Kenya and Ethiopia. A deadly combination of successive failed rains and rising food prices has resulted in the worst drought the region has seen for 60 years.

Many people have lost their livelihoods. Livestock in the region is seen as a source of income and food. For some people, their livestock is everything.

Islamic Relief is already witnessing people crossing the border from Somalia into Kenya as they attempt to flee the drought that affects their country. Islamic Relief is also seeing an increased number of families arriving in Mogadishu and other areas trying to escape the drought and find a means to feed their family.

In Kenya, the food prices are at an all-time high as a result of a decrease in livestock. The largest refugee camp in the world is in Kenya, on the Somali–Kenya border, with over 300,000 inhabitants. Islamic Relief has observed an increased number of cases of malnutrition and diarrhoea in children, which is deadly in the current conditions.

Islamic Relief has an emergency drought response project in three districts in Puntland, Somalia. This has included successful delivery of seven litres of water a day to 35,406 people for a period of one month, and the provision of essential primary healthcare services to a further 1,322 women and children.

Islamic Relief is also providing:
- Emergency primary health care services to Internally Displaced People (IDPs) and host communities in the region of Mudug, targeting 50,000 people.
- More than $350,000 worth of canned meat (60 tons) and $100,000 worth of food parcels in Puntland and Somaliland.
- Primary Healthcare for IDPs in South Central Somalia, Puntland and Somaliland.
- Emergency Healthcare and Water to IDPs in Afgooye Corridor South Central Somalia, targeting 60,000 beneficiaries.

- £14 can provide a child with high energy food supplements for a week.
- £50 can provide clean water to 1000 people.
- £100 can provide emergency food to 100 families per day.
- £150 can treat 10 malnourished children for a month.

Internet Research Activity

- **www.islamic-relief.org.uk/Aboutus.aspx**
- **www.redcrescent.org**

Visit these websites and find out more about the charities. How effective are they at fighting poverty and inequality?

Hinduism What are the main beliefs and teachings that underpin Hindu attitudes?

What beliefs underpin the Hindu religion?

Brahman is a word which tries to describe a very difficult idea. It is a Sanskrit word, which is the ancient language in which Hindu religious texts are written. Brahman tries to describe the idea of a power that may be larger than the universe. Some people translate this into English as 'God', and we might understand this as the power which supports everything, as we may think of God as the power which supports everything. Brahman is such a huge concept that Hindus usually worship one deity as a manifestation, or representation, of one part of Brahman's nature.

Hindus believe that God creates, sustains and destroys the universe time and time again. Three of the major manifestations of Brahman are Brahma who creates, Vishnu who sustains and Shiva who destroys. Other famous Hindu gods are Hanuman and Ganesha.

One of the most important ideas in Hinduism is that of **moksha**, meaning 'liberation'. It is liberation, or release, from the constant cycle of **samsara**, where the soul is constantly reborn into different bodies, both animal and human. This idea is called **reincarnation**. The next reincarnation is always dependent upon how the previous life was lived. There are good and bad actions in life, known as karma. One of the best forms to come back as is a holy person or priest. If the cycle has been broken and moksha is attained it means that that soul will no longer be reincarnated.

Why are holy books important to a religion?

Hindus have many holy books. The most important are the **Vedas**. They were originally passed down through word of mouth before later being written down. Sometimes the Vedas are called shruti as this means 'hearing', remembering that they were passed down orally.

There are four sections to the Vedas:
1 The Samhitas are the oldest of the part of the Vedas. They contain hymns and are often used at the **mandir** (temple).
2 The Brahmanas help priests in carrying out their religious duties.
3 The Aranyakas help Hindus in worship and meditation. Meditation is very important in attempting to attain moksha.
4 The Upanishads are amongst the most famous Hindu texts and contain some of the most important ideas about Hinduism.

These texts help Hindus in their everyday lives with guidance, advice and support when praying or in everyday situations.

Activity

1 Explain reincarnation in your own words.

2 Explain the idea behind the belief that there is one God but he is worshipped in many different forms.

3 Describe the Vedas in your own words.

4 Why do Hindus believe the Vedas to be so important?

5 Debate: 'Holy books serve no purpose in the modern world.'

Examiner's Tips

Learn what each section of the Vedas is about.

How and where do Hindus worship?

A lot of Hindu worship is carried out in the home where there is a shrine to perform **puja** (a religious ritual). However, Hindus also worship in the mandir. The most important features of the mandir include the **murti**, which is the image of the god to whom the mandir is dedicated. Other important features include signs such as the Aum, statues of gods and goddesses and a central shrine. The mandir is decorated with flowers. There are no seats in the worship area and prayer might be quiet (private worship) or there may be music and hymn-singing. People must take off their shoes and wash their hands before entering the mandir.

The priest looks after the murti by a carefully thought-out series of rituals including washing it and offering it food. The food is then shared amongst the worshippers when they arrive at the mandir. Communal meals like this are important.

Activity

6 Describe Hindu worship.

7 Why is the priest important?

Figure 14 Hindu temple in Neasden, London. It is Europe's first traditional Hindu mandir, opening in 1995.

What are the most important stages in a Hindu life?

How are birth and coming of age marked in Hinduism?

In Hinduism there are sixteen **samskaras** – sacraments that are marked throughout a person's life. Some of these happen during pregnancy. For children, two of the most important of these are the first haircut and the sacred thread ceremony.

The first haircut happens to both boys and girls and is associated with the removal of impurities. This is a sign that the child has been cleansed.

The sacred thread ceremony happens when a child reaches the age of about eight. The child receives the sacred thread, usually three strands of cotton cord, to symbolise three debts: knowledge, parents and society and is aimed to coincide with school. It is a sign that the child is becoming more aware of the world around them.

How are marriage and death marked in Hinduism?

Marriage

Marriage is one of the samskaras as it marks an important stage in a Hindu's life. Hindus regard the setting-up of a family as central to their faith. As puja is often carried out at home it is here that children will learn the values, tradition and history of their faith.

Figure 15 A Hindu wedding ceremony

How a marriage is celebrated varies from region to region, which is the case for all religions. However, common features can often be found. A wedding often takes place in a house. The bride's parents welcome the bridegroom and his family. The bride and groom exchange garlands and the bridegroom is offered a drink called mandap at an altar specially prepared for the occasion. Gifts are exchanged which are a symbol that both families accept the bride and groom.

A sacred fire is lit and prayers are said by the priest. Then vows are exchanged: the couple swear to be husband and wife in the spirit of dharma. The couple then walk round the sacred fire.

The next phase is the most important. It is where seven vows are made and a step is taken for each of the vows. The vows include one for wisdom. The ceremony is completed by a ceremonial knot being tied.

Death

Death in Hinduism is not the end as Hindus believe in reincarnation and souls are therefore immortal. Death is the resting of the soul before it returns to life in another form. Unless a soul attains moksha neither death nor life are permanent.

A funeral is the last of the samskaras. Hindus believe in cremation as they feel this restores each of the body's elements to its rightful place, including the soul, so it can carry on its onward journey. Where possible Hindus try and carry out a cremation on the River Ganges as they believe it is holy.

Upon death, the body is washed and then the cremation should be carried out within 48 hours, unless there are unusual circumstances. The funeral pyre is usually lit by the eldest son. A few days after the cremation the ashes are collected up and scattered in different places. They are mixed with earth, water and air to signify the return of the body to the natural elements. Rice balls are often made by the relatives of the departed so the soul can build a body for the world of the ancestors. This continues for ten days.

Activity

1 Explain the different celebrations Hindus go through as children.

2 Explain a Hindu wedding ceremony.

3 Explain a Hindu funeral.

Examiner's Tips

Remember what phase in a person's life each of the ceremonies represents. This way you will get a good idea of what is important to the religion.

Why are celebrations important in Hinduism?

How do Hindus demonstrate their attitudes, values and beliefs through their celebrations?

Hindus have two major festivals: **Diwali** and **Holi**.

Diwali

Diwali is the festival of lights and celebrates the victory of good over evil. It lasts for five days. The word Diwali comes from a Sanskrit word meaning row of lights. It is a popular festival in Britain because it is so joyous and colourful: homes are spring-cleaned, people buy new clothes to wear, buildings are lit up with a wonderful array of coloured lights.

The dates for Diwali vary from year to year. This is because the dates are set by the Hindu calendar. For many it marks the new year so it is a time to start new accounting for businesses. Diwali is also associated with Lakshmi who is the Hindu goddess of wealth. Lakshmi is guided into people's homes by these lights which are traditionally made from pottery. Fireworks are also widely used at Diwali.

Figure 16 Diwali celebrations in Shree Swaminarayan Temple in Willesden Green, London

Altars are built in people's homes. They leave windows and doors open so Lakshmi can come in. Rangoli patterns are painted on the floors of houses. These are brightly coloured designs and the paint is traditionally made from ground rice or flour, though more modern equivalents are often used nowadays. Lotus flowers are popular designs as they are associated with Lakshmi. During this time there is also a lot of eating and celebration. Gifts are exchanged. There was a time when these were often simply sweets and other foodstuffs. Nowadays, however, Hinduism has been hit by the same concerns regarding commercialism as other religions. This can be especially the case with Diwali as it is associated with wealth.

Diwali also remembers the legend of Rama and Sita. Sita, the wife of Rama, was kidnapped by the demon, Ravana. Rama had a great battle with Ravana and won. He killed Ravana and returned to become king of Ayodhya. When the king and queen returned it was dark so lamps were put out to show them the way.

Holi

Holi falls in February or March. Holi was originally a harvest festival but has now become linked with other Hindu legends, such as the legend of Prahalad and Holika.

Holi is sometimes known as the festival of colours, and people paint themselves with bright colours. There is plenty of singing and dancing. Even **caste** separation is set aside at this time. Food is often roasted on specially lit bonfires that remember Prahalad and Holika.

Because the caste system is set aside during this time, Holi is seen as a symbol of equality. People do not wear their best clothes as it is such a messy time with paint often being thrown. This means that it is difficult to tell who is rich and who is poor.

Activity

1 Diwali is an important time of year for Hindus. Why do you think other people who are not Hindus often enjoy getting involved as well?

2 Choose either Diwali or Holi and imagine you are a Hindu child writing to a penfriend, or writing a blog, describing what you are celebrating. Remember to say why it is important, the history behind it and the bits you like best.

3 Debate: 'Religious festivals are a waste of time.'

Examiner's Tips

Remember you can use another religion as an example if the question is a general one about both Christianity and the other religion you are studying (Hinduism, Judaism or Islam).

Internet Research Activity

www.bbc.co.uk/religion/religions/hinduism/holydays/holi_1.shtml

Visit this website and find out more about the legend of Prahalad and Holika. What do you think the moral of the story is?

What are the implications of practising faith in modern Britain?

What are the problems facing Hindus in practising their faith in today's society?

Hindus face many of the same problems people of any faith face in Britain today, especially if they are not Christian. These include time off for festivals in a country that is not Hindu. As we have seen already, Hinduism has important festivals. Diwali lasts five days. There are also other Hindu festivals throughout the year.

Worship at the mandir may also be a problem if there is a special service that needs to be attended. There is a good deal of flexibility in many Hindu practices such as puja but they are as important to them as prayer is to any religious person.

There may be problems getting the right materials for festivals. However, there are large Hindu communities in our bigger cities so this is more of an issue for Hindus living in less built-up areas.

On a more positive note, Hindu festivals are often fun and inclusive which means the whole community can get involved. This helps everyone understand the religion and is a very good way of educating people.

Hindus may stand out by the way they dress. However, many Hindus only wear traditional clothes when they are involved in ceremonies such as marriage. The style of dress of many Hindus is not because of their religion but because of the part of the world their family originally came from.

Activity

1 What problems might face Hindus living in Britain today?

2 Debate: 'People should be given time off work/school for their religious beliefs.'

There may be issues surrounding the lighting of bonfires at festival times, but these are issues that would be common to anyone wishing to light a bonfire. For example, people in the UK often light bonfires on 5 November. It is about ensuring people are safe and sensible around fire and fireworks. More important issues are around the regulations for cremating bodies, but this is becoming easier as it is a practice that is becoming more common in Britain among people who are traditionally Christian.

Figure 17 Hindus in Britain celebrating Diwali in Trafalgar Square, London.

How does religion impact on the day-to-day lives of individuals and families?

What are Hindu attitudes, values and beliefs about marriage, divorce and family life?

Arranged marriages are not uncommon in Hinduism. They must always be with the consent of both bride and groom, otherwise they are not in accordance with Hindu tradition. Though Hinduism allows divorce on certain grounds, it is heavily discouraged.

What are Hindu attitudes, values and beliefs about poverty and inequality?

The belief in moksha means that Hindus must work hard for equality. Attaining liberation from the cycle of birth, death and rebirth (samsara) means trying one's best for everyone. It is no coincidence that Hindus believe that poor priests are amongst the holiest people, who are most likely to attain moksha.

Hindus believe in karma, the act of building up good actions (which can be built up through lifetimes). In order to free themselves from this chain of samsara, they must try to build up these good actions. In short, doing the right thing has the right consequences.

What can Hindus do to help fight inequality?

Hindus can do all of the things that religious people can do, such as pray and campaign for change. Much of Hindu belief encourages non-violence, in the same way that Gandhi fought the British occupation of India. This non-violence is known as ahimsa, a peaceful fight against inequality.

There has been a struggle in India to fight against the injustices of the caste system (see Case Study). This has been done through the law as well as through religion. In this way it has something in common with the peaceful Civil Rights Movement in the United States of America.

> ## Activity
>
> 3 Explain why many Hindu families believe arranged marriage is a good thing.
>
> 4 Explain moksha.
>
> 5 Explain karma.
>
> 6 'Life is about doing what you want. Duty to others is no longer important.' How far do you agree with this statement? Give reasons for your answer.
>
> 7 'Reincarnation means getting another chance.' To what extent do you agree with this statement?
>
> 8 Debate: 'What goes around comes around. You get what you deserve in life.'

Case Study

The caste system in India

The caste system in India has created differences between different parts of society. Gandhi fought against treating people differently according to their place in the caste system.

Though the system defines people by the tasks they do, many people came to understand it as a way of holding on to power and wealth whilst depriving others of the same opportunities. It was probably not intended that this should be the case when the classes originally came into being. The caste system consists of: Brahmins, Vaishyas, Kshatriyas and Shudras. There is a class of people below this known as the untouchables who do jobs such as disposing of the dead. It is important to remember that this system has not always applied just to Hindus in India but also to many Christians and Muslims living there.

Judaism What are the main beliefs and teachings that underpin Jewish attitudes?

What beliefs underpin the Jewish religion?

Jews believe there is only one God. A word they often use to describe him is **Adonai**, which means 'Lord' in Hebrew.

The **Shema** is the prayer that best describes the most important Jewish beliefs. It is found in the book of Deuteronomy. The opening of the Shema states: 'Hear O Israel, the Lord is our God, the Lord is One. You shall love the Lord your God with all your heart and with all your soul and with all your might.'

The Shema also introduces us to the idea that Jews see themselves as the Chosen People. This can be seen with the reference to 'the Lord is our God'. It is important to understand that Jews do not believe this makes them more important than **Gentiles**. It is more a statement that they have a special role to perform as the priests of humanity. It is as though this was their calling. Of course the massive majority of Jews are not priests and these beliefs are from an ancient past. They can help us understand how Jews still consider that God is helping his people and that they should still try to follow the rules of their religion.

A very good example of how Jews believe God helps them if they are faithful to him is the **Passover** story. It is the story of how Moses helped rescue them from slavery in Egypt with the help of his brother Aaron and his sister Miriam. As long as the Jews remained faithful to God in this hard time, he would ensure they were saved from slavery and eventually led to the Holy Land as God and Moses had promised. You can read this story in the **Torah**, in the book of Exodus.

Why are holy books important to a religion?

The Torah is the Jewish holy book. It provides Jews with the story of creation and tells them how their religion started. It tells of the story of Abraham and Moses.

The Torah is believed by religious Jews to be the word of God. It is often translated as meaning 'teaching' or 'law'. It contains all 613 commandments Jews have to obey, including the kashrut laws, which are concerned with what foods they should and should not eat. It also features the Ten Commandments, which are often seen as the basic laws of Judaism. The first four are about religious practice and the last six about social behaviour. This is a clear indication that Jews believe religion should cover all aspects of their life and behaviour. The most important law, however, is *not* found in the Ten Commandments. It is the Golden Rule which states that 'you must love your neighbour as you love yourself'.

In worship, the Torah is treated with great care. It does not come in the form of a book. It is a scroll and is handwritten on parchment. If there is one mistake, the scribe writing it must start all over again. Before it is read it is paraded around the synagogue where the congregation touch the cover that protects it. When it is used in the synagogue it is rolled out on the bimah (platform from which the Torah is read aloud) and is never touched by human hands; a pointer called a yad is used. It is written in the holy language of Jews – Hebrew. It is read every **Shabbat** service and at important times such as a **bar/bat mitzvah**.

When the scroll is not being used it is placed in the ark which indicates the direction of Jerusalem. It is covered by a mantle and has crowns on it. When it has been worn out it is buried carefully like a human. This is because Jews see it as the word of God and it is therefore sacred.

Figure 18 Reading from the Torah using a yad

What are the main similarities and differences between Christian and Jewish worship?

How and where do Jews worship?

Jews worship in a synagogue. Synagogue is a Greek word meaning meeting place. It serves many of the same functions as a church: children can learn Hebrew; they prepare for their bar/bat mitzvah; the elderly can come together for coffee mornings and other social activities; weddings and wedding receptions may take place here too. It is also where people come and seek advice from the rabbi. One thing that is special to the synagogue is the beth din – the rabbinical court. Jews come here to sort out all sorts of problems, ranging from business disputes to divorce.

The part of the synagogue that is used for worship is special. It centres around the ark, which is where the Torah is kept. The ark indicates the direction of Jerusalem and Israel as this is the Holy Land that Jews believe God gave to them. The bimah is the raised platform from which the Torah is read.

In an **Orthodox** synagogue, men and women sit separately as men have to obey the rules regarding daily prayers but women do not. In a **Reform** synagogue, men and women sit together.

There is also a plaque with the Ten Commandments written on, as well as a plaque blessing the royal family. Above the ark is the ever-burning lamp, which indicates the eternal presence of God.

Figure 19 A synagogue in France

Activity

1 Explain why the Shema is so important to many Jews.

2 Jews are called the Chosen People in the Torah. What do they mean by this?

3 What is meant by the word *Torah*?

4 Explain why the Torah is treated with such respect.

5 What role does the synagogue play in the community?

6 Explain how a rabbi serves the local community.

7 Debate: 'The Golden Rule is the only rule a religious person needs to live by.'

8 It would be useful to find out how Judaism has influenced the Christian religion. Jesus was a Jew. Try to find out one or two things that Jews do that have influenced Christians, such as the use of flat bread at Passover by Jews. Christians use flat bread during the Eucharist. Why?

Examiner's Tips

On longer questions you may get an opportunity to compare the different religions you have studied. Make sure you know something of what they have in common and what their differences are.

What are the most important stages in a Jewish life?

How are birth and coming of age marked in Judaism?

Jews are expected to obey the commandment to 'go forth and multiply' found in the book of Genesis in the Torah. Every birth is a new Jew, as Judaism is usually passed down through the mother. Also, after all the persecution they have suffered throughout history, every new Jewish child is seen as a victory. Baby boys are circumcised at the age of eight days old following a commandment in the Torah. This is known as brit milah, which is the covenant (agreement) of circumcision.

When a boy reaches thirteen and a girl twelve they must go through a coming of age ceremony known as bar/bat mitzvah. This means son/daughter of the commandment in Hebrew. The child is now seen as an adult in the eyes of the Jewish religion. They are responsible for their own actions. The choice of age dates back to a time when people did not live as long as we do and children assumed adult responsibilities at an earlier age.

Children are taught some Hebrew; if they are Orthodox and a boy they may learn it fluently. They then read a passage from the Torah on the Shabbat closest to their birthday. After this they become an adult member of the religious community.

How are marriage and death marked in Judaism?

Marriage

As mentioned, having children is one of the most important things a Jewish person can do. Marriage is seen traditionally as the right and proper place to have children. However, attitudes are changing amongst some Jews. Traditionally, marriages were arranged; this is less the case in Britain today, though the Orthodox community may retain an element of this. As with all religions, the ceremony and customs vary according to the region from which the couple originally came.

There is no special time at which weddings are held, though they cannot be held during Shabbat and they are not usually held during festival times such as Passover. Before the service, which is usually held in the synagogue, the bride must go to the mikveh, a special pool where the woman is purified. This is usually done in the week before the ceremony. The groom also sometimes visits the mikveh. He is sometimes showered with sweets at the synagogue service closest to the wedding.

Marriage is known as kiddushin in Hebrew, which means blessing. At the ceremony itself, the bride and groom wear clothing similar to that of Christian couples, but the groom also normally wears a skull cap. Like in a Christian wedding, they exchange rings. The couple stand under a chuppah – the wedding canopy. This has four sides, representing the house the couple will live in, and the sides are open to represent that they remain part of a wider community. The ketubah – wedding contract – is signed and, nowadays, also a document saying the groom will not contest the issuing of a **get** (divorce certificate). This helps make women equal to men as men have often refused to sign a get, which means the woman cannot remarry. As with all other religions in Britain, the couple must also register their marriage at the local registry office to make it legal.

The congregation act as witnesses and dress as any ordinary congregation, although Orthodox Jews are separated men from women. In an Orthodox synagogue there is no music but plenty of music, food and drink in the big reception that follows. Seven blessings are said that represent God creating the world in seven days. The rabbi gives a sermon and the rings are exchanged. The groom does not need to have a ring but usually does. Then a glass is broken to remember the destroyed Temple in Jerusalem (when it was destroyed by the Romans and Jews were banned from Jerusalem), and that there are hard times ahead as well as good.

Funerals

A Jewish funeral must take place as soon after death as possible; within 24 hours, unless there are extenuating circumstances. The rabbi should be contacted as soon as possible. The community usually rallies around and helps with the arrangements, though this may be difficult if a family lives a long way from the nearest synagogue, as there are not many Jews in Britain. The body should be buried in a simple pine box according to Jewish law as we are all equal in death. Cremation is forbidden by Jewish law but some Reform rabbis will officiate at a cremation.

No dead person is left alone between the time of their passing and the time of their burial. The Chevra Kaddisha (sacred burial society) cleanse the body and dress it in a plain white shroud for the same reasons that a plain pine coffin is used. Men prepare men and women prepare women. Men are buried with their prayer shawls (tallit) which they wear when they attend synagogue to pray. All close relatives tear their clothing as a reminder of their loss. Mirrors are covered.

As the body is removed from the house prayers are said. These are often from the book of Psalms. People attend the burial and as the coffin is lowered into the ground more Psalms are read. The rabbi reads a eulogy to the deceased.

After the burial there is a period of seven days' mourning known as shiva. There are also different phases of mourning lasting up to a year. Members of the family sit on low stools and family, friends and the wider community come by to offer condolences as well as bring food, as the bereaved are meant to be concentrating on mourning. The bringing or sending of food is considered to be more appropriate than offering flowers.

Figure 20 An Orthodox Jewish wedding

Activity

1 Explain why a bar/bat mitzvah is important to Jews.

2 Why does the bar/bat mitzvah take place at the age of twelve/thirteen? Do you think it should change today? If so, give reasons for your answer.

3 Describe what happens at a Jewish wedding.

4 What are the main differences between what may happen at an Orthodox and a Reform wedding ceremony?

5 Debate: 'Jews believe that marriage is the best place to have children. How far do you agree with this?'

Examiner's Tips

Learning to compare and contrast is a very useful skill when studying religions.

Why are celebrations important in the Jewish religion?

How do Jews demonstrate their attitudes, values and beliefs through their celebrations?

Passover

Passover is a spring festival that reminds Jews of freedom. It remembers the time God rescued the Jews from slavery in Egypt. This was done through the leadership of Moses. God asked Moses to tell the Pharaoh (King of Egypt) to let the slaves go. The Pharaoh refused. Every time he refused, God sent a plague on Egypt, including turning the river Nile to blood and the death of cattle. In all, there were ten plagues. The last was the death of every first-born Egyptian son. The Pharaoh lost his son in this manner. The Jews avoided the massacre by painting lamb's blood on their doors, so that the angel of death knew to 'pass over' their houses. After this the Pharaoh let the Jews go.

The Jews then prepared their departure. They were in a rush so they did not have time to let the bread rise. They carried their possessions on their backs. When they had started their escape, the Egyptian army came after them as Pharaoh had changed his mind. The Jews, following Moses, got across the water as God had made a passage for them through the sea. As the army followed them, the water engulfed the soldiers and the Jews made their getaway. In the desert they were fed by **manna** from heaven, which was another miracle of the Passover.

Before the Passover festival starts each year, all **leaven** is removed from the house; products such as yeast are not permitted. This remembers having no time for the bread to rise during the original Passover, but it also symbolises that Jews should not feel pride at this time. Children take part in a game where they hunt down hidden pieces of chametz (leaven) in the house.

Passover lasts for seven days. The first and last day are the most important and they are sacred as Shabbat. The most important meal of Passover is the **seder** meal. *Seder* means 'order' and the food represents the order of events at the Passover. The youngest person present asks four questions and the oldest person replies. Jews use a special book called the Haggadah, which is a fourteen-stage retelling of the Passover containing prayers and songs.

Passover starts and ends in the home, but important services are held in the synagogue. It is a way for Jews to come together as a community. Family, tradition and law are the most important things to religious Jews.

Activity

1 Explain what happens during Passover.

2 Use the seder meal to help you write a brief explanation of Passover for a young child.

3 Design a comic strip of the Passover story.

Rosh Hashanah

Rosh Hashanah and **Yom Kippur** are the most important time of year for religious Jews. These festivals usually fall in September.

Rosh Hashanah is the Jewish new year. God sets out in the Book of Life who will have a good year and who will have a bad year. The festival lasts for two days. In the synagogue special prayers are said and the shofar, ram's horn, is blown. At home, apples are dipped in honey in the hope of a sweet new year ahead. Bread comes in a round loaf to symbolise the circle of life and the year having come full circle. Sometimes a pomegranate is used as legend has it they have 613 seeds, which is the same number of commandments Jews have to obey. Jews cannot obey many of these commandments anymore as they were to do with the Temple that was destroyed by the Romans in 70CE.

Figure 21 Rosh Hashanah celebrations

Yom Kippur

Where Rosh Hashanah is a very happy occasion, Yom Kippur is a very serious and solemn occasion. At Yom Kippur, God closes the Book of Life (which was started at Rosh Hashanah) and all decisions regarding a person's fate for the year are made final.

Even Jews who are not very religious may well make the effort to attend the synagogue on Yom Kippur. Those who have properly repented have their sins forgiven. For this to happen they must first seek forgiveness from the person they have sinned against.

Most Jewish festivals are serious fun. Yom Kippur is not. On Yom Kippur Jews must fast for 25 hours. They do not show any sign of ostentation so they do not wear perfume, do not have sex and wear no jewellery.

Another difference of Yom Kippur is that the most important aspects of the festival occur at the synagogue as opposed to in the home. Jews sing Kol Nidre, a special prayer for the festival. There are five services throughout the day rather than the normal three. At the end of the final service the shofar is blown for the last time.

Celebrating as a minority faith

Judaism suffers from all the problems facing minority faiths in Britain. Time off for festivals is difficult and many festivals last for several days, such as Passover.

The culture of materialism is affecting the Jewish faith as it is affecting all parts of society. Jewish children may not want to practise their faith with their parents as they may want to spend time shopping with their friends. They may demand very expensive presents that the family cannot afford. Orthodox Jewish families may find it harder to live a full Jewish life when there are so few Jews living in the UK, as young people may be tempted to look outside the community for things to do. There is so much advertising that, like people of all religions, they may be tempted away from what they believe. However, it is also the case that many religious Jews will continue to follow the rules of their religion despite all the temptations.

Activity

4 Explain why Rosh Hashanah and Yom Kippur are so different in the way they are celebrated.

5 Why do you think Yom Kippur is such a solemn day?

6 Debate: 'The Book of Life proves that our future has been decided.'

Examiner's Tips

Always try and put yourself, as much as is possible, in the place of a religious believer when writing about their beliefs.

What are the implications of practising faith in modern Britain?

What are the problems facing Jews in practising their faith in today's society?

Shabbat

The Jewish day starts in the evening in accordance with the story of creation found in Genesis. Therefore Shabbat starts on Friday evening when it gets dark. In the winter time this is an issue due to the need to leave school/work early. Reform Jews get round this issue by saying the evening starts at 6pm throughout the year. For Orthodox Jews, this remains an issue, not only for Shabbat but for all festival days.

On Shabbat and other festival days no work is allowed. There is a very strict definition of what constitutes work for Orthodox Jews.

- Lighting a fire is one example. This prevents Jews from driving, as this includes turning on lights.
- No cooking can be done and no electricity can be used. In these cases timers are often used, or non-Jewish neighbours may help out.
- Walking to synagogue is the most common activity on Shabbat and festival days, as well as religious activities such as reading from the Torah. This is why many Orthodox Jewish communities are so tight knit – they cannot go far from home on this day and they feel they have all they need nearby.

Figure 22 Orthodox Jews in Stamford Hill, London

Kosher food

The kashrut food laws mainly apply to the consumption of meat. Meat must be slaughtered in a certain way, known as shechitah, and the blood must be drained.

The kashrut food laws make it very hard for small Jewish communities to find kosher food, though the situation is improving. In London and Manchester it is not such a problem and in other towns and cities there are often travelling butchers. In some cities, larger supermarkets have started selling kosher foods.

Clothing and appearance

- The ultra-Orthodox wear very strict clothing. The ultra-Orthodox men have pe'ot, which are curls on the side of their hair, and they also wear beards in accordance with a commandment. This makes them stand out in British society. Reform Jews wear more modern dress.
- Adult females may well go out with either headscarves or wigs in order to keep their hair covered as uncovered hair is considered a sign of vanity. Men wear hats that are usually black.
- Men wear black and have their heads covered by a wide-brimmed hat or a skull cap, which is also used during synagogue services by all types of Jew.

Anti-Semitism

Jews have lived in Europe for over two thousand years. Since before the crucifixion of Jesus – something which Jews are often blamed for – they have been victims of persecution. Some examples of this include the expulsion of Jews from England by King Edward I in 1290. In the fourteenth century, Jews were used as an explanation for the plague. Possibly the most famous example of anti-Semitism is the Holocaust in Nazi Germany. Roughly six million Jews and other minority groups were murdered under the dictatorship of Adolf Hitler.

Whilst things have moved on since the horrors of the Holocaust, there are still parts of the world where anti-Semitism is prevalent. In these areas Jewish people often have to be on their guard against attacks on them and their property.

Activity

1 Describe what happens during Shabbat.

2 'Having a day of rest to focus on God and family is a good idea.' How far do you agree with this statement? Give reasons for your answer.

3 What is meant by the term anti-Semitism?

4 Why has anti-Semitism been such a problem for Jews?

5 Debate: 'A person's religion should not matter. We are all the same.'

Examiner's Tips

Try and imagine what it would be like to be picked on because you are different. This might help you think about how others feel, when you are answering a question in the exam. Putting yourself in someone else's shoes is a vital skill.

How does religion impact on the day-to-day lives of individuals and families?

What are Jewish attitudes, values and beliefs about marriage, divorce and family life?

One of the Ten Commandments states that 'you should honour your father and mother'. Jews are also commanded to have children. Family is the most important unit in Judaism, and Orthodox Jews still follow the traditional division of labour between men and women. For example, men are commanded to pray three times a day but women do not have to attend the synagogue as the work they have to do for the family is regarded as more important. 'Do not commit adultery' is another of the Ten Commandments, and Jews consider adultery to be any sexual relationship outside of marriage.

Reform Jews take a more modern approach to family life. Women and men tend to interchange roles more easily and it is more common for Reform Jews to work. Women are allowed to become rabbis whereas Orthodox Jews do not allow this. Amongst Orthodox Jews arranged marriage is still sometimes the case, but Reform Jews take a very modern attitude to these issues, including divorce – although it must be noted that divorce is allowed under Jewish law. If a couple has tried everything to save their marriage and it has not worked, the appropriate religious authority reluctantly signs a get. This is the case for Reform and Orthodox Jews.

Jews in Britain are subject to all of the same problems regarding family life today as everyone else. Here it must be noted that the modern approach is not always the best. Divorce rates in the more traditional Orthodox community are low.

One of the problems some Jews face is if they wish to marry out of the religion. This is especially the case if the Jew is a man as it means his children will not be Jewish. Some Reform communities do accept the children of such marriages as Jews. In the Orthodox community the future wife or husband is often expected to convert.

Family life is held with reverence. It is one of the three fundamental aspects of the religion – alongside tradition and law – and this is the reason it is the norm in many families for elderly relatives to remain in the family home. This upholds the tradition of family life, and it is the elderly who have the longest memories of this ancient religion.

Activity

1 Explain the difference between Orthodox and Reform perspectives to family life.

2 Why are the Ten Commandments important to family life?

3 What are the three most important things to many Jews? Why do you think this is the case?

4 Debate: 'Divorce should be allowed. It saves a lot of heartache.'

What are the religious and moral standpoints regarding inequality in society?

What are Jewish attitudes, values and beliefs about poverty and inequality?

The idea that 'poverty in your midst will be unceasing' is a fairly depressing one. It tells us that poverty and inequality will always be with us. Judaism is a religion that is very positive about life so it tries to recognise the problems and find solutions for them in the here and now. It is less concerned with the afterlife. Therefore, in the same passage as the above quote (Deuteronomy, Chapter 15), there is a solution that is offered so that 'there will be no poor among you'. This idea is shemitah.

This is the idea that every seven years (remember the seven days of creation), all credit and debt is cancelled. In the modern world, rock stars like Bono have signed up to a very similar idea for poor countries. So, whilst Judaism recognises that there will always be poverty and inequality it does try to deal with it.

How can religious groups develop practical responses to inequality?

What can Jews do to help fight inequality?

Jews can do all of the things that religious people can do, such as pray and campaign for change. They can pray communally in the synagogue and can remember those less fortunate at times like Passover. As above, they can also work to relieve the debts of the poorest people.

Tzedakah means 'righteousness', but is often translated as 'charity' as Jews see charity as the best way of being righteous. This can be in the way of giving money, time or other things. The best way to do so, if possible, is anonymously. World Jewish Relief is a charity that is a good example of Jews working practically to deal with suffering.

These methods do help reduce inequality, and the ultimate aim is to have a world where this is no inequality. This is not likely to happen in the near future so people must try to reduce it any way they can. It can help to know that people are praying for you. It is also essential to provide people with the ability to help themselves. This is, in the long term, the most effective way of helping fight inequality. Making sure that all children, both boys and girls, are well educated is the best way to challenge poverty and inequality.

Figure 23 Paul Anticoni, Chief Executive of World Jewish Relief, visiting a mobile health clinic in Haiti

Activity

5 'Praying will not help people who are suffering so there is no point in doing it'. How far do you agree with this statement? Give reasons for your answer.

6 'People should be given a chance by having their debts cancelled once.' Do you agree? Give reasons for your answer.

7 What would you do to fight inequality? Why?

8 Debate: 'The poor will always be with us so there is no point in helping them.'

Examiner's Tips

Exam tips

- It is common to think that one textbook will be enough to get you through the course. Make sure you read as much as you can around the subject to get different points of view.
- Ask your teacher if there is anything at all you do not understand.
- Learn key words.
- Prepare your answer thoroughly by reading the exam question carefully.
- You might think that a question is the same as one from a previous exam but this will not be the case. It may be similar, but it will be important to spot the differences in the wording.
- Make sure you write clearly at all times. Never use 'texting' language.
- Always write in paragraphs, rather than note form on the exam paper.
- If you use information from other sources, *make sure you say where you got the information from*. Write in full sentences at all times and always read the whole question.

Christianity and Judaism

To help with your preparation for the exam, make sure you know:

- the origins of Christianity and Judaism. Commenting on issues you know little or nothing about is not very wise.
- the different ways in which the religions celebrate key events such as marriage.
- the differences and similarities between the religions.
- the differences and similarities within the religion, such as the difference between Orthodox and Reform Jews.

Always remember to look at both sides of an argument. There are always two different perspectives. For example, Orthodox Jews have a very different way of adapting to life in Britain compared to Reform Jews.

Christianity and Islam

To help with your preparation for the exam, make sure you know:

- the origins of Christianity and Islam. Commenting on issues you know little or nothing about is not very wise.
- the different ways in which the religions celebrate key events such as marriage. For example, in Islam marriage is seen as more of a contract than a religious ceremony in many cases.
- the differences and similarities between the religions. Muslims and Christians both believe in the same God but they have different ideas about him.
- the differences and similarities within the religion, such as the difference between a Muslim who prays five times a day and follows dietary laws as opposed to one who does not regard themselves as religious.

A very important aspect of any religion is its holy book. This is especially the case for many Muslims who regard the Qur'an as holy and the unquestionable word of Allah. It is very important that you understand this perspective when writing about Islam.

Christianity and Hinduism

To help with your preparation for the exam, make sure you know:

- the origins of Christianity and Hinduism. Commenting on issues you know little or nothing about is not very wise.
- the different ways in which the religions celebrate key events such as marriage.
- the differences and similarities between the religions.
- the different ways in which Hindus worship in the mandir and the many different samskaras that a person will go through in their life.
- about the Hindu holy books.

Remember that Hindus believe in reincarnation. This makes their world view quite different from that of Christians and can make for some very interesting comparisons and contrasts.

Examiner's Tips

Sample question

1 Explain why Jesus used parables in his teaching. [6]

What the examiner has to say!

1
- You need to *explain* why Jesus thought that people would understand these stories better than just telling them what he thought.
- It is very helpful to use an example. You can choose any of Jesus' parables. It always looks good if you can name the Gospel from which the parable comes, but it is not necessary.
- A top-level answer will explain why Jesus used parables. The answer might state, for example, that most people at that time could neither read nor write and that these stories were popular. Backing up your answer with an example will always help.

Mark scheme

LEVEL 1 Level 1 candidates use generalised and vague comments and assertions; with basic descriptions only. For example: *Parables were a simple way of communicating a sometimes difficult message.* This answer would get 1–2 marks.

LEVEL 2 Level 2 candidates offer a more focused answer, but only one reason is referred to properly. Good descriptions should get no more than 3 marks. For example: *Parables are used as a means of attracting a wider audience than just religious officials. Jesus wanted to reach as many people as possible regardless of their background.*

LEVEL 3 Level 3 candidates offer more detailed and accurate explanation; explain with more than one reason. Candidates should refer to a parable or give an *in-depth* explanation of how Jesus used parables to explain how people should behave as Christians. Using any parable as a way of explaining the importance of his teachings would be a good way of dealing with this answer.

Sample question

2 'The most important aspect of a religion is its holy book.' How far do you agree with this view? [8]

What the examiner has to say!

2
- This is a question that asks for *opinions* – what you think about the view expressed in the question.
- You must consider more than one opinion otherwise you will not reach the highest mark band. As long as opinions are well supported by fact you will do well regardless of the opinion stated. There is no accepted correct answer. What the examiner is looking for is your ability to understand the issue.
- This question provides you with a good chance to compare and contrast the different levels of importance that religious people ascribe to their holy books. For example, one could argue that many Christians see the Bible as much more central to their faith than Hindus, who have more than one holy book. This is one possible line of argument. There are, of course, many others.
- The examples below relate only to Christianity and Hinduism; you can of course refer to the other religions you have studied.

Mark scheme

LEVEL 1 Level 1 candidates will give a generalised answer, making a few relevant points. There will be a weak quality of written communication. Candidates may agree or disagree with the statement, plus make a general comment, such as there would be no religion without a holy book.

LEVEL 2 Level 2 candidates will give a more detailed and accurate account, with an attempt at a judgement which will not be fully sustained. There will be a sound quality of written communication. As a Level 1 candidate, but will also refer to the other side of the argument, such as: *it may depend on how seriously a person takes their faith, rather than specific mention of Christian and Hindu religious practices.*

LEVEL 3 Level 3 candidates will give a detailed and accurate answer which provides a reasoned evaluation of the issue in the question. There will be a good quality of written communication. For example, both sides will be fully considered; a balanced view should be expected which considers both Christian and Hindu beliefs, but could equally address other relevant issues such as the extent of personal belief.

Sample question

3 Explain why Muslims today may have a range of different attitudes about the importance of a mosque. [6]

> My parents let me make the choice about whether I follow my religion or not. This is what Muslims are often taught. It also fits in well with life in modern Britain where most people are not religious. I do try and go to the mosque to pray and meet up with people when I have time. But I also have many friends who are not Muslim.
>
> [A young Muslim living in London]

Source A

> I was brought up in a strict Muslim household. My family moved to Britain from Pakistan when I was a child. Even though that is a long time ago and I am retired now I still remember the mosque as being the most important place in the community. It is where Muslims pray, especially on a Friday. It is where we learn about the teachings of Muhammad. In Britain the mosque is also a place where people can seek advice about living in this country.
>
> [A retired Muslim]

Source B

What the examiner has to say!

3
- The most important thing to remember in this type of question is that there are differences within religions.
- You must *explain* how some Muslims are religious but how others are not. Some Muslims may simply live a long way from the mosque.
- Another aspect of this question is understanding that the Qur'an is the most important aspect of Islam for many Muslims and that they can actually pray anywhere as long as they are clean and facing Makkah.

Mark scheme

LEVEL 1 Level 1 candidates give generalised answers; paraphrase the source; write an unfocused answer. Level 1 answers will agree or disagree; may make a general point, such as: *some people take religion more seriously than others, and people are different so we can expect differences.*

LEVEL 2 Level 2 candidates use the content of both sources well to explain the different views. For example, Level 2 candidates will look at both sides of the issue, such as the attitudes taken to worship and the need to adapt to modern society; they may make some reference to the fact that the office worker is clearly from a religious background whereas the student may have come from a less religious background.

LEVEL 3 Level 3 candidates offer a balanced answer which uses the content and reference to the authors to explain differences in views. Level 3 answers discuss the issue from two clear perspectives; there will be reference to the content and also to the fact that people are free to worship or not in the UK, though family and community can exert huge influences; the candidate will refer to how modern pressures are difficult to resist and how we may also have friends from different backgrounds.

Sample question

4 'It is sinful to live together unless you are married.' How far do you agree with this statement? [8]

What the examiner has to say!

4
- This is a question that asks what you think about the view expressed in the question.
- You must consider more than one opinion otherwise you will not reach the highest mark band. As long as opinions are well supported by fact you will do well regardless of the opinion stated. There is no accepted correct answer. What the examiner is looking for is your ability to understand the issue.
- This question provides you with a good chance to compare and contrast the different levels of importance that religious people ascribe to the idea of cohabitation. Many Christians, for example, have come to accept it even if they do not agree with it. This is a good point to make. It may be that parents would not have done this but accept that their children will as long as they are happy and committed to the relationship.

Mark scheme

LEVEL 1 Level 1 candidates give a generalised answer, making a few relevant points. There is a weak quality of written communication. Level 1 answers will agree or disagree with the statement plus make a general comment, such as: *marriage makes no difference to how much people love each other.*

LEVEL 2 Level 2 candidates give a more detailed and accurate account, with an attempt at a judgement which will not be fully sustained. There will be a sound quality of written communication. As for Level 1, but will also refer to the other side of the argument, such as: *marriage is a symbolic public display of a couple's love.*

LEVEL 3 Level 3 candidates will give a more detailed and accurate answer which provides a reasoned evaluation of the issue in the question. There will be a good quality of written communication. For a Level 3 answer, both sides will be fully considered. For example, *Whilst a wedding is a ceremony, it is a fact that married couples stay together longer, but this does not mean that feel the need to get married.* You will be awarded credit for an answer that makes references to the legal implication of being married.

Sample question

5 'The biggest problem facing religious people today is finding time to attend a place of worship.' How far do you agree with this statement? [8]

What the examiner has to say!

5 ● This is a question that asks what you think about the view expressed in the question.
   ● You must consider more than one opinion otherwise you will not reach the highest mark band. As long as opinions are well supported by fact you will do well regardless of the opinion stated. There is no accepted correct answer. What the examiner is looking for is your ability to understand the issue.
   ● This question provides you with a good chance to compare and contrast the different levels of importance that religious people ascribe to the idea of attending a place of worship. Many will do so out of a sense of tradition and duty. It is true to say that church attendances have fallen in recent years. However, many Christians still go to church and get a real sense of community and belonging from the shared experience of communal worship.
   ● For people of other religions, places of worship often provide more than simply the chance for communal worship. Mosques and mandirs, for example, frequently provide help for families arriving in the UK, offering advice on how to adapt to life in Britain.

Mark scheme

LEVEL 1 Level 1 candidates give a generalised answer, making a few relevant points. There will be a weak quality of written communication. Level 1 answers will agree or disagree; giving general statements, such as: *it is possible if you really believe.*

LEVEL 2 Level 2 candidates offer a more detailed and accurate account, with an attempt at a judgement which will not be fully sustained. There will be a sound quality of written communication. Level 2 answers begin to look at both sides of the issue, such as: *although many people might like to worship more often, it is often difficult due to other commitments.*

LEVEL 3 Level 3 candidates offer a detailed and accurate answer, which provides a reasoned evaluation of the issue in the question. There will be a good quality of written communication. Level 3 answers offer a discussion of both sides of the issue. They address issues regarding consumer culture and commercialisation. They should also note that many religious people do make a real effort to attend a place of worship. It could also be noted that Britain is not a Hindu country. Examples are given.

Exam practice

'A wedding ceremony is the most important religious ceremony.' How far do you agree with this statement? [8]

What the examiner has to say!

● This is a question that asks what you think about the view expressed in the question. It is asking you about the wedding ceremony as compared to other religious ceremonies you have studied.
● It is *not* a question about the differences between living together without getting married and being married.
● You must consider more than one opinion otherwise you will not reach the highest mark band. As long as opinions are well supported by fact you will do well regardless of the opinion stated. There is no accepted correct answer. What the examiner is looking for is your ability to understand the issue.
● This question provides you with a good chance to compare and contrast the different levels of importance that religious people ascribe to the idea of the wedding ceremony itself.

Mark scheme

LEVEL 1   Level 1 candidates will give a generalised answer, making a few relevant points. There will be a weak quality of written communication. Level 1 answers will agree or disagree, and give general statements, such as: *it is the happiest day of a couple's life and so they will remember it forever.*

LEVEL 2   Level 2 candidates will give a more detailed and accurate account, with an attempt at a judgement, which will not be fully sustained. There will be a sound quality of written communication. Level 2 answers should begin to look at both sides of the issue, such as the importance of other ceremonies like baptism and funerals.

LEVEL 3   Level 3 candidates will give a detailed and accurate answer, which provides a reasoned evaluation of the issue in the question. There will be a good quality of written communication. To give a level 3 mark, the examiner will expect a discussion of both sides of the issue. The candidate should consider the point that many people still have religious ceremonies throughout life even if they are not religious. Examples should be given here.

Exam practice

JUDAISM

1 Describe the most important features of a synagogue. [4]
2 Describe a parable you have studied. [4]
3 Explain why Jews believe Yom Kippur to be such an important day. [6]
4 Explain why Jews believe the Torah to be so important. [6]
5 'A holy book is the most important aspect of any religion.' How far do you agree with this statement? In your answer you could consider:
   ● Why a holy book is important
   ● Any other important aspects of a religion.
   ● Say how far you agree with this statement. [8]

6 'A religious marriage is more important than any other religious ceremony.' How far do you agree with this statement?
In your answer you could consider:
   ● Why people consider religious marriage to be important
   ● Any other important religious ceremonies.
   ● Say how far you agree with this statement. [8]

ISLAM

1 Describe the most important features of a mosque. [4]
2 Describe a parable you have studied. [4]
3 Explain why Muslims believe Ramadan to be such an important time of year. [6]
4 Explain why Muslims believe the Qur'an to be so important. [6]
5 'A holy book is the most important aspect of any religion.' How far do you agree with this statement? In your answer you could consider:
   ● Why a holy book is important
   ● Any other important aspects of a religion.
   ● Say how far you agree with this statement. [8]

6 'What you wear is an important reflection of what you believe.' How far do you agree with this statement? In your answer you could consider:
   ● Why people consider religious clothing to be important
   ● Any other point of view you consider to be relevant.
   ● Say how far you agree with this statement. [8]

HINDUISM

1 Describe the most important features of a mandir (temple). [4]
2 Describe a parable you have studied. [4]
3 Explain why Hindus believe Diwali to be such an important festival. [6]
4 Explain why Hindus believe the Vedas to be so important. [6]
5 'A holy book is the most important aspect of any religion.' How far do you agree with this statement? In your answer you could consider:
   ● Why a holy book is important
   ● Any other important aspects of a religion.
   ● Say how far you agree with this statement. [8]

6 'What you wear is an important reflection of what you believe.' How far do you agree with this statement? In your answer you could consider:
   ● Why people consider religious clothing to be important
   ● Any other point of view you consider to be relevant.
   ● Say how far you agree with this statement. [8]

Glossary

1964 Civil Rights Act A law that said that all American citizens had to be treated equally.

1965 Voting Rights Act A law that took away all of the tests that had been used to prevent black people from being able to vote.

AA guns Anti-aircraft guns used against German bombers in the Second World War.

Abortion The deliberate removal of the foetus or embryo from the uterus, ending a pregnancy. Abortion also refers to the range of surgical methods used.

Absolute poverty A state of poverty involving dire need, where survival is a struggle.

Adhan Call to prayer in Islam.

Adonai 'Lord' in Hebrew.

Advent Time of preparation for Christmas, where Christians look forward to celebrating the birth of Jesus and look forward to the second coming.

Affluence / affluent Having wealth and being prosperous.

Afforestation Planting trees. The opposite of deforestation.

Aftershocks After a major earthquake there are often many smaller movements as the rocks close to the break settle down in their new positions.

Agent Orange Chemical used by the USA to kill off jungle vegetation.

Allah Arabic word for 'God'.

Antithesis The section of the Sermon on the Mount where Jesus delivered his key teachings (Christianity).

Aquifers Water-soaked rock underground where water is stored and can be extracted for our use.

Arms Race A competition between countries to see who can gain a definite advantage in terms of the number or the power of their weapons.

ARP Air raid precautions used in the Second World War, like sirens to warn of enemy attacks.

Assassination A planned murder for political reasons.

Austerity Having simple living conditions with little money to spend.

Baby boom Large numbers of children born in the decade after the Second World War.

Baptism Ceremony that welcomes a person as a member into the Christian faith.

Bar/bat mitzvah Son/daughter of the commandment in Judaism.

Bathtub principle A useful way to understand how birth rates and death rates affect population. The tap represents the birth rate and the drain is the death rate. The level of water in the bath is the population.

Bay of Pigs The failed attempt by Cuban exiles living in the USA to overthrow the government of Fidel Castro.

Beatitudes Meaning 'blessings', this refers to the blessings that Jesus gave at the Sermon on the Mount (Christianity).

Beatle Mania Very fanatical interest in British pop group the Beatles.

Beatniks (1950s) Young people who rejected the beliefs of their parents.

Berlin Blockade When the USSR cut off supply routes to West Berlin.

Berlin Wall A barrier put up around West Berlin in 1961 to prevent people from escaping there from Eastern Europe.

Beveridge Sir William, author of the 1942 report. He was a civil servant and politician whose report was the basis of the Welfare State.

Bible Holy book of the Christian religion, containing teachings, stories, poems and history.

Biodiversity A measure of the amount of different types of life in an ecosystem.

Biomes Large ecosystems such as deserts or tropical rainforests.

Black Market Buying and selling goods illegally during rationing.

Black Panther Party A paramilitary group of black vigilantes who protected black communities from racist attacks.

Black Power The idea that black people live their own lives separate from white people who did not deserve to be considered equal to black people as they had started the evil of slavery.

Blackout Putting out or concealing lights that might be visible to German bombers.

Blitz A very intensive air raid or series of air raids.

Brahman Hindu name for a universal presence.

Brinkmanship Pushing your enemy so far that they can only destroy everything or give in to your demands.

Buttress roots Large roots on all sides of the base of trees, which give them more stability.

Capital intensive High levels of money are invested in a business, e.g. for expensive equipment.

Capitalism The ideology or belief that everybody should be free to make all decisions about how to make themselves as rich as possible.

Carbon footprint A measure of how much energy a person uses and therefore how much they are contributing to climate change.

Caste System of social class in India.

Central Business District The commercial heart of a city. Also known as the CBD, this is the main area of shops and offices in the centre.

Channel alteration Usually straightening or dredging rivers to make them deeper to reduce flooding.

Charismatic (worship) Free style of Christian worship with no set pattern. The charismatic movement actively invites the works of the Holy Spirit.

Christmas Important Christian celebration of the birth of Jesus.

Circumcision The removal of the foreskin of the penis, often for religious reasons.

Civil rights The rights that all citizens of a country should have.

Climate change The name given to the recent changes in climate and weather patterns that have been observed around the world and which scientists believe are because of the effect of increased CO_2 in the atmosphere due to human activity.

Climate Change Act A law passed by the government in 2008 to try to reduce the UK's emissions of CO_2 and to make the country more energy efficient.

Cohabit Live together as a couple without being married.

Cold War A conflict between two sides which does not involve direct fighting, especially relating to the state of political rivalry and tension between the USA and the USSR that stopped short of a full-scale war.

Commercial farming Farming for profit.

Commercialised The way that Christmas may be organised in a way that makes a profit, thus taking away from the Christian religious celebration.

Common Agricultural Policy (CAP) Policy consisting of all the European Union's subsidies and programmes designed to support European farmers.

Communism The ideology or belief that everyone is equal and that it is the job of the government to make sure that everyone is equal.

Comprehensive redevelopment An attempt to improve the quality of housing in the inner cities during the 1950s and 60s. Many areas of poor-quality housing were demolished and replaced by high-rise flats.

Confirmation Ceremony that confirms that a person is a member of the Christian faith.

Congestion charge A scheme to reduce traffic congestion in central London. Vehicles entering the city centre at certain times of the day must pay a fee.

Congress The US parliament that passes all of America's laws.

Conspiracy theories The idea that several groups of people worked together to organise the assassination of President Kennedy.

Constitution The set of rules that the government in America has to follow.

Consumerism Encouraging people to spend more money so that there are more jobs and people get paid better wages.

Containment American policy to stop the spread of Communism to new countries.

Contraception Any means of preventing a pregnancy from occurring.

Convectional rainfall Rainfall caused by warm, moist air rising and cooling. The water vapour condenses and forms clouds to produce rain.

CORE (Congress of Racial Equality) An organisation set up during the Second World War to help black people in America campaign for their civil rights.

Corporal punishment Physical punishment, such as a beating with a cane in schools.

Counter-culture Radical ideas that young people in the 1960s followed that were very different from what their parents believed.

Counter-urbanisation The movement of people away from cities into countryside areas in search of a better quality of life in more peaceful surroundings. It is common in many MEDCs.

Crucified The Roman method of execution, leading to a slow and painful death. Jesus was crucified (Christianity).

Cuban Missile Crisis Conflict between the USA and USSR over an attempt to put Soviet nuclear missiles on Cuba.

Cyclones The name given to hurricanes that form in the Pacific Ocean.

Dams Barriers across rivers built to store water and control river flow.

Deep Throat The secret contact who told Woodward and Bernstein, two reporters, that President Nixon was lying about the Watergate burglary.

Deforestation The process of cutting down large areas of forest. Trees are important as they absorb CO_2. Large-scale deforestation in rainforest areas is increasing the greenhouse effect and adding to global warming.

Democratic Party American political party that believes in doing more to help people who cannot help themselves.

Deterrent Making weapons so that you stop your enemies from attacking you in case you use your weapons against them.

Dharma The religious duty a Hindu should carry out in their life. Good dharma leads to good karma.

Dien Bien Phu Fortress in Vietnam where the French were beaten and forced into surrender.

Diffuse source pollution Pollution that can't be traced back to a single point due to its coming from many places or travelling long distances.

Discrimination Treating a person or a group differently, often treating them badly because of their skin colour, sex, religion, etc.

Displaced (people) People who have been forced from the place they lived.

Divorce The legal dissolution of a marriage.

Diwali The Hindu festival of light.

Domino Theory The Americans believed that if they allowed Communism to take over a country it would then have a domino effect, spreading quickly to other countries.

Draft Dodgers Men who refused government orders to go and fight in Vietnam.

Drip tips A spout-like extension on the end of tropical rainforest leaves which helps them shed water easily.

Drive-in movie cinemas Open-air cinemas where audiences went and parked in their own cars to watch films.

Easter The most important festival in the Christian calendar, which remembers and celebrates the sacrifice and resurrection of Jesus.

Easter Sunday The most joyous occasion in the Christian calendar; the day that celebrates the resurrection of Jesus.

Ecotourism Tourism that aims to have a low impact on the environment and promote local sustainable development.

Eid-ul-Adha A Muslim festival.

Eid-ul-Fitr The festival at the end of the Islamic months of Ramadan.

Embryo The name given to the young of a mammal during the early stages of its development in the womb. For humans this is until the end of the second month.

Emergents The tallest of the rainforest trees.

Epicentre The point on the surface directly above the focus of an earthquake. Places close to the epicentre often suffer the most serious effects of an earthquake.

Epiphytes Plants, also known as air plants, that have adapted to live high up in rainforest trees.

Eucharist The name of the sacrament where Christian worshippers remember the Last Supper and take bread and wine.

Evacuation The moving of population out of an area that is under threat from German bombers during the Second World War.

Evacuees People who are sent away from a dangerous or threatened area to a place of safety.

Eutrophication An effect of nitrate and phosphate water pollution from sewage and farm fertiliser runoff, causing an increase in the growth of phytoplankton which use up the available oxygen and reduces the biodiversity of a body of water.

Evaporation Heat from the sun changing water from a liquid to a gas (water vapour) which then rises up into the atmosphere.

Exploitation Using something for profit. The overuse of the world's resources, and the unfair treatment of humans and animals for individual gain.

Extensive farming Large farms where the inputs per hectare are low, e.g. Australian sheep farming.

Fair Trade A system of buying that guarantees a fair price to producers, making it a sustainable trading relationship.

Fast To go without food for religious reasons.

Favelas The name given to areas of poor-quality, slum housing found on the edge of cities in Brazil. Also called shanty towns, they are built out of whatever materials people can find.

Flash floods A sudden and dangerous flood caused by very heavy rainfall over a short period. There is evidence that climate change is leading to an increase in the type of rainfall that causes flash floods.

Flashpoint An important event that is shocking and often violent.

Focus A point on a plate boundary, often deep underground, where tectonic activity causes the rocks to break and move suddenly, causing an earthquake.

Food miles A measure of the distance that the food we buy in supermarkets has travelled. One way of reducing our indirect use of energy is to buy locally grown food.

Formica The trade name of plastic sheets known for their heat-resistant and easy-to-clean surfaces.

Fossil fuels Fuels such as coal, oil and natural gas which have formed from ancient forests over millions of years. These fuels are the major sources of energy, and burning them releases large amounts of CO_2 into the atmosphere.

Freedom Riders An organised campaign of black and white people riding on buses and deliberately breaking the segregations laws.

Funeral Ceremony that marks the end of a person's life on earth, where they are given to God's keeping.

Generation Gap When older people do not understand the things that are important to younger people.

Genetic engineering The development and use of scientific methods to modify genes. This can be used to change the development of humans, plants and animals.

Genetically modified (GM) crops Plants that have been adapted to have certain traits, such as toughness, etc.

Gentiles People who are not Jews.

Get A Jewish divorce certificate.

Gospels Meaning 'Good news', this is the name of the four books of the Christian New Testament that give accounts of the life of Jesus.

Great Society President Johnson's programme of laws intended to end poverty and injustice in the USA.

Greenhouse effect A natural process where gases such as CO_2 in the atmosphere allow the sun's energy to pass through but prevent some of the heat escaping back into space. The greenhouse effect is essential for life on the planet, but human activity is increasing the effect, leading to warmer temperatures.

Groundwater flow Water that has sunk deep into the ground and very slowly makes its way into rivers, etc.

Guerrilla warfare A secret war fought from hidden bases using 'hit and run' tactics.

Gulf of Tonkin Sea off the east coast of North Vietnam.

Halal Food prepared according to Muslim law.

Hallucinogenic A drug such as LSD that causes changes to a person's mental state.

High-yield crops Known as HYVs (high-yield varieties), these crops have been genetically altered in an attempt to increase their yield.

Hijab The head covering worn by some Muslim women.

Hippies (1960s) Young people who protested against the Vietnam War and who believed in drug-taking and sexual freedom.

Hire Purchase A system of taking possession of goods after paying a deposit and paying the rest of the purchase price in a series of weekly or monthly instalments.

Ho Chi Minh Trail The secret supply route for the Viet Cong that ran between North and South Vietnam.

Holi A Hindu festival.

Hot Line A telephone line that directly linked the leaders of the USA and USSR.

Ice ages Periods in geological history when the earth's climate was colder than it is today. During ice ages, glaciers would have covered large areas of what is now the UK.

Ideologies Ideas about how the world should be run.

Ihram The simple clothing worn by Muslims when they go on the hajj (pilgrimage) to Makkah.

Imam The Muslim who leads prayers in the mosque.

Impeachment Legal proceedings to remove a president from office for abusing the powers of his office.

Impermeable Water-proof.

Industrial estates Areas of small-scale industrial buildings often found on the edges of towns and cities.

Industrial revolution A period of rapid urbanisation in the 1800s when millions of people moved from countryside areas of the UK to work in factories in the new industrial cities.

Infant mortality The number of children who die before their first birthday. Infant mortality is high in many LEDCs.

Infiltration The movement of water from the surface to the upper layers of soil.

Inner-city housing Areas of housing close to the city centre. It is often the poorest type of housing, with large areas of terraced housing built in the 1800s and high-rise flats built after the Second World War.

Intensive farming Usually small farms where the inputs per hectare are high in an attempt to get higher outputs from them.

Interception Precipitation that is prevented from reaching the ground by vegetation.

Intermediate technology Using techniques appropriate to the skills, knowledge and wealth of the people using it.

Iron Curtain The imaginary border between Communist countries in eastern Europe and Capitalist countries in western Europe.

Islamophobia The irrational fear of Islam.

Jewish Following Judaism, the dominant religion in Israel in Jesus' time; Jesus was a Jew.

Jihad A struggle. Muslims should struggle to overcome difficulties in life, whether they be personal like drug addiction, or problems in society like poverty.

Jim Crow laws Laws that kept black and white people apart by saying that black people were 'separate but equal'.

Ku Klux Klan (KKK) An organisation of white people who used violence to stop black people from claiming their civil rights.

Kyoto Protocol A major international agreement signed in 1997 on tackling climate change. The countries involved agreed to cut their emissions of CO_2.

Land reform The transfer of land ownership from a small number of rich owners to many poorer farmers who work the land.

Land-use zoning Deciding what will be built where in order to reduce the effects of flooding, for example.

Last Supper The meal that Jesus shared with his disciples on the eve of his death (Christianity).

Leaven Anything that makes bread rise, such as yeast.

Levees Also known as dykes or embankments. A wall or raised bank either side of a river to prevent it flooding.

Lianas Woody vines that use the surrounding trees as climbing frames in order to reach the sunlight above the forest canopy.

Life expectancy The average age to which people can expect to live. Life expectancy is high in MEDCs and lower in LEDCs.

Literacy The ability to read and write. Literacy rates are very low in many LEDCs where people do not have access to education.

Lone Gunman Theory The idea that only one assassin, Lee Harvey Oswald, was responsible for the death of President Kennedy.

Lord's Prayer A prayer that Jesus taught his followers that sums up some of the most important Christian beliefs.

Lynching Hanging black people to make other black people do as they are told.

Makkah The Muslim holy city.

Malnutrition Diseases caused by a lack of food, or more usually an imbalanced diet where people do not get enough of the right sort of food.

Mandir A Hindu temple.

Manna Food given by God to the Jews during the Exodus.

March on Washington (1963) The Civil Rights Movement organised for 250,000 black and white people to protest in support of new civil rights laws.

Marriage A legally accepted relationship between a man and a woman, where they live as husband and wife. For Christians it is also a sacrament and a rite of passage.

Marshall Aid Money given to countries in western Europe to help them rebuild after the Second World War, to stop them from becoming Communist.

Matinees Film shows usually held in the morning or early afternoon.

Merseybeat The name given to the music from Liverpool in the early 1960s.

Methodist A branch of Christianity.

Minister A member of the Christian clergy.

Miracles Supernatural occurrences that are explained in Christianity as acts of God.

Moksha Release from the cycle of Samsara in Indian religions.

Monocultures Growing a single crop.

Montgomery Bus Boycott Black people refused to ride on the buses in Montgomery until segregated seating was scrapped.

Morale Keeping up people's spirits and cheerfulness during a time of crisis.

Muezzin The man who calls Muslims to prayer.

Murti The depiction of a Hindu deity.

Mutually assured destruction (MAD) What happens in a nuclear war when both sides have enough weapons to kill everyone in the world; in other words, if one side launches an attack, the other side fights back, everyone dies and no one wins.

My Lai Village where US troops infamously killed unarmed women and children while searching for the Viet Cong.

Napalm Burning jelly dropped in bombs to set fire to Viet Cong-controlled villages and jungle.

Nation of Islam Muslim organisation set up to campaign to improve the lives of black people in America.

National Association for the Advancement of Colored People (NAACP) Association set up early in the twentieth century to use legal means to challenge segregation laws.

National Government A government that contains MPs from all political parties, usually formed during an emergency as in the Second World War.

National Organization for Women (NOW) A feminist organisation set up to campaign for equal rights for women.

Nationalisation When the government takes over and controls industry, transport or trade.

NATO (North Atlantic Treaty Organisation) A defensive military alliance between the Capitalist countries of Europe and North America; they promised to defend each other if they were attacked.

Naval Blockade Using the US Navy to stop supplies getting to Cuba by sea.

New Frontier President Kennedy's programme of laws intended to end poverty and injustice in the USA.

Nikah A Muslim marriage ceremony.

Nobel Prize for Peace International award to recognise people who have worked hard to solve conflicts.

Non-violent protests Protests in which protesters did not attack others or fight back when they were attacked.

Operation Rolling Thunder The heavy American bombing of suspected Viet Cong targets.

Organic farming Growing crops without using chemical fertilisers, pesticides, etc. instead relying on techniques such as crop rotation to keep soil healthy.

Organization of Afro-American Unity (OAAU) Organisation set up to bring together black Africans and Afro-Americans to campaign to improve the lives of black people in the USA.

Orthodox The branch of Judaism that teaches strict obedience to the rules in the Torah.

Out-of-town retail parks Large shopping centres built close to main roads and by-passes on the edges of towns or cities.

Overland flow Water travelling over the surface of the land. This type of water enters rivers quickly.

Parables Christian stories with meanings that Jesus told so that people would understand his message.

Park-and-ride scheme An attempt to reduce traffic congestion in cities. People park their cars in large car parks on the outskirts of a city and a cheap and regular bus service ferries people into the city centre.

Partial Test Ban Treaty The agreement between the USA and USSR to stop testing nuclear weapons above ground.

Passive disobedience Deliberately breaking rules you do not believe in.

Passover A Jewish festival.

Pastoral The non-religious duties that a religious minister has in the local community, such as visiting schools or the sick or bereaved.

'Peace with Honour' President Nixon's plan to bring about peace in Vietnam that did not leave the USA humiliated.

Periwinkle A plant found in tropical rainforests which has been used to successfully treat some child cancers.

Permaculture A sustainable form of farming designed to work closely with nature.

Permissive society A society based on the belief that there should be as few rules as possible covering behaviour, especially sexual behaviour.

Plate boundaries The areas where two or more rigid sections of the earth's crust – called plates – come into contact. Sudden movement of these plates cause earthquakes and volcanic activity at the plate boundaries.

Point source pollution A single, local and identifiable source of pollution.

Polycultural planting Planting several varieties of crop in a single area.

Population cycle Changes to birth rates and death rates over a period of time. Many countries seem to follow a similar pattern of changes which leads to rapid population growth.

Population density A measurement of how crowded a place or country is. It is the average number of people in an area, usually measured in people per square kilometre.

Population pyramid Also known as an age–sex graph. It shows the breakdown of the population into the percentage of males and females in different age groups.

Poverty line The minimum amount of money needed to live without outside help.

Prayer book An essential aid to prayer for many Christians, used in many church services.

Precipitation Water falling from the sky in the form of rain, snow, sleet, hail, etc.

Prejudice An unfavourable opinion made about someone or something without any prior knowledge of them or it.

Primary effects The most immediate effects of a natural disaster such as an earthquake or hurricane.

Privately Some Christians prefer to worship alone in private.

Proclamation During a Christian wedding ceremony when the priest tells the couple that they are now husband and wife.

Propaganda Information in the form of posters and other material designed to persuade people to support a particular point of view.

Prophecy When something is said or written about what will happen in the future (Christianity).

Public Worship Some Christians prefer to worship with others, perhaps in a church. This is also known as collective worship.

Puja Prayer in Hinduism.

Qur'an The Muslim holy book.

Ramadan The Muslim month of fasting.

Rationing The system of sharing out goods, e.g. food, equally so that everyone has a fair share.

Reconstructed families Families where there are step-parents/brothers/sisters.

Reform The branch of Judaism that has reformed, or changed, some of the laws to adapt them to modern life.

Regenerate Redevelop and improve older city areas.

Reincarnation The belief in Hinduism that the soul survives after death to be reborn in another form.

Relative poverty A state of being poor in comparison to others.

Relief rainfall Rainfall created when air is forced to rise as it hits high land. The air cools, condenses and forms clouds which produce rain.

Renewable sources Sources of energy which do not use fossil fuels and which will not run out. Hydro-electric power, wind power and solar power are the main sources of renewable energy.

Republican Party American political party that believes in saving money, lowering taxes and encouraging prosperity to solve America's problems.

Richter Scale The scale used to measure the strength of an earthquake.

Rite of passage Religious ceremony that marks an important change in a person's life, when they move from one stage of life to another.

Rock 'n' Roll Dance music based on a combination of white people's country and black people's blues music.

Rosary beads Prayer beads used by Roman Catholics.

Rosh Hashanah Jewish new year.

Rural–urban migration The movement of people from countryside areas into cities.

Rush hour The times of the day when traffic in towns and cities is heaviest as people travel to or from work. Typically they are between 8 o'clock and 10 o'clock in the morning and 3 o'clock and 6 o'clock in the afternoon.

Sacramental (worship) Traditional form of Christian worship based on the Sacraments of the church, e.g. Baptism.

Samaritan Race of people from Samaria, holding largely pagan beliefs (Christianity).

Samsara The constant cycle of birth, death and rebirth in Hinduism.

Samskaras Lifecycle rituals in Hinduism.

San Andreas Fault A major plate boundary that runs through parts of California in south-west USA and the location of many serious earthquakes. At the San Andreas Fault the Pacific Ocean plate is sliding slowly past the North American plate.

Sanctity of Life The idea that life is sacred and special, that it is given by God and only God has the right to take it away.

Saturate Completely soaked so no more water can be absorbed.

Scribes Muslims who write or copy out documents. This was a very important job before the invention of printing.

Secondary effects Longer-term effects of an earthquake. A common secondary effect might be the outbreak of disease caused by broken sewage pipes and contaminated drinking water.

Secular Not having any connection with religion. We live in a more secular society where religion has less impact on our lives than in the past.

Secularisation As society becomes less religious, it is described as becoming more secular.

Seder The Jewish Passover meal.

Segregation Keeping different races of people apart (e.g. having restaurants for white people only).

Self-help schemes A way of helping poor people living in shanty towns to improve their houses. People are provided with basic building materials and plans that they can use to build better-quality houses for themselves.

Senate Watergate Committee Set up to investigate the Watergate burglary and attempts by President Nixon to cover up his involvement.

Shabbat The Jewish day of rest.

Shanty towns A general term for areas of poor-quality, slum housing often found on the edge of cities in LEDCs. People build the houses or shacks out of whatever materials they can find on land that often does not belong to them.

Shema The most important prayer in Judaism.

Shifting cultivation Farmers clear a small area of land, farm it then abandon it and move to another area to allow the original clearing to re-grow and replenish its soil.

Sit-in A civil rights protest where people would defy the segregation rules by sitting.

Smoking-gun tapes Recordings of conversations in the Oval Office that proved that President Nixon had known about the Watergate burglary.

The South The southern states of the USA.

Space Race A competition to get the best achievements in the exploration of space.

Squalor Living in dirty and unhygienic conditions.

Star system Encouraging the media to focus on the lives of famous movie stars as a way of promoting films and the film industry.

Stewardship Christian duty to look after the world on behalf of God.

Storm surge Very high tides caused by hurricanes that push the sea into waves which crash on to the land and cause flooding and death in coastal areas.

Strategic superiority Proving that military army is better than that of your enemy.

Student Non-Violent Co-Ordinating Committee (SNCC) University student group who organised sit-ins and other civil rights protests.

Subsistence agriculture / farming Poor, small-scale, family-run farms common in LEDCs. Most of what is grown is for personal use with little extra for trading or selling at market.

Suburbs Areas of housing on the outskirts of a town or city.

Supplication A Christian prayer asking God for help.

Supreme Court A national court to make sure that all local laws in America did not break the rules laid down in the Constitution or the ideas in the Declaration of Independence.

Surah A chapter in the Qur'an.

Sustainable Ensuring the long-term survival of the resources you are using.

Technological innovations New inventions to make cinema films more exciting – for example, films in 3D.

Tectonic activity The movement of rocks in the earth's crust, which is caused by forces deep under the surface of the earth.

Tet Offensive The surprise attack by Viet Cong on US bases throughout South Vietnam.

Thanksgiving A form of Christian prayer thanking God for all that he has provided.

Through flow Water that has infiltrated the upper soil and travels slowly into rivers, lakes, etc.

Tipping-points The points when small or gradual changes to the world's climate become irreversible and lead to major events, e.g. the gradual melting of polar ice leading to rapid and serious global warming.

Torah The Jewish holy book.

Transpiration Water lost from plants during photosynthesis, similar to evaporation.

Truman Doctrine The Americans promised to help any country that was in danger of being taken over by Communists.

Tsunami A destructive wave many metres higher than normal which is caused by an earthquake under the sea. Tsunamis devastate large areas close to the coast and cause many thousands of deaths.

Typhoons The name given to hurricanes that form in the Indian Ocean.

Urban regeneration schemes The complete redevelopment of some of the worst areas of British cities, carried out during the 1980s and 90s. Examples include London Docklands and Cardiff Bay.

Urban renewal The improvement of housing areas through a process of modernisation rather than completely demolishing the existing houses.

Urban sprawl The continued growth of cities which causes them to extend outwards into the surrounding countryside.

Urbanisation The growth of towns and cities into the countryside. Urbanisation is happening most quickly in many LEDCs as people move from countryside areas in search of a better life.

Vedas The Hindu holy book.

Viet Cong Communist army from North Vietnam who fought the forces of South Vietnam.

Viet Minh Vietnamese army who fought for independence from Japan in the Second World War.

Vietnamization The process of handing over the fighting of the Vietnam War to the army of South Vietnam.

Warsaw Pact A defensive military alliance between the countries of eastern Europe and Russia; they promised to defend each other if they were attacked.

Watergate Scandal President Nixon's security men planted listening devices in the offices of his opponents; he tried to cover it up when his men got caught.

Watts riots Violent protests against police racism in the Watts district of Los Angeles in the summer of 1965.

White Anglo-Saxon Protestants (WASPs) The ideal people that white racists wanted all Americans to be.

White Backlash Increasing white violence towards black people in response to the success of the Civil Rights Movement.

Women's Lib(eration) The name given to the movement promoting equality for women in all aspects of life, sometimes known as feminism, and the belief that women should be allowed to have the same education and jobs as men, and should be paid the same wages.

Worship To hold God in high regard. From worth-ship, showing the value that God has for people (Christianity).

Wudu Ritual washing before prayer carried out by Muslims.

Yano Also known as a shabono, a traditional Yanomami dwelling.

Yom Kippur The Jewish day of Atonement.

Zakah The third pillar of Islam.

Zone of redevelopment The old industrial areas close to the city centre. Once derelict, many of these areas are being redeveloped with new housing, shopping centres and leisure facilities.

Index